D0084824

Neoliberalism, Transnationalization and Rural Poverty

Neoliberalism, Transnationalization and Rural Poverty

A Case Study of Michoacán, Mexico

John Gledhill

Westview Press
BOULDER • SAN FRANCISCO • OXFORD

Published in 1995 in the United States of America by Westview Press, Inc., 5500 Central Avenue, Boulder, Colorado 80301-2877, and in the United Kingdom by Westview Press, 12 Hid's Copse Road, Cumnor Hill, Oxford OX2 9JJ

A CIP catalog record for this book is available from the Library of Congress.
ISBN 0-8133-2435-1

Printed and bound in the United States of America

∞ The paper used in this publication meets the requirements of the American National Standard for Permanence of Paper for Printed Library Materials Z39.48-1984.

10 9 8 7 6 5 4 3 2 1

Contents

Tables and Figures

Tables

Figures

Acknowledgments

The principal fieldwork on which this book is based was carried out between August 1990 and September 1991. I am very grateful to the Wenner-Gren Foundation for Anthropological Research for providing the funding that made this work possible. I was also able to carry out a month's follow-up work in the Ciénega de Chapala in December 1992, thanks to a grant from the Central Research Fund of the University of London, which I equally gratefully acknowledge.

My most recent visit to Michoacán was in November 1994, courtesy of an invitation to participate in two conferences from the Colegio de Michoacán in Zamora. The Colegio has provided invaluable logistical and intellectual support for my research over many years. Thanks are due, in particular, to its current president, Brigitte Boehm de Lameiras, and secretary, Heriberto Moreno, and to my other friends and colleagues, Esteban Barragán, Oscar González, Gail Mummert, Cristina Monzón, Victor Gabriel Muro, Andrew Roth, and Sergio Zendejas, all of whom made significant contributions to this book, although they are absolved from all responsibility for the analysis and conclusions I offer. I am also grateful to the generation of masters students I taught at Colmich in 1989 and again, less intensively, during my 1990–1991 visit. I hope they learned something useful from me. I certainly learned a lot from them as I advised them on their field projects, some of which introduced me to areas of Michoacán I had never previously visited.

My greatest intellectual debt in this study is to my co-worker Kathy Powell. For practical reasons our time was divided between Los Reyes and the Ciénega during the whole 1990–91 field season, but she did the real fieldwork in Los Reyes and I have drawn heavily on her deeper historical and ethnographic knowledge of this area. I have also asked her for specific information relevant to several points of interpretation, and it is no ritual gesture to state that she is in no way responsible for any defects in the arguments I present.

I have benefited greatly from supervising the Ph.D. dissertations of some excellent graduate students at University College: Victoria Forbes-Adam, Robert Aitken, Patricia Fortuny, and Margarita Zárate, to place them in chronological order. Other colleagues who work or have worked in London University, Jutta

Blauert, Sylvia Chant, Neil Harvey, Stephen Nugent, and Ann Varley, have all had a direct impact on my analysis. So have other friends in the relatively small circle of Mexicanists in Britain. I should make special mention of Alan Knight, who invited me to try out one part of the argument at his seminar in Oxford.

In Mexico, I have derived a considerable amount of inspiration from researchers attached to the University of Guadalajara and CIESAS Occidente. Humberto González invited me to try out ideas in a stimulating conference he organized in Guadalajara in 1992, where I also learned much from the other contributors. Last but certainly not least, I thank my old friends Paul Kersey and Salud Maldonado in Jacona, of whom no favor is ever too much to ask and who have been unstinting providers of valuable information and contacts over many years.

My own field research has been focused on the Mexican end of the transnational migrant circuits that link the country to the United States. Although interviews with returnees and the resident kin of migrants provide a considerable amount of information on the topic, I have, of necessity, also drawn extensively on data provided by other scholars in discussing the position of Mexicans in U.S. society, especially in Chapter Seven. I would like to express my gratitude to Cambridge University Press, The Urban Institute and *New Left Review* for granting me permission to reproduce the tables used on pages 173, 175 and 183, respectively, and to all the authors of the studies cited in the text for their stimulating and insightful contributions to the debate. Special thanks are due to Juan Vicente Palerm for his kindness in sending me copies of two of his publications.

The heaviest debts an anthropologist incurs are, however, those to the communities in which he or she works. By continuing work in Guaracha, I have accumulated debts to Jesús Prado Inocencio, Raquel Abarca and their family that I can never repay adequately. Their eldest son, Chuche, not only supplied me with invaluable information about migrant life but insisted that I occupy his room in the family house even when he was back in the village. I am also grateful to Jesús's mother, Rosa, and younger brother, Davíd, for their hospitality and friendship, and to my many other Guaracheño friends who continue to receive me with warmth and affection after so many years of dumb questions. The people of Cerrito Cotijaran were equally welcoming. I should record a special thank-you to Luis Higareda, but any empirical merit this study may possess is based on the kindness and openness of all the people I met in that community. Exactly the same can be said of Los Reyes, Guascuaro, Tingüindín, Santa Clara and Los Limones. In Los Reyes, Jorge Barajas and Josefina Canela and Rafael Andrade and Cruz Rodríguez could not have done more to make us feel at home and help us to negotiate the mundane problems of life. The Sundays on which we set out to picnic in the countryside with our friends from Santa Clara, Enrique, Nacho, Toya and the kids, remain the fondest of memories. I cannot make a complete list of the many families who invited us to meals and to family parties and deepened our understanding of life in rural Mexico, without filling up several more pages. The list would, however, include people of all shades of political allegiance and from all social classes.

This book is dedicated to them all. Its themes have forced me to dwell on some of the more negative aspects of contemporary social life in the Michoacán countryside. I do not apologize for this, because I aim to show how the circumstances imposed on the actors concerned are what undermines the warmth, sociality, tolerance and dignity with which they are so richly endowed. As a general principle, I agree with Oscar Lewis that "concern with what people suffer from is much more important than the study of human enjoyment because it lends itself to more productive insights into the human condition, the dynamics of conflict, and the forces for change" (Lewis, 1970: 252). But it is my hope that those who are responsible for current policies will recognize the lasting social damage threatened by the neoliberal model and that this book will support the diverse voices, in Mexico and abroad, that are calling for a more humane future.

John Gledhill

1

Introduction: Structural Adjustment, Neoliberalism and the Mexican Countryside

For a majority of the world's population, the 1980s was a lost decade. Even in the metropolitan countries, rising prosperity for some was counterbalanced by an escalating polarization of income distribution, rising unemployment and growth in the number of families living below the poverty line. Yet as conditions worsened in the North at the start of the Nineties, the leaders of the "First World" insisted that their policies had been virtuous. Recession was explained as a product of global forces, including the failure of the world economy as a whole to move far enough towards the deregulation and free market policies which would guarantee future growth. The North's advice to the South was to persevere with policies of "structural adjustment" despite the high social costs of those policies in countries which lacked effective public welfare systems, systems which northern governments themselves were now claiming that their own societies could no longer afford to maintain in their existing forms, in the face of fiscal crisis and ageing populations.

Even the most schematic account of the costs reveals the magnitude of the sacrifice demanded and the size of the gap a longer-term renewal of growth is being asked to bridge. In the case of Latin America, the richest 5% of the population maintained or increased their incomes through the Eighties, whilst the bottom 75% suffered a decrease. Consumption per capita declined by 25% for labor between 1980 and 1985, but rose by 16% in the case of owners of capital (Ghai and Hewitt, 1991: 21). According to a United Nations Economic Commission for Latin America study of Mexico, Venezuela, Panama, Costa Rica, Guatemala, Colombia, Brazil, Argentina and Chile, the number of people living in absolute poverty in those counties increased from 136 to 183 million individuals, equivalent to 44% of the total population (CEPAL, 1992). Increasing poverty was associated with massive rural-urban migration: in 1970, 37% of the Latin American poor lived in cities, whereas 55% were urban by 1986. Yet rural poverty remains endemic. In 1990, Mexico's National Solidarity Program (PRONASOL) identified the seven-

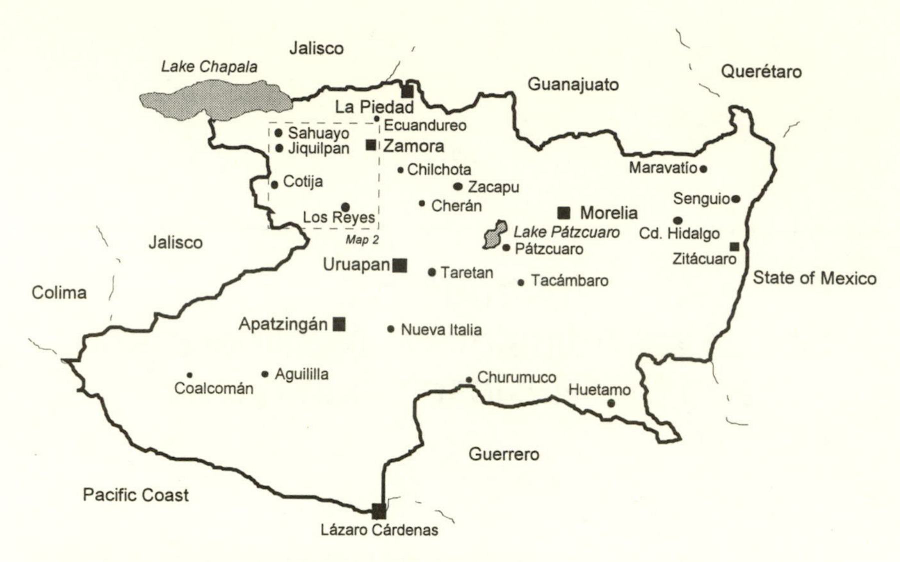

FIGURE 1.1 Map of the State of Michoacán

teen million persons living in "extreme poverty" in the country as predominantly inhabitants of rural communities. In Latin America as a whole, around 54% of the rural population were estimated to live below poverty level in the mid-Eighties (Ghai and Hewitt, op.cit.: 23) and 43% of rural households in Mexico were in this condition at the start of the next decade.

The direct impact of the stabilization policies mandated by the IMF fell in the first instance on the public sector, although the broader structural adjustment package, with its emphasis on opening up the domestic economy to the forces of international competition, also put the squeeze on small and medium sized firms in the private sector in Mexico. This was because the Mexican government opted for strong trade liberalization and reduced protection for national producers without waiting for reciprocal concessions from the country's metropolitan trading partners. Nevertheless, in the early phases of adjustment, public sector pay was cut in real terms more than private sector pay, and many public sector jobs were eliminated entirely. It is easy to denounce the unproductive nature of the massive public sector job creation associated with statist development—although there is a cruel irony in the fact that some of the most venal of former bureaucrats have been able to take their place at the forefront of the new free-market enterprise culture, whether we are talking about Latin America or the former Soviet Union.

There is, however, another side to the picture. In the first rural area which I studied in the state of Michoacán, the Ciénega de Chapala, public sector employment in manual work was the most significant form of off-farm employment for landless married men at the start of the Eighties. Almost all these jobs have now disappeared, as have some of the minor technical posts occupied by those with more

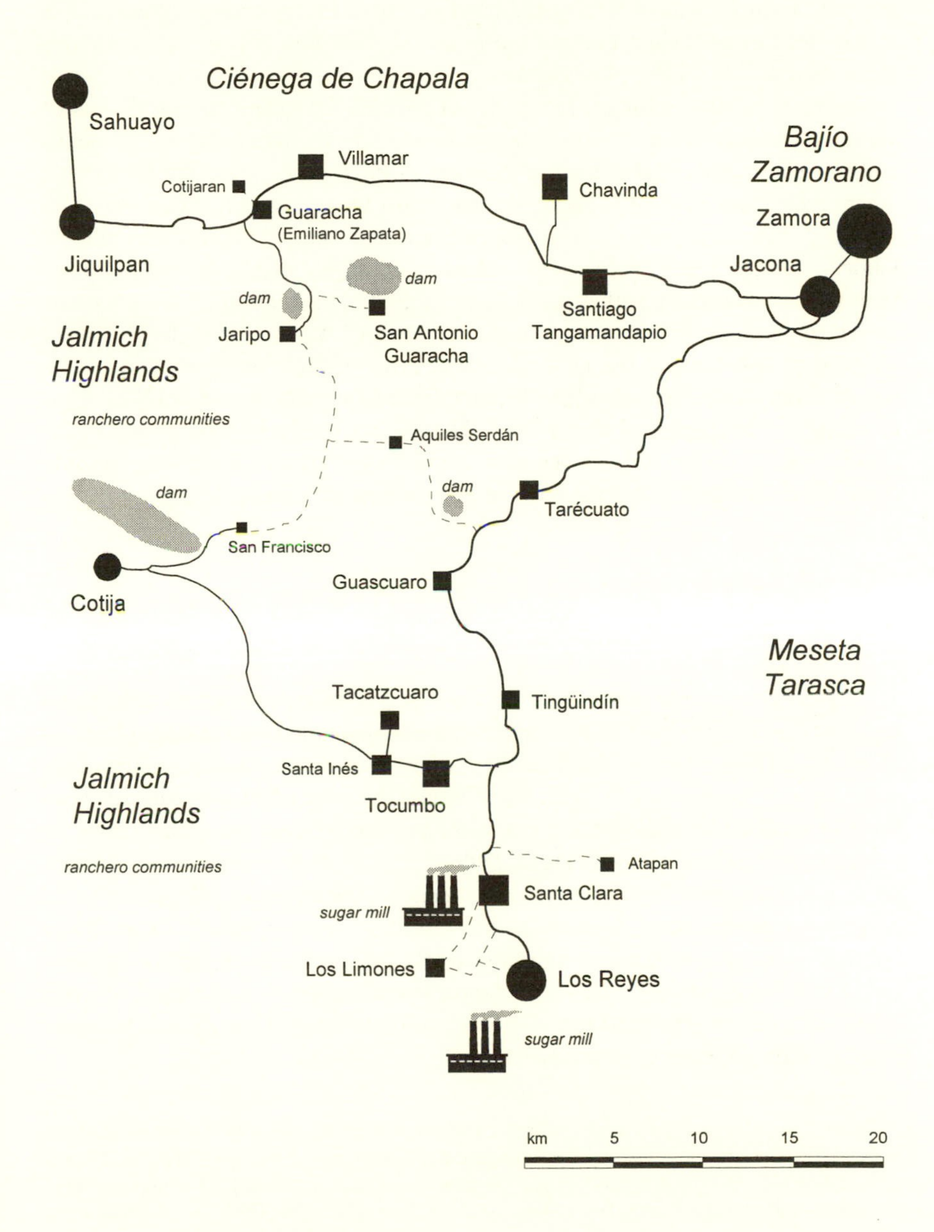

FIGURE 1.2 Map of the Ciénega de Chapala, Zamora and Los Reyes (showing places mentioned in the text and main communication routes)

education. Even those who worked in the supposed "profession" of school-teaching were earning no more than a field-hand in 1991. In some communities children lost months of education because too many teachers decided to take a working leave-of-absence in the United States.

Austerity meant a dramatic loss of social position for some families: the ECLA survey found that just over 12% of homes on the poverty-line in Brazil, Colombia and Venezuela at the end of the Eighties were former middle class families. But if the middle class lost most relatively speaking, the catastrophe was worse for working class people who had less to start with: not only did real wages fall, but labor productivity declined as well.[1] Most depressingly of all, the proportion of young people who had neither studied nor worked in the kind of job which would be recognized in official statistics as "employment" was higher at the end of the 1980s than at the end of the 1970s. Much of this youth did not even work within the secondary labor markets which proliferated under the new post-Fordist regime of capitalist accumulation which David Harvey has dubbed "flexible accumulation" (Harvey, 1989: 124). In the new world forged by neoliberalism, the once discredited concept of "marginality" at last seemed to be having its day.

Into the Nineties

The stark aggregate statistics on the costs of a decade of structural adjustment describe the consequences of rural impoverishment coupled with falling urban real incomes and declining opportunities for employment in cities in any kind of stable work, even at the lowest of wages. Yet although the costs of adjustment have been broadly similar, there are differences in the precise policies individual countries have pursued, particularly with regard to the degree of trade liberalization. Furthermore, many countries have not pursued a consistent line of policy. Within the broad parameters of structural adjustment and the shift to neoliberal policies, some countries appear to have been more "successful" than others and the jury remains out on whether extreme versions of economic liberalization yield the best long-term results in terms of stabilization and growth. Still more significantly, it is not clear how we should measure "success."

---

[1] Mexico's minimum wage lost 60% of its real value between 1982 and 1991. Although real wages in the *maquiladora* assembly plants and manufacturing industry rose in 1987, after falling by 25% and 35%, respectively, over the previous four years, aggregate real wages continued to fall up to the end of the decade whilst middle class and executive incomes recovered (Escobar, 1993: 71). The annual rate of decline of the real value of the minimum wage actually accelerated from 12% to 14% between 1988 and 1991. As noted below, hard times for working people returned again during 1993, only the *maquiladoras* manifesting any improvement in wages and benefits over the period June 1993 to May 1994.

In terms of "recovery" and renewal of economic growth, 1991 did see a general turnaround throughout the region, although the rate of increase in the number of people living in poverty continued to exceed overall population growth. Yet as UNCTAD's economists observe in their 1993 *Trade and Development Report*, most Latin American countries grew at rates which remained low in comparison with the region's post-war average in 1991 and 1992. If the primary goal is to enter a new phase of export-led manufacturing growth, Latin America has yet to achieve rates comparable to those which underlay the "take-off" into export-orientated growth of Asian countries such as Taiwan, South Korea, Malaysia and Singapore. Growth has been stimulated more by consumption than by investment, and high current account deficits cannot necessarily be viewed as a benign phenomenon of transition (caused by imports of capital need to finance the restructuring of production necessary to achieve long-term growth). Domestic savings in Mexico actually fell by 3% of GDP in the period 1988-92, and the bulk of foreign capital inflows have been destined for the financial markets rather than direct investment in production. The proceeds of privatizations and incentives to citizens to repatriate capital helped to produce a brighter short-term picture. Yet Mexico's consumer boom of 1990–92 was based on an extension of credit to individuals which the Central Bank subsequently judged imprudent in the light of stagnant real incomes, and the picture on repatriation of capital under the Salinas administration turns out to be less positive on closer inspection. During the period 1989–93, U.S.$11.6bn of flight capital was repatriated, but Mexican deposits in U.S. banks fell by only U.S.$3.8bn (*Latin American Weekly Report* 94-22: 260). Those deposits still totalled U.S.$15.8bn at the end of 1993—equivalent to 64.5% of Mexico's international reserves—making the country the largest Latin American depositor in the U.S. banking system, and the fourth largest world-wide (ibid.). A new flight of capital, estimated at U.S.$11bn, occurred in the first half of 1994, in the wake of the Chiapas uprising in January, the assassination of PRI presidential candidate Luis Donaldo Colosio in March and subsequent fears of a problematic outcome to the August elections.

The economic restructuring achieved by Salinas did not, in itself, lay the basis for sustainable growth. Mexico's commitment to the North American Free Trade Agreement (NAFTA) encouraged the government to maintain an overvalued currency and a budget surplus even though this caused growth to slow (and unemployment to rise) during 1993. Manufacturing output registered its first fall since 1987 in the second quarter of 1993. The primary sector, including agriculture, fishing and forestry, but excluding mining and crude oil extraction, continues to be the worst performer in the entire economy. Its contribution to GDP contracted throughout 1992. The official figure for open unemployment in Mexico, produced by the National Institute of Statistics, Geography and Information (INEGI) increased from 2.9% to 3.3% between May 1992 and May 1993, but using INEGI's alternative measure of "unemployment and underemployment," the proportion of the economically active population earning less than a single minimum wage, the rate rose from 12 to 13%. In the first quarter of 1994, the *maquilidora* sector showed a strong upsurge of activity, along with the steel industry, but domestically orientated industries, such as shoes and textiles, continued to contract. The particular policy tightness which caused this conjunctural slowdown is reversible, but the deeper questions posed by UNCTAD's survey remain to be answered in the longer term.

The basic presumption of structural adjustment policies is that removal of protection and subsidies from inefficient producers will, in the long term, produce a more rational allocation of national resources. Whatever the short-term costs, countries which accept the disciplines of full incorporation into the world market should be able to maximize growth and provide their citizens with a superior standard of living based on higher productivity and efficient exploitation of the potential gains from specialization in world trade (on the principle of comparative advantage). There is considerable scope for debate about the theoretical validity of this prescription in a "real world" of imperfect markets and historically entrenched unequal development. We need to ask, for example, how much of the "comparative advantage" in the production of a given type of commodity a given country enjoys (or lacks) at a particular moment reflects the accumulated result of its wider pattern of economic development to date, so that only decisions to plan for the future and ignore short-term difficulties can truly realize a nation's economic potential within the international division of labor. At this stage, however, I want to focus on the evidence provided by actual experience. In particular, the question of how far renewed economic growth will produce greater social equity remains as open an issue for the First World as for the Third.

Social and Political Dimensions of Economic Policy: A Broader View

If the performance of countries is measured in terms of the UNDP's Human Development Index rather than per capita GNP, supposed "success stories" like Mexico, Chile and Argentina are seen in a different light (UNDP, 1993). Between 1990 and 1992, Mexico fell eight places (from 45 to 53) in the world ranking on this index, which combines indicators of purchasing power, education and health. Chile and Argentina both continued to rank higher than Mexico but their absolute HDI scores declined. When increasing inequality in income distribution is factored in, the scores for all three cases decline further (by 5% in the case of Chile and Argentina and 8.5% in the case of Mexico). Equally significant is the fact that the resident Latino population of the United States would rank 35th on a global HDI scale, just above Chile and below Trinidad, which, in thirty-first place, equals the ranking which would be assigned to the Black segment of the U.S. population.[2] The results of these alternative measures of "development" immediately suggest a need to look at the deeper human and social implications of economic restructuring and to see it as a global process.

Also central to the debate about structural adjustment is the question of the proper role of the state within a market economy, as discussions of the precise conditions which brought the "Asian Tigers" economic success have illustrated (Wade, 1990). The "minimal state" concept advocated by the dominant faction within the World Bank during the Eighties, and now, it seems, under revision, is not the only alternative to the kind of interventionist state which existed in Mexico before 1982, a state which sought to run important sectors of the economy directly through public enterprises. Wade draws our attention to the more useful distinction between "hard" states which can exercise a firm influence over the holders of private economic power in civil society and "soft" states which are less effective agents of capitalist regulation. This does not correspond to a simple political distinction between authoritarian and democratic regimes. Undemocratic governments may be relatively "soft" in terms of their power to control private capital movements and investment strategies, even if they are corporatist in organization, and some relatively "soft" states seem capable of sustaining more effective industrial policies than others (Wade, op.cit.: 379). Wade argues that the United States does not belong to the more effective category, and that the shaping of the policies of agencies such as the World Bank by American conceptions of the role and competence of government is to be deplored given the unsuitability of the American model for developing countries (op.cit.: 381). Although the size of local private companies and the role played by state enterprises does in fact vary significantly among East Asian Newly Industrialized Countries (Gereffi, 1990), there is a common pattern in that region. What have undeniably been relatively "hard" states have taken a long-term view of economic development and fostered the growth of what were identified as strategic sectors, leaving the actual organization of production to local (private or public sector) enterprises but not to *transnational* capital, adopting precisely the pro-active stance on creating "comparative advantage" which recommends itself on the theoretical grounds mentioned above. This strategy of guiding the market is equally distinct from both Latin American patterns of statization of the commanding heights of the economy and also from unfettered free market policies, particularly those which depend on *current* signals from international markets to orientate national production.

If our objective is to explain the differential economic performance of countries (and the differential impact of structural adjustment policies in different national cases), then a wide variety of factors seems potentially relevant. Even within Latin America, countries differ widely in terms of natural and human resource endow-

---

2 The white population of the United States is in first place globally. When the U.S. population is treated as an aggregate, the effect of inter-ethnic disparities is sufficient to push the U.S. down into sixth place in the world HDI rankings.

ments and social and political structures. A focus on rural development must take into account the fact that the commercial agricultural systems of some countries are heavily oriented towards export markets whereas others are more oriented to supplying domestic demand, even before we begin to consider questions such as land tenure and the relationships between rural labor markets and agrarian structures. Structural adjustment policies assume *a priori* that private property relations are to be preferred to state ownership and that domestic prices should be brought in line with international prices (to encourage producers to choose more efficient techniques and switch resources to producing those products they can produce most efficiently). Yet text-book prescriptions fail to acknowledge on-the-ground realities such as the possible absence of a relationship between international prices and domestic prices,[3] monopolistic and oligopolistic distortions in the sphere of marketing, and the impact of an unequal distribution of income and access to capital. These and other factors make it far from straightforward to define a simple way of removing market "distortions."

In the case of Mexico, it is undeniable that the statization of agriculture in the period 1973–1982 failed both the national interest and the peasantry, but there are two distinct (though not mutually exclusive) ways of explaining this failure. On the one hand, we have the question of how far it would ever be possible to create a prosperous small-scale agriculture within Mexico's "bipolar" agrarian structure, so evidently distinct from the kind of agrarian structure which supported Taiwan and South Korea's transition to industrial competitiveness on the world stage (Rello, 1986). On the other hand, we have the question of how far the economic failures of Mexico's statized pattern of agricultural development reflected the nature of the country's political system. Furthermore, it remains impossible to treat economic policy in isolation from political considerations in the neoliberal era, a theme I will develop in the next two chapters.

Amplifying the problems confronting the policy-maker is the fact that orthodox economic statistics give a very inadequate picture of the real structure of the Third World economy. Even before the collapse of the Eighties, large areas of that economy enjoyed a semi-subterranean existence, linked in ways that are now better documented to the public face of private capital formation and the state sector. It is true that much of the "small-scale" sector, linked to large-scale enterprise through sub-contracting and domestic outworking, was also hit by the general economic downturn, demonstrating the degree of integration which exists within the economic process as a whole. Nevertheless, the role of the "informal sector" in adjustment to crisis during the Eighties is manifest in the 80% growth of those

---

[3] It is not necessarily the case that agricultural commodities are "tradables" in the sense of being exportable or that they face effective competition from imported substitutes, for a variety of mundane reasons, including transport infrastructure and the existence of peasant subsistence production with low to zero money costs.

working in such occupations in the period 1980 to 1987, and the increase in workers per household in both urban and rural areas. Much of the latter reflected the greater participation of women in the labor market, particularly in informal service occupations and family workshops, although the *maquiladoras* also contributed to increased employment of women (Escobar, 1993: 72; Chant, 1994: 227). There are, however, some economic activities which are relatively resilient to crisis (Zepeda, 1987) and some which are actually stimulated by growing social polarization. Mexico's popular markets, the *tianguis*, are a relatively positive example: the most negative, and most important, is the drugs business.

The ability of working people to adapt to crisis should never be underestimated. As Chant has shown, in at least some urban contexts, women not only shouldered new burdens to help their families cope with crisis, but may even have made some gains in terms of reduced male control of their labor power, greater scope for negotiation in household decision making and relaxation of pressures to marry early, although gender differentials in pay and reluctance of men to participate in domestic, reproductive labor remain entrenched (Chant, op.cit.: 223–26). Yet it remains necessary to recognize that a great many people in the cities, towns and villages of Mexico and Central America did not get through the crisis by any form of domestic economic or social adaptation: their response was to move towards the perceived center of the New World Order through migration to the United States. Complex patterns of internal migration between different rural areas have also been a feature of Latin American social reality since the colonial era, but some of the migrants of the Eighties came to resemble refugees in their own countries.

Social and Political Dimensions of Environmental Crisis

Economic and social retrocession has been accompanied by a deepening environmental crisis. In the case of Mexico, environmental questions have been given added salience through their deployment by opponents of the NAFTA. One obvious lesson to be drawn from Mexican experience is that there are limits to the sustainability of a hyperurbanized capital city which lacks water and breathable air, even without popular mobilization against the life-threatening consequences of lax enforcement of legislation on industrial contamination and toxic waste disposal. No less significant, however, is the problem of continuing deforestation and erosion of marginal agricultural land: the supply of wage-laborers to commercial agriculture at what would otherwise be starvation wages continues to depend on their supplementing the income the market offers with self-provisioning.

Environmental problems provide a paradigmatic example of the way simple macro-economic development indicators obscure important qualitative human issues. Return migrants from Mexico City I have interviewed in rural Michoacán are quite explicit about the way in which improvements in material consumption standards associated with life in the city have been increasingly eroded by deterioration in the quality of metropolitan urban life as a result of pollution, travelling to work on an overcrowded public transport system and living in fear of robbery and assault. Since the late 1960s, environmentalist arguments have been questioning the long-term costs of capital accumulation and the maximization of material civilization in the form of the ever-expanding industrialization of consumption, not only of goods but of services based on the technification of human relations. The sustainability of "development" is particularly problematic in the case of food production, and the technological "fixes" promised by biotechnology to increasingly urgent problems of world food supply may pose more problems than they resolve as far as developing countries are concerned (Buttel, 1990). Despite the high profile environmental issues have achieved in metropolitan countries, and the echoes of concern expressed by many governments of the South,[4] it is dubious whether the results to date are cause for much satisfaction. The very existence of urban concentrations of population encouraged by private and public propaganda to demand greater access to processed food products and durable consumer goods tends to set the outer limits on what is regarded as practical. Most of the benefits of Mexico City's program to reduce pollution by fixing a day on which a particular car had to keep off the streets were vitiated by promotion of new car ownership. There is, however, a peculiar cynicism apparent in the Mexican case. The government's commitment to the NAFTA led its chief negotiator, the Commerce Secretary Jaime Serra Puche, to propose the development of new assembly-plant industry in choking Mexico City. Serra Puche insisted that such "modern" industries were more environmentally friendly despite the notoriety that *maquiladoras* had already acquired for their pollution of the border region. Routine violation of environmental and labor protection legislation on the border is, however, tolerated because it is committed by "foreign investors," and central government had recently meted out repression to independent trade union organizers fighting to improve matters in Matamoros when Serra Puche made his proposal.

In agriculture, technical changes could theoretically reduce problems associated with the extensive use of agrichemicals and more determined implementation of conservation policies could help to arrest soil erosion and the exhaustion of subterranean aquifers. Yet metropolitan public opinion must be convinced that sacrifices have to be made. The problems of supplying water to the population of Mexico City have become relatively notorious, but there is less understanding of the extent of the vast hydrographic network on which the city depends and of the

---

4 The concern expressed for the environment by Salinas de Gortari was clearly related to the NAFTA negotiations. "Greenness" does, however, also have its (selective) uses in other policy areas: environmental criteria provide a convenient pretext for the decommissioning of state-owned industrial plants, allowing the social costs in terms of employment to be presented as outweighed by social advantages in terms of pollution control. It would be difficult to argue that public health criteria are applied universally or uniformly in the industrial sphere in Mexico.

problems which schemes to ameliorate the situation can create for distant regions, particularly given that there is a constant pressure to try to solve electricity generation problems in the central industrial districts by creating new hydroelectric projects in supposedly "marginal" rural areas outside the central valley. Drastic reductions in levels of consumption and population relocation are the preferred solutions, but to regard them as viable is to abstract from all the economic factors which underpin the politics of the status quo—such as investments in infrastructure which reduce industrial costs and real estate values.

Environmental problems are often the direct consequence of processes of social polarization. The concentration of income in the hands of the few can, for example, make a significant contribution to the draining of rivers as en-suite showers proliferate, whilst those segments of the rural poor which still have access to natural resources may be increasingly driven to abandon sustainable techniques for exploiting them in the interests of meeting immediate needs. It is difficult to ask peasants to abandon "non-green" strategies when these are, in fact, those which provide the best available economic returns. There are, however, some potential advantages for the environment in consumer affluence: capitalism has actually proved more than equal to the task of commoditizing "greenness," because high income consumers in metropolitan centers are willing to pay to salve their consciences. Yet the impact of such countervailing tendencies remain modest. The continuing devastation of the forest resources of Michoacán despite the existence of an extensive official apparatus for policing and enforcing conservation provides an apt illustration of the ways in which social inequality and political impunity perpetuate environmental destruction.

External demand for timber is insatiable, the profits of overexploitation are high for entrepreneurs and poorly paid state functionaries make poor policemen. Those who run the illegal logging operations are notorious for their excellent connections with leading members of the ruling party in the capital and are frequently to be found playing the role of the principal bosses (*caciques*) of the ruling Partido Revolucionario Institucional (PRI) within the regions in which they operate, if not openly, then as leading power brokers behind the scenes. At a lower level, many indigenous communities have faced extreme difficulties in combating the despoliation of their own and their neighbors' forests by local-level *caciques* whose political credentials entitle them to protection from above even in apparently hopeless situations of large-scale community mobilization. Should they rid themselves of these oppressors, they then discover that the latter were merely the last link in a chain leading to a higher level of the power structure in which capital and politics are still more closely, but less visibly, intermeshed. There has been sustained mobilization on the part of indigenous communities to defend their forest resources in recent years. In 1991 in the community of Atapan, near Los Reyes, Michoacán, judicial police acting for private interests physically assaulted indigenous women attempting to block the exit of trucks carrying contraband timber. Yet many people are fighting to defend their rights to a livelihood, not nature itself. As in the case of cultivation of marijuana, the poor can scarcely be expected to do anything other than seek the maximum income available within the limited series of opportunities available, and as all green intellectuals must concede, it is much easier to concern oneself with the long-term when the present is relatively comfortable and secure.

From the Local to the Global

Environmental issues and the goal of "sustainable development" are clearly central to the development debate today but I do not believe that they can or should be the starting point either for analysis of the development process or for its critique. It is not simply a matter of debating what is determinant and what a dependent variable—self-evidently a meaningless exercise given that changes to resource bases and the physical environment participate dialectically in concrete processes of social transformation—but of identifying all the human issues involved in current developments. If the forests are suffering, so are the people, but not simply in terms of the obvious material economic indicators. In the case of the indigenous communities of Michoacán, for example, beyond the violence of the *caciques* and the intra-communal violence and alcoholism of the *pueblos* lies an even greater systemic social violence, a poverty imposed by a class system which has a specific "ethnic" dimension premised on notions of racial distinction. As I argue in more depth in Chapter Seven, this system is now transnational rather than local, and the "ethnicization" of class is not so much a "legacy of history" as an ongoing trend in late capitalist civilization in both "core" and "periphery."

Despite up-beat pronouncements on future prospects for growth in a more liberalized world economy in the Nineties, the economic and environmental trends of the 1980s raise obvious questions about the sustainability of the emergent global order. The way that order is structured as a global order seems to compound the problems. At the end of the 1980s, what had previously seemed, at least in ideological terms, to be a bipolar order based on the rivalry of two total systems of civilization, the capitalist and socialist, collapsed into an apparently unitary system. Despite continuing ideological resistance to "Western hegemony" from some quarters, the socio-economic paradigm seems increasingly uniform, with such diverse cases as Iran and China yielding little to the West in their pursuit of market-orientated, technocratically managed development. For some, this represents the end of history and the consummation of the Triumph of the West. Yet it is difficult to be triumphalist about a civilizational system in which large segments of the population not only remain excluded from full enjoyment of the Good Society but may, indeed, face deepening immiseration. This is not simply a problem of the underdeveloped "periphery" in the late 20th century, since ever larger numbers of people from "peripheral" regions are relocated within the core as members of an ever-expanding class of workers who are desired as labor power but rejected as persons (Kearney, 1991: 58). Some of the current political disorder of the "New World Order" might be regarded as an inevitable consequence of the collapse of empires, but national states are now locked in conflict with forces which threaten their survival in many parts of the world, whilst dominant "majorities" are becoming increasingly intolerant in both the North and the South. Growing social polarization is a serious enough problem in itself, but it takes on a new dimension when the more fortunate demonize the poor and explain their poverty in terms of "race."

In the chapters which follow, I look through the lens of the small fragments of social reality I can observe as an anthropologist at some of the cracks in the world order of late capitalist civilization. I explore the increasingly problematic nature of sociality within local rural communities swept up in the restructuring of the Mexican economy and questions of social identity and solidarity within the "transnational communities" formed by international migration. I emphasize the way these changes are resonances of a larger conjuncture of crisis in the New World Order. It will become apparent that I might have started that argument in a different place, not in Michoacán but in Los Angeles, and not with the crisis of the periphery, but with the crisis of the center into which the Michoacán periphery was imploding at an accelerating rate by the end of the 1980s. Ultimately the analysis I offer will steer us away from talk of centers and peripheries altogether, towards a bleaker language of global crisis and restructuring. My focus on the qualitative social and political implications of recent developments will suggest the need to work with different measures of "success" and "failure" than those enshrined in conventional macro-economic indicators of economic performance.

This is not, however, to suggest that economists are necessarily blind to the need to consider the social costs of different development strategies or to ignore the considerable amount of debate which exists even within institutions such as the World Bank on how to ensure that future growth improves general social welfare. In the case of Mexico, it is perhaps particularly important to begin with the debate about the economy. For some, everything that has happened under the auspices of neoliberalism presages greater social polarization and a definitive abandonment of the progressive programs enshrined in the ideology of the Mexican revolution. For others, particularly foreign commentators, economic change will itself prove "progressive" in the long-term, whatever its short-term social costs, because it will eventually prove the catalyst for political change in the direction of real democratization. Those within Mexico who see the NAFTA as the way forward for the country tend, of course, to be those who argue that democratization is already underway, but the most striking characteristic of their rhetoric has been its vagueness on the mechanisms which will translate economic openness into improved social welfare for the mass of the population.

As far as agriculture is concerned, it seems possible to identify two basic schools of technocratic thought which argue that the capitalist future is bright, both of them somewhat simplistic. One is that agriculture is not important to Mexico's future at all, and that the NAFTA will open the way towards a more dynamic industrial and service-based economy which will be able to absorb any surplus labor released from the agricultural sector. The other is that the amendment of Constitutional Article 27, which regulates Mexico's three basic forms of land tenure—rights in land reform communities (*ejidos)*, communal land and private property (*pequeña propiedad*)—will produce a beneficial restructuring of the Mexican rural economy as inefficient peasant subsistence farmers are replaced by dynamic commercial farmers who can make better use of what agricultural resources the country has to offer. The NAFTA will therefore promote agricultural growth as well as growth in other sectors, even if the major benefits lie in the growth of export markets for specific crops in which Mexico possesses a comparative advantage. Such thinking reveals little grasp of what rural Mexico was really like prior to 1991—the complexity of its agrarian structures and the equally complex synergies which exist between marginal rural zones and agricultural and agroindustrial centers, not to mention the damage done even to capitalist agriculture by the policies of the Eighties.

It also bespeaks scant reflection on the implications of an immediate reinforcement of American power over the Mexican food system and rural employment, let alone the longer-term implications of a biotechnological revolution. The latter may not simply strengthen the global power of transnational agrichemical and biotech corporations but even imply a progressive loss of markets and rural employment for developing countries, as agriculture is relegated to production of biotechnology feedstocks—much of which will be concentrated in metropolitan countries—and factory-made substitutes displace field crops (Goodman et al, 1987; Kennedy, 1993: 79–80). In principle, Mexico ought to rank as one of the Newly Industrialized Countries best able to develop its own biotechnology industry and research and development programs. It may well prove that only countries which do this will reap any net benefit from developments in a field where, despite relatively low start-up costs, northern corporate capital has striven to keep new discoveries in the private domain by in-house research and by patenting and licensing results of university research (Buttel, 1990: 165–6). A great danger of present neoliberal policies of privatization and economic integration with the North is, however, precisely that they undermine the country's capacity to make strategic moves of this kind.

Agricultural Crisis, 1982–1990

Mexicans experience "crisis" in two distinct ways, as concrete problems of daily living and as a culturally and politically constructed discourse about the experience of "development" and "modernization" (Gledhill, 1993). In both senses, crisis has been a regular feature of the life of the Mexican masses for many decades, but whereas the discourse of crisis has ebbed and flowed, the concrete experience of crisis has been a more permanent and oppressive condition for substantial numbers of people through the entire period from the early days of post-revolutionary social transformation to the present.

In the case of rural Mexico, José Luis Calva has argued that the period from 1982 to the end of the decade represented a period of profound and deepening crisis, reversing the brief period of relative recovery from the decade of agricultural recession provoked by the policy of *desarrollo estabilizadador* achieved in the period 1977–81 (Calva, 1991a: 41–2). The absolute volume of national production of basic grains for human consumption fell by over 20% between 1981 and 1988, by which time the per capita harvest had declined to two thirds of its level at the start of the decade. Gross public fixed investment in agriculture declined 68.2% between 1982 and 1986. By 1988 its real level was actually lower than prior to the oil boom. This prejudiced not only levels of new investment in infrastructure but the maintenance of that already in existence: the area under irrigation fell by 22% between 1981 and 1988, widening the gap between the 10 million hectares of land potentially irrigable and those actually irrigated once again to more than 50%. The real value of agricultural credits offered by the national development banks and the commercial sector also declined to levels below those of the early 1970s. At the same time, the once subsidized or even negative real interest rates charged by the state development banks had risen to what Calva describes as "usurious real levels" by April 1989, when cultivators of basic grains were paying 32.4% and cultivators of other crops 35.9%, with nominal rates of 4.2–4.5% three times that of the monthly rate of inflation (Calva, 1991b: 6).

By the end of 1988, 750,000 cultivators of basic grains were unable to cover the costs of their credit from the proceeds of their harvests because of the "cost-price" squeeze imposed on the farmers from 1982 onwards. The real guaranteed price of maize (deflated by the *Índice Nacional de Precios de las Materias Primas de la Actividad Agrícola*, a measure of all agricultural input prices) fell 43.7% in the period 1982–1988, and that of beans by more than 50%. At the same time, input subsidies were reduced, those for fertilizer falling from a total of 9,756 million pesos in 1982 to 7,069 million in 1988, and those for irrigation water from 4,581 million to 1,308 million, measured at 1980 price levels (Escalante, 1993). Producers therefore faced a serious deterioration in the relationship between the real prices of agricultural outputs and the real prices of inputs. Small producers were hardest hit, since operating credit not merely became increasingly expensive but also in increasingly scarce supply as far as they were concerned, but all producers were affected by the cost-price squeeze.

A similar collapse occurred in per capita production of forage crops and fresh milk, and the figures for pork and beef production per capita were even more adverse: the level for the former in 1988 was 46.7% lower than the 1981 figure (Calva, 1991b: 4). Falling domestic production was accompanied by unprecedented levels of importation. The 3,058 million dollars spent on food imports in 1988 represented more than half the sum earned by Mexico's petroleum exports in that year, and more than twice the savings in interest payments on the international debt achieved under the Brady Plan in the following year (Calva, 1991b: 3). The country continued to export other agricultural products, offsetting some of this hemorrhage of foreign exchange, but by 1990 the deficit in the trade balance with the exterior in agricultural, pastoral and agroindustrial products had reached $1,530 million (Alcocer, 1991: 38). Mexico became a net importer of products such as sugar which had previously figured prominently in the list of the country's exports to the world market.

The deterioration in the agricultural trade balance was aggravated by the removal of protection for domestic producers. Mexican farmers who had crops to sell in 1990 found their prices deflated by the flooding of the markets with cheaper imports. In many cases, the crops being imported had been released from U.S. reserves, so that Mexican producers who were being asked to absorb increasing local costs of production were trying to compete with an imported product priced at a level appropriate to U.S. production costs four years earlier.

In the case of sorghum, the 1989 market price on the western side of the Ciénega de Chapala region of Michoacán had been 350,000 pesos a ton (equivalent to the national average rural price), but this fell to a new low of 280,000 pesos in November of the following year, and never recovered its level of the previous year, since regional *acaparadores* refused to honor the "precio de concertación" of 414,000 pesos per ton supposedly established by agreement between the government, the National Peasant Confederation (CNC) and the private sector buyers after this crop had been removed from the system of guaranteed prices.[5] Even at the rather better market prices achieved in the region of La Piedad, 360,000 pesos per ton, a producer with 3.5 hectares who achieved a harvest of 6 tons per hectare in 1990 still had to cope with a 100% increase in production costs relative to 1989, and could expect to receive a net income little higher than the minimum wage for his six months of labor. Even this miserable situation was, however, idyllic in comparison with that faced by farmers who sowed sorghum in the Ciénega de Chapala in 1990. They earned even less per ton on average yields of between 3 and 3.5 tons per hectare.[6] Though it is undeniable that U.S. sorghum farmers, on average, have a productivity advantage over the average Mexican producer, the difference is slight, at 10%, and the irrigation districts of Michoacán figure in the

---

[5] CONASUPO had ceased intervention in the sorghum market in this part of Mexico at the beginning of the De la Madrid administration. In practice, the guarantee price had long been a dead letter. When farmers asked the private merchants for the "precio de concertación," they were told to "go and ask the government to buy their grain." There may be longer-term lessons to be learned from this experience. Dependence on "precios de concertación" as a means of creating and stabilizing regional markets for agricultural products remained a cornerstone of the new policies for farm support announced in 1993.

[6] The majority of the peasant producers of the western Ciénega in fact fared considerably worse than these averages would suggest in 1990, since most failed to achieve even 1 ton per hectare.

ranks of the most productive zones nationally (Martínez Fernández, 1990: 939). More significant is the fact that between 1982 and 1989 U.S. producers of sorghum were receiving subsidies to the tune of 32% of their total income, whilst sorghum imports were unrestricted and subject to a zero rate of import duty in 1989 and 1990 (Alcocer, op.cit.: 38).

Producers of rice in Veracruz and Colima experienced similar difficulties with cheap U.S. imports, again a reflection of a higher rate of subsidy on the American side, which the SARH estimated at $85 per metric ton. The recently privatized sugar mills of Los Reyes, Michoacán, found themselves equally uncompetitive against imports despite extracting a record quantity of sugar from their cane in the 1990–91 *zafra* (Powell, 1994). In the spring of 1991, milk producers throughout western Mexico were repeating the complaints of the arable farmers in the face of declining prices and demand for their product on the part of a national dairy industry increasingly meeting its needs from powdered milk imports. Roads were blocked to traffic and milk poured onto the highway. The official response was that imports had been increased to cope with an expected shortfall in domestic supply, and that the situation would be "normalized," though no promises were made on future prices and small producers were left with the problem of feeding cows whose milk could not, at present, be sold outside the village market.

Government liberality towards imports wiped out much of the benefit which might have accrued to the nation from the fact that 1990 was a year of good rainfall nationally, a factor which reversed the tendency of the previous two years towards an overall contraction of the gross agricultural product in physical terms (Alcocer, op.cit.). Table 1.1 illustrates the relationship between falling levels of production and falling real average guaranteed prices which was the general pattern nationally in the second half of the 1980s. In this case the real values of the guaranteed prices are calculated using the consumer price index (*Índice Nacional de Precios al Consumidor*) as the deflator, a measure more appropriate to peasant farmers, whose income from farming is primarily orientated towards consumption and for whom the rural-urban terms of trade are of crucial significance.

The process of agricultural recession the table depicts was not, however, simply another phase of crisis for the peasant producer, since the profitability of private capital was also diminished, a process reflected in falling sales of tractors and fertilizers (Calva, 1991b: 9–10). Nevertheless, whilst all types of agricultural enterprise were prejudiced by increasing production costs and deteriorating rural-urban terms of trade, the position of peasant farmers who failed to secure an income sufficient to cover their debts to credit institutions was qualitatively distinct given the neoliberal state's eagerness to shift credit policy to more "commercial" principles of operation.

The 1990 rainy-season (Spring-Summer) cycle coincided with the ending of the system of agricultural insurance previously administered by the parastatal ANAGSA. Its successor, AGROASEMEX, did not carry out its functions in a manner which could have liberated peasants who had secured poor harvests from

TABLE 1.1 Levels of Production of Selected Crops in Relation to Real Guaranteed Prices, 1985–1989

Crop	Year	Real Guaranteed Price	Production (1000 tons)
Maize	1985	3,026	14,104
	1986	2,870	11,722
	1987	2,280	11,607
	1988	2,332	10,607
	1989	2,272	10,509
Beans	1985	7,500	912
	1986	7,380	1,085
	1987	6,330	1,024
	1988	4,952	878
	1989	6,638	629
Rice	1985	3,363	808
	1986	3,289	545
	1987	3,330	591
	1988	2,560	415
	1989	2,655	534
Wheat	1985	2,407	5,214
	1986	2,400	4,770
	1987	1,737	4,415
	1988	2,096	3,658
	1989	2,231	4,379
Sorghum	1985	1,897	6,596
	1986	2,014	4,882
	1987	1,969	6,298
	1988	1,961	5,691
	1989	1,977	4,977
Safflower	1985	3,938	140
	1986	3,796	163
	1987	3,258	170
	1988	3,516	243
	1989	3,841	135
Cotton	1985	2,504	311
	1986	2,172	228
	1987	3,185	339
	1988	2,907	470
	1989	2,429	268

Source: Solis Rosales, 1990: 930–931, 932, Tables 1 and 2

the burden of debts they were patently incapable of repaying. There were press reports of complaints against the way AGROASEMEX operated from many regions, and the CNC announced that it would legal action against the enterprise on grounds of fraud in the case of the State of Mexico potato growers. I can, however, speak to the case of the Ciénega de Chapala on the basis of direct observation. The *ejidatarios* were asked to sign a paper agreeing that their premiums should be paid by BANRURAL to ANAGSA's successor while the issue of the new arrangements was still unresolved. Signing the agreement committed the *ejidatario* to the new principle that BANRURAL would be paid in full and compensation would be sought subsequently from the insurers, though this was not clearly explained by the bank officials at the time. The information that AGROASEMEX would only cover 75% of any loss was also not provided to its clients until a much later stage. No *ejidatario* received a written contract explaining the terms of the cover they now enjoyed.

In practice, AGROASEMEX's operation consisted in the arrival of one young and inexperienced employee at harvest time to deal with a region covering three *municipios*. His estimates of likely harvests were generally overoptimistic but also varied substantially between individual *parcelas* on grounds which were seldom if ever agronomically self-evident. Those who complained were told that they would have to stop the machine after harvesting the first hectare and arrange for the inspector to remeasure the yield on that basis, something that was practically impossible since he was not available on site and an interruption of the harvest for possibly several days would have increased its cost substantially. Few found it feasible to follow the procedures. This enabled AGROASEMEX to disclaim responsibility. In practice, the *ejidatarios* were told by BANRURAL that they had to repay the sum borrowed in full and were given no information about how to make a claim with the company's office in Morelia, the inspector having long since disappeared. Most took the view that the *seguro* had been a fraud, made no effort to pursue the matter and refused to pay BANRURAL, giving the bank the pretext for declaring the whole region one in which the accumulated debt of the *ejidos* made further lending impossible.[7] BANRURAL proceeded to close seven of its sixteen branches in Michoacán in July 1991, removing credit facilities from the vast majority of the producers of the agricultural regions they had previously served, declaring that its diminishing resources would be concentrated on those who had proved their capacity to repay.

The ideological justification for this policy centered on "ending paternalism" and promoting "responsibility" on the part of farmers who receive credit. The

---

[7] The AGROASEMEX employee told me explicitly that he saw his mission as part of a concerted strategy to lay the ground for a replacement of peasant by capitalist farming. His performance of his job was certainly consistent with this belief, although it was clear from the outset that he would be unable to cope efficiently with the volume of work required.

system managed by ANAGSA was certainly riddled with corruption and encouraged peasants to cooperate in fraudulent transactions from which bureaucrats were the primary beneficiaries (Gledhill, 1991). Yet it is difficult to lay the blame for these defects at the door of peasant farmers. As Gustavo Gordillo, later to become one of the architects of Salinas's rural reforms,[8] argued, the statized system run by BANRURAL functioned in a way which prevented peasants from achieving any self-sustaining process of capital accumulation and decision-making autonomy (Gordillo, 1988). Some peasant communities were able to mount an organized struggle against the kind of tutelage to which the state and its bureaucratic agencies subjected them, but the fact that many more became accomplices in maladministration is a reflection of the way the power infrastructure which the state commanded inhibited and fragmented grassroots activism to improve matters (Gledhill, op.cit.). As a member of the Salinas administration, Gordillo continued to stress that state "paternalism" towards the *ejidos* was pernicious rather than benign (Cornelius, 1992: 4). Yet as he showed in his own analyses of Sonora, the failure of many peasants to defend themselves effectively was largely a consequence of the regime's own strategies for inhibiting peasant empowerment, strategies which Salinas himself exploited with consummate skill throughout the sexennial in engineering consent to his reforms and dividing potentially recalcitrant forces through selective deployment of federal patronage. Peasant views of the problem of their debts to BANRURAL in Michoacán mirrored Marilyn Gates's account of the conviction of a broad spectrum of commercial and subsistence producers in Campeche that:

> *ejidatarios* should not be held in default, either specifically in terms of debts owed to the credit bank for failing to produce in misguided government projects or more generally as scapegoats for the failure of state policies. Rather, *ejidatarios* believe that the government has defaulted on its constitutional contract with the peasantry to deliver social justice in the countryside (Gates, 1993: 7).

The policy shift carried through in the period 1990 to 1991 was a "wager on the strong," a redirection of the remaining public resources targeted at agriculture towards commercial producers, but with the main emphasis on leaving private capital to fill the gap created by the overall reduction in state support for the farm sector. At the same time it was a policy of "economic triage" (Gates, op.cit.: 59), which left peasants unable to continue financing production for the market with few options beyond a retreat into subsistence production ("repeasantization") or

[8] Gordillo was initially Undersecretary of Agriculture and subsequently Undersecretary of Agrarian Reform in the Salinas administration. As a militant of the Left, he was adviser to the Coalition of Collective *Ejidos* of the Yaqui and Mayo Valleys in Sonora. Along with the anthropologist Arturo Warman, he belonged to a populist "pro-peasant" *(campesinista)* faction within the administration, whose position is discussed in more detail in the next chapter.

rental of the land and total dependence on the earnings family members could obtain through local wage labor and migration.

The statistics on the Mexican farming, fisheries and animal husbandry sectors lead us to diagnose the development of a general, sector-wide crisis through the 1980s. Reduction in government support for domestic producers was far more drastic than the policies of "deregulation" pursued in the metropolitan countries—often in a largely rhetorical manner, as evidenced by the mutuality of the recriminations exchanged between European Community and American negotiators through the Uruguay Round of the GATT. Even before Salinas announced his intention to amend Article 27 of the Mexican Constitution in November 1991, and by doing so, raised the specter of still more radical changes in the countryside, critics of his agricultural policy like José Luis Calva were predicting a massive flight of population from rural areas as more peasant farmers fell victim to the "cost-price squeeze" imposed by withdrawal of subsidies and liberalization of imports (Calva, 1991a).

From Economy to Politics and Society and Back Again

In the chapter that follows, I measure the prognostications of Salinas's critics against reality with a more detailed survey of the twists and turns of agricultural policy and rural "reform" during the sexennial, focusing primarily on economic issues. I argue that both supporters and critics of the regime have tended to base their analyses on an oversimplification of reality. A focus on "economic development" and "economic problems" is, however, too narrow. We should judge the successes and failures of neoliberalism against a broader set of criteria, which include the quality of social life as well as more tangible measures of social welfare like income distribution, literacy and health.

In Chapter Three I tackle the issue of the politics of *Salinismo*, using evidence primarily but not exclusively from Michoacán. I explore the question of whether the neoliberal economic project was pushed through simply by revamping "traditional" means of political control and also provide an analysis of the political opposition's failure to deal with Salinas's offensive. I suggest, however, that close scrutiny of the facts takes something of the shine off the triumphalist image the regime projected before 1994. The second objective of this chapter is to explore the deeper roots of the ebb and flow of popular mobilization in the countryside and the bases of hegemony in a regional society. I offer a comparative analysis of different zones of Michoacán to illustrate the social heterogeneity within this regional space and how politics is influenced by differing local cultures of class. In more general terms, I consider how political practices reflect the way a past "transition to modernity" in Mexico brought only the formal adoption of liberal principles of governance and equality under the law, and also review the contributions of violence to the country's much vaunted political stability.

This discussion provides the framework for Chapter Four, where I begin to examine what appears to be an individualistic response to crisis which could be seen as an alternative to collective political resistance to neoliberalism: international migration. I suggest that a more nuanced distinction is appropriate, since migration is a socially organized process which also has profound social consequences. I argue that the best framework for tackling the broader issues raised by the study of international migration is to focus on the different ways in which contemporary class relations have become transnational. I also examine explanations for differences in patterns of international migration between communities and regions in Michoacán and the relationships between migration processes and social differentiation. Consideration of the way peasants are involved in transnational processes offers further grounds for rejecting the notion that the Michoacán countryside has yet to experience "modernization."

In Chapter Five, I offer a detailed analysis of recent patterns of international migration from two case-study communities, selected not for their "typicality" but because they enable me to make some general points about long-term trends which I relate to a broader literature in the two chapters which follow. This chapter pays particular attention to the impact of the Immigration Reform and Control Act and raises further issues about the precise sense in which U.S. policy seeks to "regulate" migration.

Chapter Six discusses the relationship between international migration and social change, with particular reference to gender issues and questions of identity. Its message, like that of much of the rest the study, is that trends are not simple or unilinear, and that this is a reflection both of differing local conditions and of the existence of different kinds of articulations between parts of Mexican society and parts of U.S. society. Although it makes sense to talk of international migration as a process which creates "transnational communities," we need to continue to use the plural: the impact of the transnationalization of social relations on social life within Mexico is not uniform. In interpreting this material, I also emphasize the need to recognize that the power relations involved in gender and constructions of the person and sexuality have a degree of autonomy.

Chapter Seven addresses the question of the position of Mexicans within the United States and explores the historical foundations and contemporary determinants of the culture of Anglo power. The brush-strokes are inevitably broad, but my aim is to relate Mexico's crisis and restructuring to America's crisis and restructuring, and Latin American neoliberalism to U.S. neoconservatism. Just as I emphasized the need to consider the politics of development in Mexico, I explore the politics of the crisis of the inner city and stigmatization of the "underclass" in the North, drawing out homologies between American policy towards the Third World and domestic society. At the same time, I show how the victims of these processes may be drawn to interiorize elements of the hegemonic discourse in a way which divides the subaltern classes and reinforces the symptoms of social crisis. I also draw here upon work which emphasizes the continuing significance of movement between rural areas of Mexico and the farm sector in the United States. Rural poverty in Mexico is articulated to what is a growing problem of (Mexican) rural poverty in the United States, which is influenced by very much the same political factors and social processes as the problem of inner city poverty in the North, although immigration policy has also had a specific impact. My analysis highlights the way in which national units remain important in a globalized political economy, since it is the political construction of the American nation which underlies the continuing rejection of Mexicans as "persons" by Anglo society. I end, however, with some discussion of whether the transnational character of contemporary class relationships may enhance prospects for the collective empowerment of Mexican migrants and whether there are alternatives to the ethnic wars of California.

The discussion offered in the book as a whole suggests the need to understand what is happening in Mexico as both a specific process (related to the peculiarities of Mexican history and the country's specific geographical relationship to the United States) and as an aspect of a global process. In the concluding chapter I review the specific consequences of neoliberalism and transnationalization for Mexican rural society and emphasize the continuing value of a class perspective on these processes. I argue that the Mexican Center-Left now faces an uphill struggle against the regime's "politics of exclusion" and needs to address the immediate problems of working people more directly and seize the opportunities available for building alliances across national boundaries if it is to break the hegemony of the Right. Although I try to avoid taking the position that everything being done by neoliberal governments is to be deplored, I argue against optimistic assessments of the prospects for a diminution of social inequality and strengthening of democracy under their auspices. Such pessimism can, I think, have positive consequences if it focuses our attention on the issues which are vital to securing an alternative future.

2

On Audacity and Social Polarization: An Assessment of Rural Policy Under Salinas

Many commentators have seen the modification of Constitutional Article 27 as a watershed in the history of post-revolutionary Mexico. Wayne Cornelius judged *ejido* reform "probably the most politically audacious step to be taken by Carlos Salinas during his presidency thus far," given the *ejido*'s role in maintaining the regime's control over the peasantry (Cornelius, 1992: 3). He went on to suggest that the constitutional amendments "passed with only the feeblest of dissents," not simply because the political opposition was weak but because there was "widespread recognition, even among the most fervent defenders of the *ejido*, that something had to be done to modernize and stimulate this sector of Mexican agriculture" (ibid.).

Given the regime's adeptness at engineering consent from the leaders of peasant organizations, such a conclusion might seem premature *a priori*, and doubly so in the wake of the Chiapas uprising. Nevertheless, the heterogeneity of Mexican rural society guarantees diversity in the way that *ejidatarios* view the implications of the reform and respond to it. As Zendejas and Mummert (1994) observe, in some local contexts the *ejido* is much more than an economic institution, and may have a social and political value to people who are not themselves *ejidatarios*. There are certainly areas where commercially successful elements within *ejidos* are already pushing for full land privatization. Yet even where something approaching the neoliberal ideal of how *ejido* reform should be conducted in areas of high commercial potential enjoys politically effective local backing, responses will still be influenced by the wider effects of economic policy and the expectations they engender.

As Cornelius rightly argues, there are a number of good structural reasons why a massive sell-up of peasant land is not likely to occur in the near future, ranging from the fact that the new legislation largely gives *de jure* legitimacy to *de facto* practices on tenure and alienation to the limited interest of modern agribusiness in land ownership as such (op.cit.: 7). Yet the other side of the new agrarian law, the removal of the legal basis for most petitions for new land redistribution and extension of new guarantees to owners who convert pasture land to arable, has deeper implications than Cornelius acknowledges: it impedes struggles by the rural poor to wrest subsistence resources from existing latifundists and expansionary cattle ranchers, undermining the viability of semi-proletarian modes of life. How ordinary peasants view the matter is important. As a symbol, the reform of Article 27 is one of a series of developments fostering negative expectations about the future.

Pace Octavio Paz (1994), the uprising in Chiapas was not a fading and anachronistic trace of the "great shipwreck of the revolutionary ideologies of the 19th Century." It demonstrated the consistency between longstanding popular projects and the new politics of identity of the postmodern world, and was also a specific consequence of the exclusionary tactics of neoliberal politics (Collier, 1994). Chiapas is admittedly an extreme case in terms of the entanglement of dominant class economic projects with oppression premised on racist ideologies (Rus, 1983). Peasant visions of "alternative modernities" and willingness to die for them will again vary from region to region. Yet at the more mundane level of individual strategies, the changing pattern of international migration from both rural and urban areas of Mexico in the Eighties reflected a sea-change in perceptions of life chances within the country. During the crisis, the geographical and social composition of international migration became more heterogeneous (Cornelius, 1990). Migrants from the established rural sending regions, including Michoacán, were joined by relatively uneducated people from metropolitan cities and people from more marginal rural areas who would previously have moved internally, including young male and female migrants from indigenous communities with little past tradition of international movement. This produced a situation in which it became possible to talk about the transnationalization of the opportunity structure of the Mexican "popular sector" as a whole (Escobar, 1993: 75–77).

It also makes little sense to talk about "modernizing the *ejido*" in abstraction from the international political economy of food production, particularly in the case of Mexico, which has long been integrated into transnational systems of production *and* social reproduction. From this point of view, the *ejidos* as they exist today are already "modernized." Indeed, as I will show in Chapters Four and Seven, they have played an important role in the evolution of transnational class relations which link rural poverty in Mexico to rural and urban poverty in the United States. In this chapter, I will restrict myself to one basic issue: the way that the Salinas regime's apparent "audacity" on the question of *ejido* reform was accompanied by a less decisive approach to agricultural policy as a whole. The rest of the analysis of the book will demonstrate its inadequacy as a response to the social and economic problems posed by a continuously evolving transnational political economy of food production.

Campesinistas and Technocrats

Cornelius accepts that the *ejido* reform itself is not without contradictions. He ascribes this to divisions within the regime between the "campesinista" faction, led by Gustavo Gordillo and Arturo Warman, and "modernizing technocrats." As I noted in the previous chapter, for the former, state tutelage over the *ejidos* was a dead hand which inhibited potential capital accumulation by sections of the land reform peasantry capable of producing commercial surpluses. Wedded to neoliberalism, this diagnosis invites us to make a leap of faith: that peasants can reorganize themselves as effective market agents within a system which is dominated economically by transnational corporations and remains subject to politically reinforced structures of private economic power domestically. In practice, the model only appears plausible with continuing indirect state intervention to regulate markets and control the use of non-economic power for economic ends.

The *campesinista* perspective does, however, embody an important truth which distinguishes it from the technocrat position. Producers sowing marginal land which is of no interest to capitalist farmers have been able to supplement family income deriving principally from off-farm activities, wage employment and migration. Nothing would be gained from eliminating such "marginal" production. The labor expended on it and resources used by it have no competing uses in the short- and medium-term. It makes low rural wages sustainable and restrains permanent out-migration.

The technocratic viewpoint focuses on the fiscal costs of producer subsidies and the need to make Mexican agriculture more competitive internationally. Salinas proclaimed early in the sexennial that food policy would be qualified by the principle of comparative advantage, stating that:

> La política alimentaria del país tiene como objetivo fundamental alcanzar la *soberanía alimentaria*, entendida ésta como *el aprovechamiento eficiente de las ventajas comparativas* con que cuenta el país para la producción agropecuaria y forestal (*Ley Federal de Reforma Agraria*, 1991: 741–43, emphasis added).[1]

It was the potential implications of this proposition which stimulated José Luis Calva's apocalyptic predictions of a massive flight of population from rural areas as peasant farmers faced an insuperable "cost-price squeeze" following withdrawal of subsidies and liberalization of imports.

Looking at the aggregate figures for the disparity between U.S. and Mexican average productivity figures for maize (4.35:1), many other commentators concluded that this meant that Mexico would deepen its food dependency on imports.

---

1 This statement originally formed part of the decree approving the *Programa Nacional de Modernización del Campo 1990–1994*, published in the *Diario Oficial* on January 14th, 1991, and was added to the Agrarian Reform Law as an appendix.

According to the figures supplied by the SARH in the NAFTA negotiations, less than 8% of Mexico's corn farmers were competitive at international prices in 1990, and only 35% were growing maize at a profit with the existing domestic price. The issue of food dependence was central to the debates about Mexican agriculture long before Salinas became president (Barkin and Suárez, 1985), but Salinas's approach provoked renewed debate around the long-term economic and political dangers of abandoning real "food sovereignty" (Barraclough, 1992). Many technocrats have argued that Mexico should meet its maize needs from imports, concentrating agricultural development efforts on fruit and vegetables for export. Even Cornelius, a commentator who was much more sympathetic to the Salinas regime than Calva, suggested that this prescription only made sense if the "safety-valves" of migration to the United States and urban informal sector in Mexico remained open (Cornelius, 1992 : 5–6).

At first sight, some of the fears expressed in the first half of Salinas's sexennial appear exaggerated. Escalating dependence on basic food imports was reversed in 1991 and 1992. The following year the regime announced a new system of direct producer subsidies (PROCAMPO) which would include marginal corn farmers. Nevertheless, if we look more closely at underlying trends in the rural sector, the picture remains disturbing, although it is important to be more precise about what those trends in production, profitability and migration actually are. There has been some further abandonment of the countryside, but not on the lines suggested by either Calva or Cornelius. The 1970s witnessed a substantial growth of medium and smaller sized cities, reducing the predominance of the three metropolitan cities (México, Guadalajara and Monterrey), and the three bigger cities of second rank (Puebla, León and Ciudad Juárez), in the overall pattern of urbanization in relative terms (Verduzco, 1989: 20). During the 1980s, migration to the United States increased, but it was the medium-sized cities of the Center, West, and northern border which became the foci of internal movements (Escobar, op.cit.: 74). We must ask what kind of infrastructure and job opportunities smaller urban centers will be able to provide in the Nineties, particularly if the NAFTA increases economic polarization between the North and Center-South. Rural towns which remain dependent on the prosperity of an agricultural hinterland have been devastated by agricultural recession combined with the collapse of public sector salaries and employment.[2]

What happened over the Salinas sexennial suggested the absence of any coherent strategy for "agricultural modernization." Mexican agriculture was not perceived as a core sector in the technocratic project of export-led development and economic

---

2 It is important to recognize the special salience of what happened to the public sector in many provincial areas, since public employment was the main basis for social mobility and the consolidation of a middle class able to consume services. Many lower middle class public sector professionals in Michoacán turned to small business, but suffered heavily when recession hit again in 1993.

integration with the United States. Nor was it central for the Mexican transnational capitalist interests with most to gain from NAFTA. The reason that policy appeared improvised, was not, however, so much a reflection of factional conflicts within the regime as a consequence of strong objective constraints, both political and economic.

From Structural Adjustment to Procampo

Although the agricultural situation which Salinas confronted on entering office was dismal, the situation was alleviated to some extent by developments in 1990–1992. In those years, agriculture did sustain some positive growth. National production of six of the ten principle crops, including wheat, rice and soya, continued to decline, but maize and beans production improved quite significantly, enabling the country to cut back its imports of these basic staples to quite insignificant levels in 1991 and 1992 (Escalante, op.cit.).[3] This turnaround reflected the impact of a deliberate government policy to preserve a guaranteed price for maize and beans, whilst prices of other crops were allowed to fall to international levels. Although the maize and beans prices set in 1990 were not modified in the ensuing years, they remained at a level double international prices. This fostered a process of crop substitution. Nationally, some 1.6 million hectares were switched to maize from other crops, and this shift included a substantial amount of movement out of wheat and forage crops by the most heavily capitalized irrigated commercial farms in Northern Mexico. Fruit and vegetable production also increased, and private sector investment did compensate for some of the reduction in state funding. This "success" was, however, deceptive.

In December 1992, I sat in the office of the SARH in Sahuayo interviewing the director, accompanied by an *ejidatario* friend who came from the same village and had known the official since childhood. After delivering a brief discourse on the end of paternalism and the need for *campesinos* to pay attention to prices in the futures markets,[4] the director turned to my companion and urged him to sow maize and beans, since these were obviously the best bet commercially. Since he, along with two of his neighbors in the *ejido*, had rented half his own land to a commercial grower for a planting of beans in the previous cycle, and was now surrounded by maize fields sown by a group of commercial renters from Zamora, the point was

---

[3] Sorghum cultivation nationally recovered in 1992 after a large fall in production in 1991.

[4] In fairness, I should point out that the SARH does offer information on national and international prices for different crops to anyone who wishes to consult them, though the usefulness of this information to most peasants in this region is limited by the fact that they depend on intermediaries for commercialization, assuming, of course, that they can produce any surplus for the market in the first place.

not lost on him, though it was hardly of much relevance, since his only source of finance for cultivation was remissions from a migrant son in the United States.

The raw data for the irrigation district provided to me by the SARH for the spring-summer cycle of 1991 showed that maize was the most significant irrigated crop in all but one of the *municipios* within the district. Maize and beans combined occupied 50% of the irrigated area, compared with the 28% sown in sorghum, a change relative to the situation a decade earlier, when sorghum was the predominant crop. Some of the maize sown represented peasant production, and some of it represented a peasant sowing only a fraction of the parcela to meet family subsistence needs, the rest remaining unsown or being rented to a third party. The overall picture in 1991 and 1992 confirmed, however, that the increase in national production of maize and beans in these years came principally from commercial producers.

Crop substitution by the commercial sector in response to relative price changes reflects the experience of López-Portillo's *Sistema Alimentario Mexicano*, which sought to use price incentives to promote food self-sufficiency. Production of maize, in particular the high yield varieties, carries higher money costs and risks than heavily mechanized crops like sorghum, in regions like the Ciénega de Chapala where peasant cultivation of the latter is viable. Only those poorer peasant households which were in a particularly good position to substitute labor for capital responded to the incentives offered by the SAM (Gledhill, 1991: 311–25). Attempts to foster maize and beans production through market incentives also entail social costs, since poorer rural households tend to be net purchasers of maize. Many households which sell maize they have grown themselves at harvest time also make purchases later in the year. Consumer subsidies in Mexico have been concentrated on the (metropolitan) urban poor, so that using market incentives to foster production of staples actually makes life more difficult for many rural people.

By 1993 it was becoming clear that price support for maize and beans was a transitional measure designed to cushion the impact of liberalization, with the added attraction of providing a short-term rebuttal of the argument that the government favored food dependence on the United States. Its impact on peasant farmers was limited by the difficulties many had financing production. On October 4th 1993, Salinas formally announced a new policy, based on direct cash subsidies to producers, which it was claimed would extend government support to 2.2 million peasant farmers excluded from existing programs, and cost 11,700 million new pesos in the calendar year 1994.

Official literature promoting PROCAMPO belatedly recognized disequilibria in the international grain market arising from the producer subsidies enjoyed by farmers in metropolitan countries. Indeed, it stressed that the scheme would bring the level of state support received by Mexican farmers in line with that enjoyed by farmers in the U.S.A and Canada in terms of percentage of GDP. Equally belated was its recognition that policies based on price support are regressive from the standpoint of low income consumers. At the same time, the regime justified PROCAMPO as an extension of policies designed to remove domestic market distortions by encouraging competitive commercialization and establishing prices reflecting regional comparative advantage. The introduction of direct subsidies to producers was, however, to be accompanied by a progressive reduction in the indirect subsidies provided by the guaranteed price system. PROCAMPO therefore only offered some aid to producers as they weathered the additional long-term negative impact of NAFTA implementation.

Any farmer—title-holder or usufructuary—registered in the agricultural census as a producer of maize, beans, sorghum, wheat, rice, soya or cotton would receive a cheque for 330 new pesos ($103 U.S.) per hectare for the 1993–4 season, to be paid in March 1994 (a provision which was not helpful to the cash-starved). The subsidy would increase gradually until the autumn-winter cycle of 1994/5 and thereafter be maintained at a constant real value until the eleventh year of the program, which would mark the beginning of its progressive elimination over five years. Farmers were not obliged to continue sowing grains, and another claim made for the program was that it would encourage abandonment of grain cultivation on forest land where it caused erosion, promoting an ecologically desirable diversification of rural production.

PROCAMPO is specifically designed to include *campesinos* who produce mainly for subsistence, and represents something of a windfall for farmers in this category. This, the anti-poverty side of PROCAMPO, may be its most significant aspect in political terms. Calculations made by Neil Harvey suggest, however, that the subsidy offered will not compensate small farmers for whom market sales of maize are a significant component of income for the combined negative effects of declining output prices and rising input costs. Nor does it does offer them sufficient financial resources to switch to more profitable crops. Given that 67% of the maize grown by the social sector is marketed even in Chiapas, PROCAMPO's ability to halt rural impoverishment should clearly not be exaggerated (Harvey, 1994: 14–17).

Despite the protestations of Agriculture Secretary Carlos Hank González that PROCAMPO was a logical development of earlier policies, it requires an effort of will to ignore the significance of the 1994 presidential elections for what appeared to be a straightforward attempt to give some income back to a peasantry being marginalized by ongoing neoliberal "reform." Disbursement of PROCAMPO funds was reserved for the SARH, through its network of Centros de Apoyo al Desarrollo Rural (CADER's), although other agencies and state government offices could act as intermediaries in the inscription process. Peasant organizations (including the CNC) were explicitly excluded from playing any role. Nevertheless, past experience, including experience of the political manipulation of PRONASOL funds in rural areas, does not encourage optimism concerning the impartial and transparent administration of the program.

Given the chaotic nature of land registration, opportunities abound for manipulating the system at the inscription stage for a variety of ends, despite the control apparatus established to accompany the program, much of which is also pertinent to the *ejido* reform. Local practice appears to vary on the question of whether the implementation of PROCAMPO should be linked to what is supposedly the voluntary entry of *ejidos* into the program for overhauling and regularizing land tenure, PROCEDE (Programa de Certificación de Derechos Ejidales y Titulación de Solares Urbanos). In practice, however, establishing a linkage seems utopian in the light of the Herculean task facing the PROCEDE bureaucrats. They face the prospect of confronting foot-dragging and delaying tactics by opposition groups even within *ejidos* which enter the program (Pisa, 1994), and thus far seem to have avoided problems by beginning with *ejidos* where potential for conflict seemed minimal (Carlos, Gutiérrez and Real, 1994). Given the size of the existing backlog of unresolved land petitions (*rezago agrario*) in many regions—much of it a legacy of previous strategies of political control over the peasantry as well as a product of peasant struggles against *caciquismo*—and the extreme gaps between juridical theory and actual land tenure practice which have long characterized many *ejidos* which possess resources worth engrossing, this massive new state bureaucratic intervention in agrarian affairs is likely to be deflected into the same pragmatism and accommodation with local power relations which has characterized the entire history of agrarian reform. PROCEDE apart, however, functionaries are in a good position to use allocation of PROCAMPO funds as a means of political manipulation, and wealthier members of the community may well benefit disproportionately.

It is true that PROCAMPO, like PRONASOL, is structured in a way which should reinforce central government control relative to local and regional power holders. Its implementation is, however, likely to reflect the way that centralization is compromised in practice by continuing dilemmas of maintaining political control in rural regions under sustained crisis conditions, and by the way the regime's policies have strengthened a variety of forms of class power, some of them beyond the margin of "legality." I will have more to say about these issues in the next chapter, but for the present wish to stress another feature of PROCAMPO. Cutting out peasant organizations as intermediaries between the state and the *campesinos* places each claimant in the position of confronting the official apparatus as an individual. Those, like Cornelius, who see the role of the *comisario ejidal* as a local power broker able to regulate access to land and resources as one of the principal failings of the old system (Cornelius, 1992: 5), are forgetting that the leverage such agents acquired arose from the fact that they handled the internal distribution of resources to beneficiaries who were deliberately individualized (Martínez Saldaña, 1980; Gledhill, op.cit.: 309–10). PROCAMPO cuts out the middle-man only to restore the dependence of *campesinos* on bureaucratic agents and increases their vulnerability to manipulation, or exclusion, by those controlling local levers of political and economic power.

There are therefore ample reasons for being skeptical about the kinds of claims made for PROCAMPO as a social and environmental policy. Even if the program is implemented according to the letter of its norms, the actual economic effects of putting cash in the hands of rural people are quite unpredictable: the subsidy might, for example, be used to finance migration, which might or might not have a beneficial long-term effect on agricultural production. Yet PROCAMPO did seem to be a policy U-turn, which drew fire from technocrats and free-marketeers as well as from the political Left. Its long-term survival in its present form under the Zedillo administration is not guaranteed, but at the time of writing, speculation about the future is less important than a more rigorous assessment of what caused the regime to embrace it. Politics is part of the answer, but not perhaps the whole of it.

The Crisis Continues

The primary sector contribution to GDP declined throughout 1993. Agriculture remained particularly unattractive to those few foreigners who are willing to invest in production. Domestic investment in the sector was clearly not encouraged by the uncertainty surrounding the NAFTA negotiation and ratification process, and sectoral confidence was not enhanced by the extensive concessions Clinton made to the farm lobby in the course of securing ratification. Then came Chiapas, negotiations with the EZLN, and an apparent weakening of the regime's resolve on agrarian issues, which may well have had wider repercussions on expectations amongst more prosperous domestic commercial farmers. Reactions to rural policy were not, however, restricted to relatively marginalized groups.

In 1993, Guadalajara and the Bajío agricultural cities witnessed another summer of farmer protests, organized by the *El Barzón* movement which crystallized around the mounting discontent of those medium sized commercial producers in the private sector whom free-market policies were supposed to galvanize. The *barzonistas* blockaded highways with their tractors in protest at their inability, under existing policies, to repay the loans which they received from the commercial banks, and reinforced their campaign with occupations of bank offices. Many of them had been PRI loyalists until they found themselves facing ruin and foreclosure, but the movement's militancy increased further after its leaders were subjected to repression following an attempt to mount tractor protests in Mexico City on the day of the *destape* of Luis Donaldo Colosio as the new presidential candidate of the PRI. The *barzonistas* articulated a discourse which countered much of the government's line on "paternalism": embracing the role of enterprising, "responsible" producers, the *barzonistas* argued explicitly that they are not looking for hand-outs, but demanded that the government accept *its* responsibility to provide a level playing field in terms of subsidies, which would enable them to operate under conditions comparable to farmers in other countries. This message of "fair competition" also proved congenial to a broad spectrum of *ejidatarios* in regions like the Ciénega de Chapala. Together with the movement's militant tactics, it promoted a broadening of the movement's initial social base and increased its potential political significance, although many peasant producers remain skeptical about the value of allying themselves with farmers whose class position remains radically different from their own and are intensely fearful about accepting any form of credit which would involve putting up their land or homes as collateral.

The rise of the *barzonistas* not only suggests that the process of "economic triage" was taken too far, but that it produced few tangible benefits, even from a technocratic viewpoint which focuses on the need to increase production and reallocate resources to more profitable uses. As I noted earlier, the improving balance of agricultural trade since 1990 reflects an increase in fruit and vegetable exports as well as a reduction in maize and beans imports. Once again, however, it is necessary to ask what this modest improvement in the aggregate picture actually represented. The Ciénega de Chapala has been an important area for the commercial production of tomatoes, onions, potatoes, cabbage, lettuce and other vegetables, sown on private ranches and on rented *ejido* land. The data I gathered from within the *ejidos* in 1990–91 and 1992 showed significant changes in the structure of production.

Firstly, there had been a shift from production of fruit and vegetables towards maize and beans on the part of many of the smaller-scale commercial growers. Better-off *ejidatarios* who owned machinery and rented the land of others were forced by rising costs and shortage of capital to shift downward in the hierarchy of commercial production and switch from vegetables to grains. Some passed land they rented to outsiders with whom they had commercial relationships.

Secondly, there was a notable diminution of activity by growers who were sub-contracted by the wholesalers in the *mercados de abastos*. No tomatoes were sown at all in the rains of 1993 or 1993–94 winter cycle, depriving the local communities of the wage-incomes generated by labor intensive production. The overall picture from this region is therefore one of a complex pattern of polarization, which is indicative of both a greater concentration of capital in the rural sector and also of the decline of *ejidal* enterprise.

Many *ejidatarios* who were previously producing a commercial surplus have abandoned cultivation altogether, or simply maintained a small amount of subsistence production. This is a reflection of the withdrawal of BANRURAL credit. The decline of peasant cultivation has not, however, thus far been matched by a major inflow of new capitalist renters capable of galvanizing local agriculture. Most of the new renters I have recorded in recent years are essentially speculators.[5] They have some capital and ties to the wholesale food markets or agribusiness of the region. A few others are individuals who have acquired capital from past migration. None are not making big profits and a general air of continuing recession hangs over the whole region.

---

5 I do not use this term in a pejorative sense. It is simply intended to capture the idea that this is a kind of capital which can move in and out of agricultural production according to market conditions and a kind of investor who is unlikely to establish long-term roots in any particular zone.

As an illustration, I will provide some quantitative data on the Emiliano Zapata (Guaracha) *ejido*, which is one of the principle case studies used in this book. The bulk of the land of this agrarian community is irrigable and of interest to commercial producers. In the Spring-Summer cycle of 1992, 5% of the *ejido*'s plots (*parcelas*) were left completely uncultivated, and 37% were rented, more than half of them to people from outside the community. Of the 65 *parcelas* rented by outsiders, 35% were sown in vegetables by three entrepreneurs who specialized in this kind of trade and a fourth individual who was an experienced sub-contractor for a large Guadalajara merchant. Five *parcelas* were sown in irrigated maize by a group of agronomists, former public sector professionals now working on their own account within Zamoran agribusiness. They were associated with a leading *ejidatario* entrepreneur. The larger part of the land rented by outsiders was sown in grains, as well as virtually the whole area rented by people who belonged to the *ejido*. Almost a third of the land rented to outsiders was rented to *ejidatarios* from neighboring communities, with two wealthy individuals who had accumulated capital outside the local region predominating. They too sowed grains.

In the Winter Cycle of 1992–93, 52% of the land of the *ejido* was left fallow, and 40% of the land which was cultivated was sown by renters rather than the beneficiary of the *parcela*, 60% of them outsiders. Only a quarter of the land sown by outsiders was sown in vegetables in this cycle and two of the commercial vegetable growers sowed half the land they rented in wheat on this occasion. The sub-contractor was reduced to sowing chick-peas rather than tomatoes on three of the four *parcelas* he rented. The *ingenieros* from Zamora now controlled eight parcelas: seven of them were sown in wheat, the relative price of which had now improved, and one in irrigated beans.

In comparison with the situation I observed a decade ago in the same *ejido*, today's agricultural panorama is relatively gloomy, and the actors themselves, including the most dynamic commercial actors, do not manifest buoyant expectations. Uncertainty is great and market-led production patterns are unstable. Many of the commercial farmers who have replaced peasant farmers are not particularly dynamic. In 1990–91, I had a number of conversations about the implications of government policy with another "speculator" from Zamora, whom I will call Alfonso. Alfonso rented twelve hectares and sowed irrigated beans, boasting to the peasants who rented their land to him that he would give them an object lesson in how to make the *ejido* produce. He claimed to have had extensive experience in commercial agriculture, though he too had originally been a professional in public service. Yet he failed to pay sufficient attention to the rising curve of input costs in making his calculations, and frequently sought technical advice from the *ejidatarios* working for him. In the end, he produced a very average harvest and lost money. He did not persevere in the *ejido* thereafter, but the Alfonsos of this world can prove more enduring, given a little better luck (and management). They are, however, unlikely to spearhead major leaps forward in productivity relative to the peasant farmers they are displacing.

There was talk in late 1992 of the establishment of new contract-farming systems in the region, following the privatization of an ejidal agroindustrial facility located in the town of Venustiano Carranza, north of Sahuayo, though in the event nothing concrete materialized during the Salinas sexennial. Such vertical concentration in marketing and processing might indeed act as a more powerful agency of both technical modernization and transformation of agrarian class relations. Rumors about the Venustiano Carranza facility did not, however, provoke a negative response in principle on the part of peasant farmers, who saw contract farming simply as a new source of credit and technical support, hopefully free of the corruption of the old statized system. "Capitalist" was applied as an epithet with negative connotations only to some of the speculators, who were seen as merely parasitic beneficiaries of peasant misfortune. This again highlights the importance of subjective factors in mediating the relations between capital and peasant producers. Contract farming seemed to offer the chance for *ejidatarios* to recover their capacity to produce, on the assumption that all landholders could participate and secure what would be judged fair returns to labor by peasant producers, measured in terms of living standards: opinions would clearly change were contract farming to promote strong differentiation and reinforce "economic triage."

The data from western Michoacán suggest that the macro-economic evidence for agricultural recovery, modest as it is, is deceiving because recovery has clearly been stronger in some regions than in others. Furthermore, not only do we need to disaggregate the data to identify the regions which have benefitted most from recent policies, but we also need to identify the specific kinds of social and economic actors who have benefitted from those policies within any given region. Given the continuing rise in input prices, the long-term profitability of agriculture is far from guaranteed. Although private investment has been able to compensate for the reduction in state support for agriculture to some extent, part at least of this new private capital entering agricultural production may prove ephemeral in the absence of a sustained climate of profitability.

It will, of course, take a substantial amount of time for the full consequences of the structural changes introduced during the sexennial to work themselves out, particularly those arising from the Amendment of Article 27 and the PROCEDE process. Even one important part of the first phase of Salinas's program, the decentralization of control over irrigation systems to the users, has yet to be completed. Under the new system, the National Water Commission remains responsible for maintaining the dams and other major water sources, but the users become responsible for maintaining local networks of ditches and drains through which water is carried to their fields, and should ideally pay for the precise amount of water they consume. In practice, however, measuring facilities capable of supporting such a system have yet to be installed in many irrigation districts, and until they are installed, fixed charges by area sown and crop type will have to be maintained. The policy should theoretically encourage conservation, and price increases are justified on those grounds. It was presented by its original promoter,

Gustavo Gordillo, as another strategy for giving producers greater autonomy vis-à-vis the state. Yet the new system will disempower some people: wealthier users have always been able to secure preferential treatment and have often been able to circumvent measures necessary for conservation. Users' committees representing rich and poor consumers are unlikely to function in a very satisfactory manner. In the Ciénega de Chapala, however, officials regarded the target of implementing the new system before the end of the sexennial as unrealistic. The major preoccupation of all producers was simply the escalating cost of irrigation. For the first time in many years, abundant rainfall had left the dams close to full capacity for the winter sowings of 1992–93, but demand proved strikingly modest.

The Death of the Peasantry?

In the light of the problems of implementing reform, the low profitability of much of Mexico's private sector agriculture and the dearth of foreign investment to date, the prospects of renewed growth in the agricultural sector might seem limited. There are, nevertheless, strong arguments against making apocalyptic predictions about the extent to which peasants might be expected to abandon the countryside in the short-term, even if they face still further impoverishment.

Firstly, it can hardly be assumed that peasant farming *as such* was sustaining a majority of rural households in Mexico economically at the start of the Eighties. The impact of abandonment of cultivation on migration patterns in any particular region or community will depend on how cultivation fitted into broader strategies of household economic behavior. It will be increasingly difficult for peasant farmers growing grains on *temporal* (rain-fed) land to produce for the market. The long-standing conflict between *temporal* subsistence farming and commercial cattle-raising will continue in some regions, but many *temporal* farmers occupy land which is of no interest to commercial cultivators. Much *temporal* farming is orientated principally to making up the gap between consumption needs and money income, and may be combined with other forms peasant production, including raising calves for the meat industry and small-scale exploitation of forestry and fishery resources. Marginal peasant cultivation does not correspond to the economic logic of capitalist production, and is likely to be maintained—providing there is no alternative allocation of peasant labor time and resources which would bring a return of higher subjective or monetary value, and that it remains possible to grow food for less money cost than would be involved in purchasing it.[6]

---

[6] Many who combined subsistence farming with agricultural wage-work around the towns of Los Reyes and Santa Clara refused to enter the PRONASOL "créditos a la palabra" program on the grounds that they were uninterested in putting money into what was essentially a subsistence activity, particularly at the cost of compromising themselves politically by accepting the patronage of the PRI.

Secondly, as far as the issue of the relationship between rural immiseration and migration is concerned, a very large number of rural Mexicans are already living in conditions of extreme poverty. When we look in more detail at who these people are, it becomes obvious that a large proportion have past experience of migration—often to cities and of work in sectors such as construction as well as to zones of commercial agriculture—and yet have not emigrated permanently. A more precise argument is needed to justify the case that a new wave of mass expulsions from the countryside is inevitable and that emigration is viable for the people concerned.

A third line of objection to predictions of a mass rural exodus is that some of the processes of crop substitution which are expected to result from present policies should absorb greater quantities of labor as well as capital per hectare, and may thus actually improve the employment prospects of the rural poor. This latter argument may, however, also be simplistic. As I suggested earlier, the much stigmatized low productivity peasant corn-farmer has become a symbol of Mexico's agricultural backwardness, but might be better seen as a precondition for the continuing provision of cheap wage-labor to commercial agriculture and some sectors of the urban economy. Indeed, as I emphasize later, the siting of labor force reproduction within rural Mexico remains of enduring significance for U.S. capitalism as well as for Mexican capitalism (Palerm and Urquiola, 1993).

Peasant production of subsistence staples is of crucial significance for the dynamics of rural wages and migratory behavior between rural areas as well as between the countryside and cities and between countries. What will happen if the market encourages further crop substitution has to be understood in the context of the whole set of synergies underlying regional rural economies (Linck and Santana, eds. 1988). Expanding production of some tradables will entail increasing competition for land and water between different social and economic sectors. In some cases, overall gains in potential rural employment from an expansion of crops which are both capital and labor intensive may disturb the delicate balances between paid work and various marginal rural production activities on which the households supplying the labor depend. As I noted in the last chapter, progress in biotechnological research may also reduce agricultural employment, when *in vitro* production of laboratory substitutes in the North replaces existing export crops produced in tropical zones.

In the case of the Ciénega de Chapala, some *ejidatarios* who produced commercial surpluses in the past are now using the parts of their land they can still afford to sow for subsistence provisioning and striving to "hang in there" while their children migrate. Yet this pattern has the appearance of a temporary coping mechanism, which is unlikely to persist in the long-term because of negative expectations about the quality of rural life in the future. Here, however, we have to recognize that migration possibilities are socially selective to a high degree, as I will demonstrate in greater detail in Chapter Four. In western Mexico, rural communities can be ranked in a hierarchy according to the degree to which they can gain access to U.S. labor markets. Whilst some young people from more marginal communities, in particular indigenous ones, are now participating more in international migration than in the past, this does not prevent others remaining relatively trapped in a kind of "underclass" situation within rural communities or in less remunerative inter-regional and rural-urban migratory circuits.

Talk of an immediate mass exodus from the countryside may therefore be premature. On the one hand, those who do live in the countryside are already involved in various kinds of migration. On the other hand, any processes of emigration will be related to the prospects for non-agricultural employment which emerge outside the region, and also, to some extent, to the quality of life in other places, in particular large cities. In the case of Aguascalientes, urban assembly manufacturing has developed on the basis of drawing on a "commuter" labor-force remaining resident in rural villages around the city. The "industrial corridor" between Guadalajara and La Barca in Jalisco represents an industrial colonization of a largely rural space, and there is an established pattern of extending manufacturing production by domestic outworkers into a number of rural areas of western Mexico and the Bajío (Arías and Durand, 1988; Wilson, 1990). These kinds of cases may not provide a model for any "typical" pattern of future development in Mexico, but they do serve to remind us that a contrast between the "industrial" city and "agricultural" countryside is simplistic under modern conditions.

It remains far from clear, however, whether the restructuring of rural economy which the Salinas government set in train can avoid deepening social polarization and absolute poverty in rural areas. Not only does the principle of "comparative advantage," in the context of globally mobile transnational capital and world market pricing, imply a continuing downward pressure on rural wages, but redistribution of income from labor to (transnational) capital is to date the *general* pattern in the latest round of restructuring of the global capitalist economy. From a global perspective, it is this restructuring which is forcing a rise in household labor market participation rates as more women enter part-time employment, along with the growth of low-wage jobs and insecurity of employment for almost all categories of employees. In Mexico, the *Solidaridad* programs have been presented as the key to cushioning the shocks of adjustment, followed by PROCAMPO. I have already questioned the effectiveness of these programs in social policy terms. Like Dresser (1991), I take a skeptical view of PRONASOL as a "neopopulist solution to neoliberal problems," and the next chapter offers some concrete examples of the ways in which the *Solidaridad* program in Michoacán was implemented in a politically selective manner which conflicted with social welfare objectives.

Anti-poverty measures benefit marginal peasants and semi-proletarians primarily, and therefore subsidize labor reproduction costs, but the crucial question remains whether the Amendment of Article 27 will promote a new concentration of landholding and increase the number of families primarily dependent on wages. The new agrarian law does maintain legal limits on private landholdings, and safeguards designed to prevent individuals acquiring more than 5% of the land of any *ejidos* which opt for full privatization. Past experience demonstrates, however, that legal controls on land tenure practices have never been effective: private *latifundios* of significantly greater size than the legal maximum have been expropriated from time to time since the revolution, but the number of such entities which have survived untouched is vastly greater (as was conceded, albeit as a "special case," during the negotiations between Manuel Camacho Solis and the EZLN in Chiapas). Illegal leasing of *ejido* land to outsiders, and effective land concentration within *ejidos,* have also long been commonplace in many regions.

Conceding such points, the Salinas administration has argued that the new transparency created by the legalization of pre-existing de facto illegalities both protects the interests of the private investor and protects *ejidatarios* from exploitation by private firms (Cornelius, 1992: 5). Whatever skepticism one might feel about these claims, it is true that much *ejido* land is of no interest to commercial farmers, and only likely to be threatened by an expansion of ranching, a situation which existed before the Amendment of Article 27 and was a major source of rural conflict. The significance of the constitutional change here is that it may help to legitimize a more aggressive stance on the part of the *ganaderos* (cattlemen), at the same time as it further disempowers land claimants denouncing illegally large holdings.

A secondly constraint on the rapid transformation of the *ejido* is the fact that the on the ground situation with regard to land tenure is a complete mess as a result of past illegalities. As Cornelius notes, only around ten per cent of *ejidos* are parcellized into properly demarcated parcelas. Even in those cases, the allocation of titles to the land in question may remain subject to dispute. In the 1940s in Michoacán, there were cases where outsiders turned whole *ejidos* into their personal domains by the simple expedient of massacring the beneficiaries. But we are no longer in the 1940s. Whilst violence continues to play a role in the reallocation of farm resources, particularly to marijuana cultivation, and still figures from time-to-time in contemporary disputes over land within parcellized *ejidos*, more complex processes of transformation are to be expected.

In some areas, such as the Oaxaca-Veracruz borderlands, there will be continuing conflict between expanding capitalist interests and organized groups of *campesinos*, around *production* and marketing issues as well as access to land. In other areas, like the Ciénega de Chapala, poorer *ejidatarios* have not been organized effectively (though the influence of the *barzonistas* might change that situation), and have solved their problems as best they could through other strategies, primarily international migration. Yet in this kind of case, commercially exploitable *ejido* land is in the hands of a quite heterogeneous group of social actors. Land acquired a commercial value, even if this was not previously a full free market value because sales lacked legal validity. As commercial rental of land increased, values rose and purchasing a title became beyond the means of persons without capital. After it ceased to be possible for most international migrants to accumulate the funds to buy land, the main purchasers were professionals and other persons with substantial incomes from non-farming activities.

This may make it quite difficult for agrarian communities to reach the required level of consensus on the future disposition of their resources. Individuals who wished to sell their land were able to do so (illicitly) without the reform of Article 27, and did so. Some *ejidatarios* who welcomed the *ejido* reform—in the sense that they welcomed the chance to become full proprietors, like the majority of the cane-growers of the Los Reyes region—remained antagonistic to Salinas's agricultural policies, suspicious of the intentions of private agroindustrial capital and worried about the future open to their landless children. They tended to see retaining the land as a guarantee of minimal security in a threatening world. It may therefore be more useful to ask what kinds of *initiatives* private capital is likely to take which might promote a transformation of the *ejidos* in the short- to medium-term.

What happens to *ejidos* will be influenced by the kinds of economic deals on offer to *ejidatarios*, and the kinds of articulations established between outside agencies and individuals capable of engineering a "community majority." One word for such articulations might be *caciquismo*. Cornelius may be correct to insist that large-scale agribusiness will seldom be interested in buying up land, rather than leasing it and employing the *ejidatarios* as workers. Yet despite the publicity given to an operation of this type in Nuevo León, announced by the Mexican food company Gamesa on the eve of its purchase by Pepsico in 1990, even this has not proved a widespread pattern to date. It seems more likely that large-scale capital in Mexico will concentrate even more than in the past on packing, processing and marketing operations, leaving local growers to organize production, compete for the business offered by the processing firms, and bear the lion's share of the risks associated with market and output fluctuations.

For geographically mobile transnational companies, substantial direct investment, even in processing facilities, carries risks which may still remain unattractive under the new conditions created by the reform of Article 27 and the NAFTA, particularly while continuing agrarian conflict seems likely. The risks of direct investment in production are even greater. It is true that corporate operation has largely superseded owner operation in Californian farming (Palerm, 1991: 79), but it is less likely that foreign corporate capital will be eager to undertake much direct management of production within Mexico. The profitability of processing plants does, however, depend on reliability of supply and quality guarantees. This generally favors the establishment of partnerships between transnationals and regional agribusiness capital, or contract farming systems, although less close relations with producers are needed by more flexible facilities capable of processing a wide variety of fruit and vegetables: this latter type of operation can adapt more easily than a specialized plant to demand and supply fluctuations, and is less dependent on the performance of particular local suppliers.

Large-scale Mexican agribusiness capital is already integrated into transnational marketing systems, but it is notable that it too has tended to depend on local intermediaries or sub-contractors to organize production, because the effective management of land and labor has required skills in management of "face-to-face" relationships at community level and knowledge of the local idioms of class culture.[7] Within a framework of vertically concentrated agro-export expansion, there would certainly be scope for individuals to concentrate landholdings within parcellized *ejidos* if they were working as contract farmers, since this would enable them to overcome some of the production diseconomies of parcellization. Even under the old system, it was possible for individuals to control more than one *parcela* permanently, by assigning titles to minor children or other relatives as well as by renting on long-term contracts. In the case of *ejidos* in which plots were never legally demarcated and assigned, I have come across individuals enjoying undisputed and open control of more than 40 hectares of irrigated land. Nevertheless, a generalized transformation of rural production towards a more purely capitalist model at the expense of existing peasant producers would also depend on the development of means of disciplining labor beyond traditional corporatist arrangements, and still stronger repression of agrarian demands.

The amendment of Article 27 undoubtedly does make it easier for both outsiders and existing *ejidatarios* with capital to create larger farming units within *ejidos*, should there be an economic motivation for them to do so. Even the agrarian structure of the Porfiriato was not focused exclusively on the giant *latifundio* (Gledhill, 1991), and an increase in land concentration and a conversion of former *ejidos* into a series of medium-sized private farms is a quite probable scenario *in some cases*. Where there are strong economic motivations to reorganize production, there may also be conflicts over such reorganization, and use of local political power networks to enforce restructuring. Thus, whilst critics of the reform may be wrong to argue that there will be a rapid and universal dissolution of the *ejidos* in favor of large-scale, wage-labor based, capitalist farms, it would be equally simplistic to argue that the constitutional change is insignificant. It removes the legal basis for demanding land redistribution, and it establishes the juridical and pragmatic-ideological framework for a policy which could sharpen class divisions and the concentration of control of resources in the countryside even more, in what is already a heavily inegalitarian and polarized society.

Another factor which might contribute to this process in the longer term is the interest of the younger generation in the land. The revised legislation does weaken the rights of potential heirs to ejidal plots, by assigning rights of alienation unambiguously to the current holder, but in some cases it is possible that males of the next generation will simply not be interested in inheriting, either because they have committed themselves to a more permanent kind of wage-labor migration or because they see the returns on farming as subjectively inadequate to justify the

---

[7] It is common for the large merchants in the *mercados de abastos* to use kin as production managers in principal supply zones which are, in fact, their own regions of origin. This highlights the importance of considering the way the organization of capitalist activity reflects the specific character of rural societies.

expenditure of their time and effort. This will by no means universally be the case, for the reasons already noted, and the continuing demand for land among younger people in Michoacán was evident in their continuing participation in militant organizations which organize land invasions during the Salinas sexennial, in particular the Unión de Comuneros "Emiliano Zapata" (UCEZ). Nevertheless, younger people in established *ejidos* do not necessarily attach the same symbolic weight to the land and the *ejido* as a form of social organization as their parents and grandparents, and the future of the land reform sector will be crucially affected by the amount of pressure potential heirs are willing to exert against alienation of the family plot. Since widows and daughters may also inherit, the politics of land alienation within the community will also have a gender dimension. This is a matter of no small significance, given the frequency with which women are found to be the real activists in contemporary struggles over land, sometimes committing themselves to a public role in defiance of their husbands. In surveying the process of "repeasantization" provoked by the crisis of the past decade, I have also observed women insisting that their husbands do not alienate other assets which form a basis for a subsistence livelihood, in particularly dairy cows.

The Fate of Capitalist Enterprise Under Salinas

As I have stressed, some elements in the Mexican government see the *ejido* reform as the best way for the state to wash its hands of the fiscal burden of supporting peasant agriculture, and do not regard agriculture as a whole as a strategic sector in the model of Mexico's economic future enshrined in the NAFTA. Assuming, however, that the government is still attempting to pursue a positive agricultural policy, the principal justification for "reform" is that it is a necessary step towards securing the sector's recapitalization. Few private investors took up the possibilities for association between private capital and the *ejidos* offered by López-Portillo's *Ley de Fomento Agropecuario*, and it could be argued that the more fundamental changes in the agrarian law were essential to improve matters. Yet, as we have seen, it is not only "underproductive peasants" who have found the *Salinista* economic climate too austere: in some regions at least, the most entrepreneurial of existing *ejidatarios* have experienced decapitalization. Furthermore, major agroindustries are also in deep crisis. It is therefore questionable where the capital to finance restructuring will be found, if foreign investors continue to fight shy of direct investment in the agricultural sector.

The famous strawberry agroindustry of Zamora, for example, has long since ceased to be the "strawberry imperialism" of which Ernest Feder wrote (Feder, 1977). Most of the U.S. companies withdrew and sold the processing plants to local businessmen. There are some signs, following the ratification of the NAFTA, of renewed interest on the part of U.S. companies in setting up the less specialized kinds of plants mentioned above, to process other fruits and vegetables grown in the region, and Zamora's local agribusiness might eventually benefit from the kind of shake-up present policy is producing. The decline of the strawberry industry through the Eighties reflected problems of product quality and entrepreneurial inertia, and it accelerated in the early Nineties. The case suggests that it is important to look at institutional factors influencing responses and the nature of local business and financial organization, but it is also vital to consider how potential performance in export markets is affected by the organization of marketing and distribution in the United States. One of the problems the Zamoran processing plants faced after the American companies withdrew from direct involvement in production in Michoacán was that they remained dependent on American brokers for access to U.S. markets. Not only were there problems with the prices they received for their produce, but effective business planning was inhibited by the fact that managers had to make fruit purchases and ship processed produce without knowing with certainty what price they would ultimately be paid.

Strawberries are an example of a crop where there is probably no great potential for further gains for Mexico under the NAFTA. If we turn to consider sugar, the picture seems no more encouraging, despite the fact that U.S. sugar producers were at the forefront of the anti-NAFTA lobby on the farm side. The U.S. industry was worried about Mexico developing its refining capacity, once it had the stimulus of unlimited access to the U.S. market six years after ratification (in contrast to the fifteen year delay imposed on raw sugar exports from Mexico). It was also worried that Mexico could relabel and then re-export sugar imported from third countries for its soft drinks industry, which is already imitating U.S. practice and using more maize syrup as a sugar substitute. This growing tendency to use substitutes for both cane and beet sugar as sweeteners is, however, one of the main reasons to doubt whether there is scope for developing a substantial market for Mexican sugar in the United States, particularly since laboratory-produced substitutes such as isoglucose are becoming increasingly important.

The bulk of the Mexican industry remains in poor shape because of the failure of the statized regime to make the capital investments which were one of the major justifications for taking the industry into public ownership, and there is still a good deal of cane with low yields in the countryside. Michoacán's main sugar-producing zone does, however, offer potential cane yields which are particularly high by international standards, and actual yields are surprisingly good, given the under-capitalization of most producers and the fact that marginal land is also cultivated. Since privatization, there has been some long overdue investment in the mills and the initial shake-out in the workforce was probably justifiable. Yet the transition to privatization was impeded by price and import policies that led to huge accumulation of unsold stocks. Record harvests did not protect the cane growers from the impact of changes in the official pricing structure or from extending delays in payment from the mill. Further lay-offs in the industry and changes in the credit system are simply managerial responses to lack of profitability. The resulting decline in worker and peasant incomes has depressed a local urban economy which exists mainly to provide services to those who gain their livelihoods in the sugar sector.

Here it is worth re-emphasizing the point that threatening the small producer has implications not only for rural wage workers in both agriculture and agroindustry, but also for small urban enterprises whose existence is premised on supplying rural populations with goods and services. Despite the relative (but not absolute) diminution of Mexico's rural population provoked by urbanization, the inhabitants of rural villages and provincial towns sited in a largely agrarian landscape still constitute a vital component of a potentially greatly expandable domestic market, both for wage goods and capital goods. The shift towards export-orientated policies is in serious danger of neglecting this market. The examples given earlier suggest that rural populations can participate in the development of new manufacturing and assembly industries, but in the absence of such developments, rural town economies may find recovery difficult, particularly if new agribusiness development is based on depression of wages and a greater share of the profit generated locally is exported to more distant centers.

Sugar is also a significant case because the state still plays a direct role in setting the prices received by growers, and has not pursued policies which help potentially viable actors in the sector survive and modernize (Powell, 1994). The appropriateness of this particular mix of state intervention and leaving matters to the market is questionable, given Mexico's inability to meet its domestic needs and continuing dependence on imports for the refined sugar which is an input into its processed food exports. Despite the fears of the U.S. industry, little effort seems to be being made to foster the development of the refining capacity which would help the sector take what advantage it could from the NAFTA. In the case of the region of Los Reyes, doubts about the strategy increase once we consider the secondary effects on the larger local economy, living standards and capital formation and, indeed, on the distant and economically marginalized indigenous communities in Guerrero which have supplied seasonal migrant labor for the *zafra*.[8] It does not seem beyond the Mexican state's bureaucratic capacity to conduct studies which would trace these connections, and enable it to make a planning intervention to guide market forces. Under Salinas, however, Mexico has combined a heavily politicized form of state intervention with deregulation in a way which may well ensure the worst of both worlds: high social costs and little strategic economic direction.

The case for a more strategic approach on the part of the state would seem justified on economic as well as social welfare grounds. Although domestic investment in agriculture in mid-sexennial prevented the state's withdrawal from being catastrophic, the positive benefits to agriculture of Salinas's policies in the

---

8 The Nahua communities of the Upper Balsas region were, in fact, threatened with total destruction by a hydroelectric dam project before they reminded the neoliberal state of their existence by a spirited campaign of resistence (Hindley, in press).

long-term remained more matters of faith than actual accomplishment. There was, however, a general presumption that any positive developments must, in the long-term, lie principally in Mexico's exploiting its (climatic and geographic) "comparative advantages" in fruit and vegetable exports. The most obvious point to make about fruit and vegetables is that the bulk of Mexico's past success in developing exports of such products to the North has been based on the seasonal complementarity of Mexican and U.S. production rather than on competition (Sanderson, 1986). Florida tomato growers were already demanding action from the Clinton administration against "unfair competition" from the Mexican side within months of the NAFTA ratification. The assumption that fruit and vegetable exports could grow much further under the NAFTA may be problematic, and the problems can be highlighted further by taking an example which seems a particularly favorable case.

With 45% of world production, Mexico is the world's largest producer of avocados. The country is also the world's largest consumer. Within Michoacán, avocados of low quality are available cheaply, sold door-to-door to peasant households beyond the avocado cultivation zones by women traders from indigenous communities, who collect fruits which have fallen from the trees. There is substantial scope for increasing U.S. consumption of fresh avocados, but at present unprocessed imports from Mexico are prohibited on phytosanitary grounds, and have to pass to their principal northern market in Canada in sealed trucks. Only California can produce the high grade Hass variety of avocados, and expansion of production within California is blocked by the price of land, which has a competing urban use (Cook et al, 1991: 143). Michoacán, the main production zone, has orchards coming on stream which could meet an increased U.S. demand, and there is still scope for further expansion, albeit at the expense of greater deforestation and loss of subsistence production.

Within Michoacán, the problem is the extreme variability of quality. This reflects the organization of the sector, in which peasants as well as large growers participate, but it also reflects the fact that avocados are widely consumed by people on lower incomes. Major investments, some foreign, have been made in packaging and processing facilities in recent years and there is expansion in other markets world-wide besides the U.S., which currently only takes the processed product. Yet the avocado boom has always been a mixed blessing (Linck and Santana, 1988). It helped many peasants become a little more prosperous than they would otherwise have been, but it also distorted other aspects of regional agricultural development and prices were not stable. Most of the power in the sector is heavily concentrated in the hands of a cartel which is recruited from the elite of a region much broader than the production zone—a mixture of politicians and businessmen whose capital was derived in other activities, not necessarily in agriculture. Despite, or perhaps because of, this structure of production and investment, reports from the region I received in the first half of 1994 indicated a marked absence of revival of activity after the NAFTA ratification. Prices remained depressed, and commercial orchards were being sold off at bargain prices.

The position of the United States on the phytosanitary question is not totally groundless, but it is grossly exaggerated and inflexible, a reflection, perhaps, of the cultural logic of the politics of U.S.-Mexico relations at all levels which I explore in Chapter Seven. It is also serving as a useful pretext for a campaign on the part of big business, backed by state agencies, to eliminate smaller growers from the market place within Mexico. What happens with avocados could prove an illuminating test-case of how far the United States will continue to limit access of Mexican producers to their market by non-tariff barriers, and it also illustrates the way the game of modernizing Mexican agriculture is likely to become even more biased towards the holders of substantial political and economic power.

Last but not least, it illustrates the other long-standing problem of agricultural development via market forces, the fact that production is shaped by those with higher disposable incomes. It would be ironic, but not without precedent, if the future success of Mexican avocado producers were measured by the fact that its product corresponded to American standards of quality, whilst those who picked the fruit ceased to be able to consume *guacamole* on a regular basis.

3

Social Life and the Practices of Power: The Limits of Neocardenismo and the Limits of the PRI

It is particularly difficult to divorce economics and social change from politics in Mexico, but analysis of the country's political system often takes a "top-down" view, focusing on institutional politics rather than the sociological and cultural dimensions of power. This reflects emphasis on the "corporatist" model of the Mexican political system, an unreflective view of the "strength" of the Mexican post-revolutionary state (Knight, 1993), and what, from a provincial perspective, often seems an exaggerated notion of the capacity of that state to stamp its authority on local power holders (Rubin, 1990). Yet the ruling *Partido Revolucionario Institucional* does have a distinctive relationship with civil society in comparison with the regimes of other Latin American countries, for its tentacles run deep into social life throughout national space and even, as we will see in Chapter Seven, beyond it. In this chapter, I will focus on the way the nature of society at regional level shapes politics and the way politics shapes social life, emphasizing the less formal processes which enabled the PRI to recover at least part of the ground it lost in 1988. This will lay some necessary groundwork not only for understanding the results of the August 1994 presidential elections, discussed in the concluding chapter, but also for understanding how the experience of political life has had a profound and subtle influence upon Mexican ideas about social relationships and about the possibilities of changing society through collective action.

Like many other neoliberal regimes, the Salinas government talked the language of "decentralization" whilst pursuing strategies to reinforce centralized, executive power. At first, these strategies appeared resoundingly successful. Not only was the NAFTA pushed through with a minimum of effective debate, even within the PRI itself, but the regime controlled potential dissidence on the part of the leaders of the corporatist sectoral organizations. It moved from a position of weakness to triumphalism. Salinas's prestige abroad rested on his economic reforms, coupled with the assumption that he had restored political stability, by rebuilding PRI hegemony in the electoral arena, defusing the challenge of the PRD, and establishing an effective *modus vivendi* with the post-Clouthier PAN. This bred a domestic confidence which enabled the regime to talk about modernizing the revolutionary project itself, on the new-old principles of "social liberalism."

Then came the economic downswing, Chiapas, and the assassination of Colosio. The political coup achieved by the EZLN reanimated the divided forces of the Mexican Left. Colosio died at a moment when his rhetoric had taken a populist turn. Observers noted that the candidate was eschewing *priísta* tradition by conspicuously failing to surround himself on the campaign trail with local PRI bosses and the "dinosaurs" of the official organizations, an innovation which his successor, Ernesto Zedillo Ponce de León, equally conspicuously abandoned. In the aftermath of the assassination, intellectuals began to debate the consequences of the PRI candidate's failing to secure a convincing mandate and, by July, were talking about the need to secure consensus on a "transition regime" modelled on the Moncloa Pact which set Spain on its path to democracy after the death of Franco (*Mexico and Nafta Report*, 94-07: 1). At the same time, however, with polls continuing to proclaim Cuauhtémoc Cárdenas a distant third in the presidential race, the PRD was denouncing preparations for fraud. The Alianza Democrática Nacional coalition backing Cárdenas endorsed the call by the umbrella organization of the Indian and Peasant movement in Chiapas for mass mobilization in defence of the vote (*Latin American Weekly Report*, 94-28: 334). Some polling organizations discovered high levels of skepticism amongst the Mexican public on the transparency of the new electoral system. Such suspicions were not calmed by the attempted resignation of Jorge Carpizo, the politically independent former rector of the National Autonomous University and head of the National Human Rights Commission (CNDH), who was brought in as Interior Minister and head of the Federal Electoral Institute (IFE) in the wake of the Chiapas uprising.

Suddenly, it seemed, triumphalism had given way to a new political crisis. Tensions within Mexico's normally solidary political class became relatively public. In the event, the system proved more resilient than many commentators had anticipated, but the precise grounds, nature and costs of this resilience may be what is important in the longer term. The place to begin is with the regional political scene prior to the Chiapas rebellion.

Towards a More Skeptical View of *Salinista* Politics

Firstly, we should ask how far the reconstruction of PRI hegemony depended on opposition weakness. The sexennial's electoral high-point, the August 1991 congressional elections, involved very high rates of abstentionism. Admittedly, this was a contest which most Mexicans regard as relatively insignificant in comparison with presidential, gubernatorial and even municipal elections, but the rate of abstentionism remained high in subsequent contests.

Secondly, Salinas's method of managing gubernatorial elections through negotiation with the PAN and intransigence towards the PRD appeared politically astute, but produced some anomalous situations. The executive often found itself in conflict with the PRI at state level, and sometimes had limited room for maneuver because only regional power brokers could deliver the vote. In Guerrero, the accession of Rubén Figueroa Alcocer, latest in a long line of political bosses from the Figueroa family, was not an inspiring signal from the point of view of the new commitments to democratization made by Salinas in his 1992 *Informe de Gobierno*. With 67% of registered electors abstaining, Figueroa gained 63.5% of the vote to the PRD's 27%, in a contest distinguished for violent incidents. The promotion of Patrocinio González Gárrido to the post of Interior Minister was, given his record as governor of Chiapas, virtually an endorsement of repression as a means of resolving agrarian problems. In Michoacán, the PRI gubernatorial candidate was unable to defend his supposed triumph against popular protests, despite the fact that his campaign expenses exceeded the entire PRONASOL budget for the Meseta Tarasca zone. He asked for "leave of absence" and was replaced by an interim governor, Ausencio Chávez. Chávez renewed his mandate in 1993 without holding extraordinary elections by a transparent manipulation of the PRI majority in the state congress, but had already thrown the regional party into disarray by auctioning municipal presidencies and honoring personal political debts to persons who did not present its more respectable face. A considerable amount of political power in both Michoacán and Guerrero now gravitated into the hands of elements of the regional bourgeoisie who were popularly believed to have links with the drugs trade. In the Michoacán municipality of Villamar, the victorious PRI mayor had previously served a gaol sentence for misappropriation of public funds.

Although turnout remained low, at 40% in the countryside and 25% in the urban centers, the respected independent regional weekly newspaper *Guía* reported that the unusual lack of voter interest in the December 1992 municipal elections in Michoacán contrasted with the frenetic activity of electoral "carrousels" of voters trucked to polling stations by the PRI. As far as *Guía* was concerned, what most distinguished these elections was the unprecedented scale of suborning of votes for the PRI through the use of the resources, vehicles, personnel and programs of the federal and state governments. In a highly organized campaign, involving over a hundred persons acting as "promotores sociales" in each *municipio*, the resources of the *Solidaridad* and *Vivienda Digna* programs—including the *Niños en Solidaridad* scholarships and credits for corn production—were used for the outright purchase of votes.

In the period since 1988, the PRD has tended to fractionalize at municipal level, and its loss of control of many town halls that were won in 1989 reflects the manifold contradictions of its position, discussed in more depth below. Yet there has also been fragmentation within the PRI itself. In 1992, dissident factions put up independent PRI candidates in some *municipios*, including the town of Jacona. In the aftermath of the official results, which sustained PRI victories impugned by both the PAN and the PRD, there was considerable cross-party negotiation between *priísta* dissidents and the opposition, aimed at ensuring the ungovernability of those *municipios* which were left in the hands of PRI officials who were unacceptable to local people.

Local factionalism is nothing new in Mexican politics. Rival factions have long used party labels as a way of pursuing personal and sectional goals and providing a banner for their clienteles. Party affiliations do not necessarily have any great ideological significance even if the faction in question constitutes a distinct social interest group. Party organization beyond the locality may be virtually an irrelevance. Nevertheless, the local-level conflict which the Salinas sexennial generated did foreground issues of civic responsibility, respect for democracy and the need for genuine political reform, and it produced some realignment of regional political forces. Nor was it simply states like Michoacán, Guerrero and Chiapas which presented problems of governability.

There is no doubt that economic difficulties had some political impact. As I noted in the first chapter, the short-term social cost of NAFTA included renewed pressure on the middle class as well as on working people, and the long-term cost will be to shift the economic center of gravity of the country northwards, a point which is already apparent to many small businessmen. There was also growing political fall-out from the state's changing relationship with the corporatist organizations. The *Salinista* state continued to intervene strategically in the social sector, but it severely reduced the quantity of resources circulating through the old corporate channels. The regional leaderships of corporate organizations, in particular, the National Peasant Confederation (CNC), became more selective in allocating patronage, concentrating on core clienteles at the cost of diminishing the overall weight of the organizations in local political life.

PRONASOL can be interpreted as a strategy for rebuilding regime power by dispensing with intermediaries and refocusing state clientalism on the presidential executive, as distinct from the PRI apparatus (Harvey, 1993: 18). This strategy deploys limited resources more efficiently and makes the faction controlling the state less dependent on the survival of the official party. In practice, however, the allocation of PRONASOL and SEDESOL resources did not necessarily by-pass existing local power brokers and municipal administrations. Federal officials did not intervene in many PRI-governed *municipios* in Michoacán, but the state-level PRI pursued a policy of setting up *Solidaridad* committees in PRD-governed *municipios* with an exclusively *priísta* membership, in order to reconquer local power by rigorously excluding opposition supporters from access to federal programs. Medardo Méndez, head of the Development Program for the Meseta Tarasca, was accused by the independent press of conducting a systematic campaign to foster factionalism in indigenous communities by such means. He was subsequently "fingered" by the governor for the post of federal deputy for the Los Reyes district, against the protests of many local *priístas*.

During fieldwork in 1990 and 1991, I observed flagrant violations of the official norms of PRONASOL by the *priísta* authorities in Villamar, whose election in 1989 was heavily contested (Gledhill, 1991: 375). These included organized misappropriation of the funds allocated to the *créditos a la palabra* program. With the full cooperation of the municipal authorities, wealthier farmers succeeded in getting credit by hiring landless workers as *prestanombres* (front-men), spent them on purposes other than cultivating maize, and failed to repay the loans. This frustrated the next stage of the program, which mandated that the repaid loans should be used to provide public works of benefit to the whole community, under the administration of a non-partisan *Solidaridad* committee. Lack of official action against such abuses in PRI-controlled communities contrasted with the situation in the PAN-controlled *municipio* of Sahuayo. There the mayor denounced abuses of the *créditos a la palabra* program within the local *ejido*, suspended further disbursement of funds, which were deposited in a bank, and forced federal PRONASOL officials to conduct an official audit, although no action was ultimately taken to castigate those responsible.

There was also political manipulation of PRONASOL-sponsored public works projects in Villamar. The *ejido* authorities and *encargado de orden* of the small community of Cerrito Cotijaran were *perredistas*, and the community was known to have voted solidly for the PRD in 1988 and 1989. The *perredista* leaders succeeded in negotiating for PRONASOL to drill a new well for drinking water. The work was completed in time for the August 1991 elections, but the engineers were ordered by the municipal authorities, backed by the state-level officials, to seal the well with concrete until the community had recorded a unanimous vote for the PRI. The political returns from PRONASOL could thus be secured in a coercive manner, albeit at the cost of further delegimating PRI rule. The people of Cotijaran expressed anger at their treatment: it exploited their lack of a basic resource, to secure which they had paid a substantial amount of money.

In considering the role of PRONASOL in national terms, it is important to concede that regional experiences varied. PRONASOL could sometimes function in a non-partisan manner, and even create spaces for genuine grassroots participation, whether or not this was intended or desired by the regime itself. Jonathan Fox (1994) has analyzed a particularly favorable case, the administration of the Regional Funds program by the National Indigenous Institute (INI) in Oaxaca. What made the case favorable was the conjunction of strong local indigenous organizations and good faith on the part of the INI functionaries. This led to a higher level of participation by popular organizations in the program's management and greater pluralism in the distribution of its resources, but Fox also stresses the factors which made the outcome different in states like Michoacán: the opposition of authoritarian regional elites and governors, less cohesive popular movements, and different behaviour on the part of INI officials. Even in Oaxaca, central government adopted a more interventionist position after indigenous organizations manifested reluctance to approve the reform of Article 27. Respect for those organizations' autonomy on the part of local INI functionaries diminished as they were brought into line by their political masters. Although popular movements in Oaxaca may be strong enough to continue a "war of position" for broader social reform, it is important that positive results also depend on the stance of local *Solidaridad* promoters with respect to regional and national power structures. In the case of central Veracruz, for example, close relations between INI and CNC functionaries worked to exclude the most representative peasant organizations of the region (Olvera and Millan, 1994). One of PRONASOL's more subtle means of restoring the regime's hegemony in terms of popular representation was its recruitment to the *Solidaridad* campaign of activists from those Maoist-inspired sections of the Mexican Left which had argued for the primacy of direct work at the grassroots over electoral politics (Moguel, 1994). The Salinas regime's inclusion of such activists furthered its strategy of fragmenting potential forces of opposition, but what they could achieve in practice was constrained by the broader distribution of power, however genuine their personal commitment.

Even in Michoacán, PRONASOL was undoubtedly perceived as a more positive form of patronage in some communities, and aided PRI recovery even when it was manipulated most cynically. Nevertheless, the resources provided did not compensate for the social impact of the regime's broader economic strategy, and PRONASOL was not relevant to all the actors in rural society. Getting a share of diminishing government resources encouraged a variety of groups to organize themselves politically, including *pequeños propietarios* who were previously content to keep their heads down, working within informal channels through local organizations of the PRI which they did not control. Furthermore, given the way PRONASOL was implemented in contexts like Michoacán, to what extent can it be said that *Salinismo* really changed anything in Mexican politics in the countryside?

Judith Hellman contends that Mexico under De la Madrid and Salinas became even *less* democratic (Hellman, 1994: 138). Not only did electoral violence and fraud continue after 1988, but the regime pushed through policies "destined to transform the Mexican economy and culture" without consulting even economic elites in sectors like textiles and electronics which stood to be affected by the changes. Hellman also argues that regime's success in implementing policies so damaging to lower class Mexicans demonstrated the continuing success of established mechanisms of social and political control (ibid.). It is, of course, necessary to define what we mean by "democratization." The political science debate has focused mainly on possible change in the structures of political representation, with liberal democracy as the ultimate ideal. One of the more optimistic scenarios considered realistic early in the Salinas sexennial was what Cornelius, Gentleman and Smith (1989) termed "partial democratization," a continuing PRI government at national level, but with greater participation by the PAN, which would be allowed to win local and state elections with regularity. The limitation of this kind of discussion is that it abstracts from crucial differences between North and South, in the relationship between legislatures and executives, in the salience of the rule of law in everyday social life, and, above all, in the organization of civil society (Dunkerley, 1994: 5).

Confronted with evidence of continuity in terms of electoral manipulation and clientalism, it is tempting to argue that the new economic model has been installed via established political practices, updated technologically, but not changed in essential ways. Yet a *plus ça change* perspective seems unsatisfactory. It ignores the way the end of the road of transformation entails a new kind of model of the relationship between the national community and the state, a model in which the "place" of the members of Mexican national society is no longer defined according to the logic of corporatism which was central to the ideology of the old regime (Gledhill, 1993). In particular, it ignores the deeper social consequences of what George Collier (1994) has termed the "new politics of exclusion" manifest in the regime's intransigence towards the PRD and the popular interests it represents.

Political Cultures in Regional and National Space

Political scientists tend to focus on the "high politics" of the state rather than the "deep politics" of popular responses to domination in social life (Gledhill, 1994: 102–3). One of the reasons local- and regional-level analysis is important for understanding political change is that it gives us otherwise unavailable insights into "deep politics" and the ways hegemony is actually effected in a complex and socially heterogeneous society. Anthropologists stress the value of examining the role of local actors in shaping the conditions of state intervention (Arce, 1993), the meanings they attribute to developments and situations, and their particular forms of historical consciousness. As Daniel Nugent shows in the case of the "revolutionary" *pueblo* of Namiquipa in Chihuahua, the contemporary social identity of the Namiquipenses is based on a popular construction of "rights" to land, which is in turn linked to particular constructions of social dignity and masculinity (Nugent, 1993). This construction, which has some affinities with the *ranchero* ideologies of Michoacán I discuss later, is rooted in the colonial past, but it has been reworked in response to more recent state interventions so as to "imaginatively contend with a capitalist present" (Nugent, op.cit.: 101). Once one understands the Namiquipense mind set, it becomes clear that their "popular" view of the meaning of the Mexican revolution contests the "official" version, and that their apparent "individualism" is not of the capitalist variety.

This is not, however, an argument for redrawing rigid cultural boundaries around local societies (Roseberry, 1989: 49–50). It is a matter of devising new ways of thinking about regional societies in relation to national society, and new ways of thinking about both the local and the national in relation to the global and transnational. As I argue in more depth in later chapters, the "new" politics of identity and ethnicity now so visible around the world, for example, cannot be understood adequately without considering the impact of global and transnational processes.

Mexican society has not been standing still during the years of PRI rule. "Campesinos" may have remained a significant politico-ideological category, but the class situations of rural people have changed quite radically. Along with the new class situations, and new kinds of class relationships, have emerged new local class cultures and "cultures of social relations," which articulate those class cultures within regional systems of hegemony (Lomnitz-Adler, 1992). Furthermore, international migration from Mexico to the United States has produced new kinds of "deterritorialized" migrant communities of persons who reside in the North but are not completely incorporated into Northern society nor cut off from their roots in Mexico. Mobile working populations which cross the borders between political units on a regular basis complicate one of the primary functions of the modern national state: definition of the identities of the members of national society through their bureaucratic classification and the integration of difference within a hegemonic project of "national unity," via social control effected through modern surveillance-based power technologies (Giddens, 1985; Kearney, 1991). Under these conditions, the formation of social identities becomes a transnational process which may pose threats to the hegemonic systems associated with states.

There is, however, still some value in beginning with a comparative perspective on how national cultures differ, and in particular on how Latin American societies differ from those of the Anglo-Saxon North, not so much in terms of their "non-modernity" but in terms of the way that "modernity" has been implanted within them. In addressing these issues, Roberto DaMatta (1992) has focused on the relationship between hierarchy and individualism in Brazil, and Lomnitz-Adler (1992) has stressed the continuing tensions between "rational-bureaucratic" and "particularistic-personalist" practices in Mexican politics. Both writers use the work of Louis Dumont to highlight the paradoxes of Latin American "modernity."

Under Latin American social conditions, the adoption of liberal constitutions and legal systems in which citizens are notionally equal created anomalies. One was the problem of women's status (Arrom, 1985), and another was the classification of the different "castes" which made up the hierarchic order of colonial society in terms of race and mixtures of blood. The solution in both cases was to naturalize and essentialize difference, by focusing on spiritual difference in the first case, and by separating the body and the soul in the second. A third problem lay in the exercise of justice in a society which retained hierarchic principles of social organization at the level of daily social practice. Under such circumstances, formal equality under the law actually perpetuates inequalities: as DaMatta puts it, the law in Brazil is for "individuals," the marginalized and powerless. Individualism is a disempowering and unwelcome condition. Those who remain "persons," by virtue of the social connections they can mobilize, routinely circumvent legal sanctions, demanding recognition of their personhood from the agents of law enforcement with the stock phrase of authoritarian rituals: "Do you know who you're taking to!" (DaMatta, op.cit.: 180–1). Even better-off people may, of course, sometimes be victims of abuse, but since they generally possess the means to save themselves, the practical advantages of their collective situation limit pressures for reform.

There are, of course, significant historical differences between Brazil and Mexico. Alan Knight (1992) has argued that the post-revolutionary state in Mexico is distinctive within Latin America for its "inclusionary" quality. It re-established an holistic-hierarchic model of society in the sectoral organization of political representation (Lomnitz-Adler, op.cit.: 278). The actual practices of hegemony by the political class went beyond mere state clientalism, and could draw on a richer base of ideological legitimations. Nevertheless, there remains a fundamental similarity. When universalistic law is deformed into a weapon of privilege, patron-client relations continue to act as survival strategies for the relatively powerless. Faced with total exclusion, the latter may be drawn into a potentially violent, and certainly solidarity-inhibiting, struggle for recognition as a "person" within their own peer group (Linger, 1993). Because it does not establish a true "rule of law," the Latin American state is also unable to complete the task of "penetrating" civil society, particularly in the countryside.

Lomnitz-Adler highlights this point in his explanation for the persistence of *caciquismo* in Mexico. Because national space is highly socially heterogenous, the hegemonic project of the national state is perforce effected in the first instance through intermediaries who articulate two or more local "intimate cultures" of class. González Santos, boss of the Huasteca Potosina, for example, secured leadership over the dominant local elite of *rancheros* by making claims to legitimacy in terms of *ranchero* values: wealth, intellectual superiority, and *machismo*. He encouraged his lower-class followers among the *mestizo* peons in their belief that he owed his success to a pact with the Devil. At the same time, he behaved in a hierarchical and paternalistic form towards Indians, building this constituency on a completely different basis to the liberalism on which his leadership of the *rancheros* was founded (Lomnitz-Adler, op.cit. 301–2). He related to the national political elite through a further transformation of a liberal populist style, speaking bluntly and, indeed, brutishly, to assert his regional power base through an exaggerated display of its *machista* culture. Because political control requires the articulation of distinct regional class cultures, Lomnitz-Adler argues, *caciques* are a necessary instrument for the modern state to penetrate local societies sufficiently to establish a bureaucratic structure of governance.

The *caciques* can then, normally, be incorporated into bureaucratic structures, and are eventually detached from their original constituencies by promotion. The local population now ceases to enjoy a personalistic link with the state apparatus. Access to state resources increasingly becomes a matter of wealth, of *social* power. At this point, Lomnitz-Adler suggests, a certain indifference to state institutions develops, but not a situation of complete delegitimation, since it tends to be accompanied by a fetishization of the state in the person of the President. Nineteenth century *caudillos* became fetishes of nationality in a national state system yet to be successfully constructed. The completion of the state-building process established the president as the single figure standing above the selfishness and venality of ordinary politicians (Lomnitz-Adler, op.cit.: 307–8). This is, however, a reflection of the continuing personalism of power relations within the system. Making contact with the President is the way people renew their place in society or the nation. Furthermore, the transition at regional level from *cacicazgo* to bureaucratic-plutocratic domination is never stable. As society changes, older intimate class cultures move from a core to peripheral position, and lose their coherence: new classes are formed, and new class cultures emerge. This allows new forms of local organization to emerge to contest the maldistribution of resources. New *cacicazgos* develop on the basis of these constituencies, renewing the cycle and forcing the center to renegotiate the conditions for hegemony.

These anthropological analyses start with social life as it is historically constituted in the Latin American setting. They invoke some of the peculiarities of regional systems of status honor and their connections with racial models of social difference, as well as an analysis of economic class relations. The way power is asserted and contested reflects the culturally specific ways in which persons are constituted in local societies. It also reflects the existential dilemmas members of the lower classes face in negotiating their way through life. National political institutions have to colonize and hegemonize this space, but the manner in which they hegemonize, and the limits of the hegemony they establish, are influenced by their inability to effect a total transformation of the social conditions which generate the practices of power. This reflects the inability of elites to deliver either a more socially equitable distribution of resources or the rule of law. The root of the Mexican dilemma is not merely the persistence of extreme poverty but the persistence of extreme wealth. The political "system" in a broad sense is a set of practices concerned with defence or acquisition of privileges at various levels.

One implication of this interpretation is that Mexican notions of "legitimacy" are not particularly demanding. There is nothing particularly indecent in favoring kin and clients, or in self-enrichment through public service, providing everyone gets some benefit. "Civic consciousness" and notions of good governance are in no way alien to popular political culture in Mexico. Indeed, as Knight has argued, *popular liberalism* is an important element in Mexican history (Knight, 1992: 121–2). It would, however, be mistaken to equate Mexican civic conceptions with the most austere Anglo-Saxon variants on the theme. Mexicans also have good reason to value "social peace" in the light of a turbulent modern history. People anticipate a degree of arbitrariness in the exercise of power, particularly by central government. In many ways, the problem in analyzing popular politics in post-revolutionary Mexico lies more in explaining persistent cycles of popular mobilization than explaining acquiescence. Yet once we move from the macro-picture of a stable and adaptive regime to what happens "on the ground" in particular localities, a less orderly picture does emerge.

Hegemony in Regional Space

The state of Michoacán is a political unit, but its definition as a region in social terms poses more of a problem, particularly as the definition would have to vary historically. We might take Mexico City as its political center, but the economic center might, depending on the locality, equally well be Guadalajara or Los Angeles. Even in political terms, links other than to Mexico City can be important, as witnessed, for example, by the impact of the "El Barzón" movement, or the support *neocardenismo* received from migrant colonies in California. There are substantial social and economic differences between the eastern frontier of the state with the state of Mexico, the *Tierra Caliente*, which has a border with Guerrero, the Meseta Tarasca highlands, where the Purhépecha population is concentrated, the Jalmich highlands, bordering Jalisco and (sparsely) populated by *ranchero* communities, the western region which links to Guadalajara through the Chapala corridor, and the northern region, which links up to the Bajío through La Piedad (see Figure 1.1, page 2). The agribusiness center of Zamora is the focus of economic networks extending westward, eastward and northward, and Zamora is the most important service center after Morelia, serving the east, and Uruapan, serving the south. Nevertheless, the picture can be complicated almost indefinitely, since Michoacán is a multi-centric space from the point of view of understanding the organization of the regional elite.

As Forbes-Adam (1994) has pointed out for the case of the commercial town of Sahuayo, elite ideologies of localism can disguise the way their businesses and investments are highly spatially dispersed. The leading figures of the sleepy *ranchero* town of Cotija are similarly wide-ranging in their economic interests, whilst the citizens of the even smaller but prosperous community of Tocumbo have become key players in the *paletería* (ice-lolly) business nationally (see Figure 1.2, page 3). High rates of international migration, and transnational agribusiness penetration in some zones, have also led to a multiplication of the ties with the North which are significant for local economies, societies and cultures. Specific kinds of businesses have developed to cater for the emigrant population, and emigrants continue to feed investment back into the region, although capital generated in the countryside within the state frequently ends up in real estate investment in metropolitan cities outside it.

Nevertheless, in contrast to the case of Morelos, as described by Lomnitz-Adler, Michoacán possesses a diversified regional elite which plays an important role in the affairs of its various sub-regions. Morelia, the state capital, is not, however, a hegemonic center in socio-economic terms so much as a seat of intermediate bureaucratic and politico-administrative power. Its population did grow enormously during the Seventies, at a time when dynamic agribusiness centers like Uruapan were experiencing zero or negative growth (Arroyo Alejandre, 1986). This growth was associated with the expansion of public employment. Whilst new residential construction continued during the Eighties, so did the state capital's articulation to the national capital, as new transport systems made it convenient to run businesses from Mexico City and for middle and lower class migrants to commute. The political impact of these processes is visible in the political life of *municipios* in the eastern part of the state.

The *municipio* of Senguio will serve as an example. The *cabecera* is an architecturally pristine Porfirian town, founded through the displacement of the indigenous population to the social and political periphery. The marginalized Indians are now heavily dependent on undocumented migration to the United States, and suffer from such visible social maladies as a high rate of alcohol abuse. Land reform was accomplished through the preemptive fractionalization of small *haciendas* into *pequeñas propiedades*. The local *cacique* was a former *hacienda* administrator. The decline of his power with age was reinforced by conflict between ranchers and *ejidatarios*, the latter faction gravitating from the PPS to the PRD after 1988. Yet all this was something of a "war of position," in which control of the municipal committee of the PRI remained a key prize, of as much interest to those who militated in the PRD as other factions. The behind-the-scenes power brokers of the 1980s were no longer authority figures associated with the traditional agrarian order, but owners of illegal saw-mills with political patrons in Mexico City. Their control of the local PRI was contested by a group of professionals, who had made their own peregrinations to the capital. The logic of class differentiation is therefore overlain by two other structures: firstly, by the division between *pequeños propietarios* and *ejidatarios* in terms of channels of political representation, modes of resource acquisition and possibilities for mobilizing clienteles, and secondly, by the possibilities for factionalization created by the impacts of past migration and the political networks individuals could establish outside the locality.

Within those parameters, alliances are generally necessary, since in terms of pure social power, the timber barons are in a highly advantageous position and the professionals relatively marginalized. Whilst local political control is obviously a convenience for the former, it is the key to social advance for the latter. In Senguio, party affiliations are situational, contingent and shifting, as alliances and blocs reshape themselves. The *ejidatarios* are (typically) socially heterogeneous, but more significantly, have never been able to make the *ejido* a key point of articulation in municipal politics. Too much of the local economy and patronage system gravitates around private property.

By way of contrast, I now turn to the western part of the state and the tranche of territory which runs down from Lake Chapala to the *Tierra Caliente*, bounded by the Jalmich *ranchero* borderlands on the east, and the Valley of Zamora and the Meseta Tarasca on the west. This sub-region has some historical unity, although its internal relationships have been reshaped by both economic changes and changes in communications infrastructure in the post-revolutionary period. Here local society is constructed through categorical oppositions between "white" *rancheros*, *mestizo* "peons" and indigenous *naturales*.

In the post-land reform era, ethnic distinctions correspond to social distinctions based on forms of property and dependence on the state (Barragán, 1990). *Mestizo* land reform beneficiaries, for example, are seen as state-dependents by the inhabitants of the *ranchos*, traditionally pastorally orientated hill communities owning or renting private land; *ejidatarios* are seen as incapable of either economic initiative or defending themselves against the depredations of power-holders. As I suggested earlier, *ranchero* views on private property should not be seen as having any direct affinity with a capitalist ethic: notions of self-sufficiency and freedom from domination, bound up with a cult of masculinity, can be strongly resistant to capitalism, state and private. The Jalmich *rancheros* also emphasize their European roots, purity of blood and whiteness of complexion.

These oppositions constitute a dialectic of social distinction which fosters interiorization of stigma by the mediating group, the *mestizos*, whose "intimate class culture" is thereby deprived of coherence in Lomnitz-Adler's sense (op.cit.: 37–39). *Mestizos* shift contextually between identification with the *ranchero* pole versus the *indígenas*, and identification with the *indígenas* versus national elites, which are perceived as "foreign" (Spanish), or even "French" (more foreign) in expressions of extreme antagonism. In the case of the former *peones acasillados* of the ex-*hacienda* of Guaracha, it was the *hacienda* itself which continued to form the core identity for a majority in the community well into the land reform period, and this has remained a problem despite the fact that the Eighties presented them with an opportunity to reinvent themselves as *cardenistas* (Gledhill, 1991).

Land reform and *cardenismo* in fact provide many of the region's *mestizo* communities with a possible anchor for identity and dignity within the revolutionary tradition. Yet this is the root of their dilemma, since their post-revolutionary history is one of continuing inability to secure economic reproduction within the confines of regional space. In contrast to the Huasteca Potosina, the *ejido* became the dominant form of land tenure throughout much of the region, with the ranchers confined to the periphery. There is therefore not necessarily any direct relationship of class domination between the two social categories. Nevertheless, the post-Cárdenas era subordinated the *mestizo* peasantry within the *ejidos* to a new regional agrarian bourgeoisie of *acaparadores* and neolatifundists, which could be described as a "peasant bourgeoisie" in Frans Schryer's sense, an exploiting class preserving a rustic cultural style (Schryer, 1980: 7). It also forced a massive shake-out of population to the metropolitan cities and a high level of temporary migration towards the United States, which was already developing into a more permanent emigration before the crisis of the Eighties. The respite from direct domination by capital provided by the statization of *ejido* agriculture during the 1970s did not inhibit emigration or produce a general recapitalization of the peasantry (Gledhill, 1991), but the new round of state intervention (and consolidation of bureaucratic domination) was not a wholly negative process. It brought increases in public sector employment and improved educational opportunities, along with commercial development in urban centers. Teachers and other educated professionals were important actors on the regional political scene during the 1980s, albeit not in a uniform way, along with various elements of the small-town bourgeoisie. Some of the latter switched from the PAN to the PRD as a means of contesting local power after 1988.

In the Ciénega de Chapala, peasants expressed their antagonism to abuse by state agencies by contrasting the situation of the *rancheros* with their own dependence, but local leadership of the *cardenista* reaction to neoliberalism came principally from the beneficiaries of public sector expansion and public education. The alternative ideological vision offered by this group was largely a refashioning of the old system on more socially equitable lines. The limitations of the politics they have been able to pursue reflects their continuing dependence of availability of public sector resources. Where power was won at the local level, delivery of resources to constituencies proved problematic, even where leaderships were willing to negotiate with the PRI.

In the absence of a strong "subaltern culture of resistance," it is difficult to maintain popular support without delivering resources. This problem is, however, aggravated by the way personalism is seen as integral to political activity: the local PRI itself was able to exploit the suspicions which followers invariably harbored about the self-interested motivations of leaders to undermine the position of those who chose the route of negotiation. A striking example is provided by the case of Cerrito Cotijaran mentioned earlier. When the *perredista* leader of the *ejido* entered into negotiations with *priísta* officials to secure PRONASOL resources, and agreed to organize community contributions to get the well project off the ground, he opened himself up to a subtle form of "black propaganda." The wife of one of the community's minority of PRI loyalists went around among the other women suggesting (quite groundlessly) that he had "sold himself" politically in order to pocket his share of the money. The "fragmentation" of popular forces therefore also reflects the way external power intervenes in community life. The irony here is that the PRI can exploit popular skepticism created by its own history of coopting leaders and misuse of public resources to delegitimize its opponents.

In some parts of the wider region, however, notably the sugar-growing area around Los Reyes, the core of the *ejidos* formed in the 1920s was provided by *ranchero* share-croppers rather than *peones acasillados*. These sugar *haciendas* were owned by commercial companies established by Guadalajaran capital. Their internal social relations of production were less burdensome for *peones* and *medieros* than those of both the vast Guaracha *hacienda* to the North and the smaller grain and cattle-producing *haciendas* which lay between the Guaracha and the Los Reyes valley, which coordinated their systems of labor control with Guaracha. After the initial land reform in Los Reyes, both land and water were relatively freely available, attracting new settlers from the *ranchero* periphery who then became *ejidatarios*.

With many of these people, asking questions about "the Revolution" produces recollections of the *Cristiada*. Their agrarian communities were and are socially differentiated, but their members are less psychologically burdened by the legacy of stigma generated by *ranchero* culture. Those who worked on the *haciendas* before land reform were not subjected to the kind social humiliation inflicted on *hacienda* dependents in the Ciénega de Chapala and its environs, and many of the new *ejidatarios* were newcomers from the *ranchero* zone. Some families continue to possess property in the upland communities today as well as *ejido* land. Nevertheless, it was impossible to exorcise the *ranchero* ideological critique of the *ejido* entirely. This has produced a significant symbolic transformation, which is mapped out on local social space.

The *ejidatarios* in the core communities of the valley see themselves as embodying a positive pole of *ranchero* values, and have turned the uplands into a negative pole, associated with brutishness and lack of "civilization." Communities which are physically situated on the margins of the *ranchero* zone proper are (unjustly) ascribed *ranchero* cultural characteristics of the *negative* kind, as *broncos*, people who are prone to violence. Of late, the negative pole is marked by a linkage between peripheral communities and the *narcos*. These constructions are entirely relational. The spatially peripheral communities are indignant about their characterization in these terms, and some, at least, have responded by organizing themselves sufficiently to challenge the communities of the valley core for control of local agrarian organizations. All the actors draw on elements of the *ranchero* identity in projecting a positive self-image of themselves, whilst engaging in further cultural production within this encompassing value-system to combat the stigma attached to state dependence, downgrading the communities which can present themselves as more "authentic" bearers of *ranchero* identity in terms of political and social autonomy.

In the Los Reyes area, *ejidatarios* do experience their dependence on the (now privatized) mills as a problem, and many are fearful of the consequences of *ejido* reform within a capitalist framework. Yet they are also antagonistic to contemporary agrarian movements in the region, which they see as menacing their own security by inviting political repression (Gledhill, 1992).

There are also conflicts between contemporary land claimants and members of *ejidos* which are run by rancher *caciques* with substantial amounts of private property.[1] As an ideological system, *ranchero* culture binds together very poor and relatively rich members of the upland communities beyond the *ejidos*. It also penetrates the social sector itself in three distinct ways: some *ejidatarios* are *rancheros*, some are not *rancheros,* but see themselves as more or less socially

---

[1] The land claimants are dismissed by existing *ejidatarios* as "squatters," and attention is frequently drawn to the presence within such movements of persons who have jobs as mill workers and other forms of livelihood. Rancher *caciques* are well connected politically in Morelia and are leading figures in the private ranchers association at state level. This situation can lead to conflict between state-level functionaries and federal power, since the ranchers use their political influence with the state administration to thwart successful land petitions.

equivalent to *rancheros*, whilst a third group of *ejidatarios* see themselves as distinct from *rancheros,* and experience *mestizaje* as a socially incapacitating condition in a manner which derives from *ranchero* ideology. Some members of the latter group were already speculating about the possibility of the state ending agrarian reform and converting them into real proletarians at the start of the Eighties.

All these groups may express antagonism to more powerful social elites and the state. Yet the principle antagonism expressed by the wealthy ranchers under Salinas was directed at what they perceived as the indecisiveness of the regime in carrying through the abolition of the *ejido*. There is not, however, a single *ranchero* class position, and there is therefore not a uniform attitude. The devastation wrought in the upland communities by the drugs trade and the economic problems facing small pastoral producers in recent years have provoked a new wave of emigration from the highlands, and considerable resentment about the destruction of a way of life. Struggling for dignity in this devastated social space is frequently at one's neighbor's expense.

Big cattle ranchers have come into conflict with both landless *mestizo* peasants and members of indigenous communities over control of land suitable for grazing and subsistence cultivation. Such land includes *agostadero* within the boundaries of *ejidos* which was sold off decades ago to private interests in illicit deals by ejidal authorities. The established *ranchero-ejidatario* system of social distinction based on status honor does not erase conflicts which are seen explicitly in class terms. In fact, neoliberalism is highlighting class by highlighting the issue of economic power in relation to politics. It is not simply, as everyone has always known, that those who possess wealth possess political influence, and that political connections are key to accumulating wealth in certain forms—plundering forest resources or possessing ill gotten gains to invest in avocado orchards. It is a matter of denial of a structured place in a hierarchic order: if the fate of the poor is to be left to market forces, then everything will have its owner and the poor will have nothing.

At this point, however, we should consider the position of the indigenous communities. The raw materials for the discourses on status honor and the relationships between ethnic groups I have discussed are clearly drawn from the estamental categories of the colonial period, but they have been reworked ideologically through history, first in the 19th century, and then in terms of the new situation created by the 1910 revolution. The latter re-established an holistic, hierarchic model of Mexican society, but one which was premised on a reappraisal of the *mestizo*, Indian and Spaniard. As Lomnitz-Adler points out, the new imagining of the nation based on *mestizo* nationalist ideology continued to valorize "whitening" and indeed "modernization," but under the aegis of a protectionist state and a party which stood for the majority of Mexicans (op.cit.: 278–9). The Indians would eventually be assimilated, but their souls were the souls of the nation and their bodies would receive the material benefits of the transition to modernity the encompassing state would secure. The continuing power of this model is demonstrated by the fact that the forces of opposition to neoliberalism initially crystallized around *neocardenismo* (Mallon, 1992). In the light of this, a paradox of local history, that the staunchest *cardenistas* are found in the indigenous communities (Becker, 1987), becomes less perplexing.

Indigenous "identity politics" may pose a special problem for neoliberal regimes, because of the threats posed to indigenous communities by the irrigation projects, logging concessions and colonization projects which accompany "development" (Blauert and Guidi, 1992). In recent years, some Purhépecha communities in the Meseta Tarasca have mounted sustained popular attacks on local bosses, many of them centered on illegal logging, and these struggles have tended to pit the communities against the state because of the political value of some of the bosses to the PRI. In the community of Tanaco, in the *municipio* of Cherán, for example, villagers occupied the show-piece communal saw-mill, after denouncing successive *comisarios de bienes comunales* over a period of eight years to no effect, not only to the state authorities but to the President of the Republic. Although the current *cacique* enjoyed the protection of hired guns, he was also able to maintain his control by arbitrarily jailing opponents, with the connivance of the local political and judicial authorities. His loyalty to the PRI made Tanaco the official party's only redoubt in an opposition *municipio*, winning him unconditional support from government at all levels.[2] The Meseta has, however, also witnessed a growth of ethnic revindication politics, which is not invariably socially radical. One important feature of Purhépecha ethnic politics has been its frequent assertion of the distinctiveness of *Purhépecha* identity versus "Nahua-Aztec" indigenous identity. This has pragmatic value in terms of demanding special programs, but it is also a significant political construction because it asserts the dignity of the provincial periphery against the national center.

Those who are leading the constructing are mostly professionals. Some have always been marginal to official power structures, and some aligned themselves with the PRD after 1988, but many are intermediaries who play significant roles in community political representation and in institutional politics beyond the communities (Zárate Hernández, 1994). In general, *profesionistas* have displaced traditional elders in community leadership roles, precisely because they are best fitted to mediating community-state relations. The cultural politics of Purhépecha revindication therefore plays a legitimating role in terms of the claims of these intermediaries to speak on behalf of their constituencies and perform functions of political representation vis-à-vis the state. It also provides a significant discourse on unity

---

2 State officials continued to present the communal enterprise as a "model of efficiency and organization," turning a blind eye to the *cacique*'s illegal exploitation of the forests of neighboring communities and the fact that the saw-mill was unaccountably operating at a loss. The boss was declared re-elected in 1989 by an official of the Ministry of Agrarian Reform despite protest from the community assembly (*Guía*, 23rd October, 1990).

for an indigenous society which has been characterized by a high degree of inter-village and intra-communal factionalism historically. Nevertheless, in the Meseta Tarasca we also encounter some of the problems which Lomnitz-Adler has discussed in examining the role of "internal-articulatory intellectuals" in the Huasteca.

Lomnitz-Adler argues that, in searching for a "pure" Indian culture parallel to, but distinct from, European culture, such intellectuals either have to downgrade it, or posit it as the basis for an alternative hegemony, an alternative to the existing "culture of social relations" (Lomnitz-Adler, op.cit.: 240). As I noted earlier, by culture of social relations he means hegemony in a specific *regional* setting, the symbolic field through which relations between "intimate" class cultures are established. In the case of relations between peasants and *políticos* in Morelos, for example, the latter use their official mythification of the 1910 revolution and its symbols as a basis for claims to legitimacy, whereas the peasants can continue to see themselves as the authentic heirs to Zapata, and at the same time negotiate concessions from the bureaucracy by appealing to the fetishized symbols the bureaucrats have alienated from them (op.cit.: 29–30). The problem here is envisaging how Indian culture could establish *itself* as hegemonic.

Another problem is noted by Charles Hale in a recent discussion of the inability of the *popular* and *indígena* factions to resolve their differences at the Quetzaltenango *Encuentro* in 1991 (Hale, 1994). This is the problem of the essentialization and naturalization of indigenous culture embodied in notions of radical difference. Hale suggests that *popular* resistance to dominant creole and *mestizo* elites has been conducted from within the frame of the dominant culture, without directly challenging its premises. For *populares*, striving for equality within society means striving "towards increased social and symbolic difference from Indians" (op.cit.: 27). *Indígenas* respond by emphasizing their own value in terms of radical difference, spirituality and "nation-hood," which replicates the same justifying myths and same cultural logic of state- and nation-building.

The *indígena* position entails making demands for recognition by the national state. Such demands can to some extent be satisfied without threat to the broader hegemony underlying the political constitution of the nation and threatening dominant class interests. Nevertheless, indigenous demands can raise intractable issues of control of resources and models of "development." Such issues remain prominent in the Meseta Tarasca, because of the influence of an independent peasant movement which combines "ethnic," "class" and "anti-imperialist" discourses, and which recruits *mestizo* peasants as well as members of indigenous communities, the UCEZ. The discourse of the EZLN also struck a responsive chord among some Michoacanos, including the workers and cane growers of Puruarán, where the local mill was closed by its new private owners.

In underscoring the value of analyzing hegemony at the national level through the optic of differentiated regional spaces, I have stressed the need to understand the enormous amount of cultural production which shapes on the ground political practice. A national political class in which a transnational capitalist elite has become dominant is taking great risks in dismantling the basis on which hegemony has been established at the level of the state since the revolution. On the other hand, the question remains whether it is still possible to construct popular alternatives to the neoliberal future from below, rather than relying on more civilized members of the political class to rediscover social democracy.

Wealth, Power and the Realism of the Popular Classes

Emphasis on the state's political control of the masses in the shaping of postrevolutionary development has tended to distract attention from the analysis of class power in civil society. It is, however, important to note that the levels of active participation by entrepreneurial groups in politics have increased in the past two decades. In some cases, activism seems initially to have been motivated by contradictions created by the development of large-scale "entrepreneurial" public sector *cacicazgos* in the Echeverría period (Leyva, 1993). Neoliberalism has brought the role of business in Mexican politics into more public view, highlighting the immense economic power enjoyed by a comparatively small capitalist elite at national level, and its transnational character. Lower-class views of the wealthy are, however, still shaped by the fact that the post-revolutionary sectoral model did not allot a positively marked position to entrepreneurs, submerging them in the amorphous "popular sector." What poorer citizens could most readily observe was the connection between wealth and politics, at all levels of the stratification system.

The conversion of political power into private wealth was not peculiar to the "presidentialist" economics run by Echeverría and López Portillo (Zaid, 1987), which are popularly viewed as epitomes of corruption. Lázaro Cárdenas certainly left office a far richer man than when he entered it, and was a covert *accionista* in a number of private sector projects which he promoted in Michoacán in the years following his presidency. Miguel Alemán seems fully comparable with his notorious "statist" successors, and the emptiness of Miguel De la Madrid's rhetoric of *renovación moral* was apparent within months of his leaving office. Neoliberal reduction of the economic role of the state and social polarization may actually have diminished popular willingness to fetishize the president. It was commonplace for people to remark that the only next sexennial would provide the full measure of the extent to which Salinas had benefitted personally from his privatization policies. Even before he left office, there was widespread speculation about which of the businessmen involved in the more lucrative of these transfers of public assets were the president's *prestanombres*.

Looking towards the bottom of the hierarchy, at the level of provincial *municipios* with a substantial rural population controlled by the PRI, it is commonplace to observe a blatant banditry on the part of officials. The wealthiest local citizens operating profitable private businesses often shun public office, even when invited, though they generally play an important role in the local organization of the PRI, influence the selection of candidates, and contribute handsomely to campaign funds. The advantages such people derived from the political system became apparent where *perredista* administrations secured election at municipal level: in the case of Los Reyes, it transpired that the wealthiest citizens of the town had been absolved from their liabilities to local business taxation. Where businessmen do become office-holders, they have tended to do so in organizations more directly associated with their business interests, associations of cattlemen and farmers, chambers of commerce, and producer unions. In some cases, major local businessmen are *panistas*, but this seldom prejudiced their business interests providing they solidarized with their *priísta* peers on questions of economic interest and restricted their political activity to the purely electoral field.

To some extent, the origins of wealth in the provinces continue to have provincial roots, in the possession of private landed property unaffected by agrarian reform, the generation of new agrarian capital on the basis of the exploitation of the *ejidos*, investment in transport and in real estate and commerce in local urban centers, and, of course, the clandestine sectors of the economy. Since, however, wealthy families often invest in educating their children, who may then move to larger population centers and enter politics at a higher level, the family's direct participation in politics may be real but not manifest at local level. There has, however, been a strong tendency for older money to gravitate towards the larger cities. This gives rise to the formation of new local wealth holders, as absentees seek administrators for local assets they no longer manage directly, or finance a client or kinsman in some venture. The opening up of new agro-export activities has given rise to an ever-extending chain of ownership and finance, in which local agents, managers and representatives of metropolitan or even foreign capital move up in the wealth scale in the local community.

Neoliberalism should reinforce the extent to which private capital formation benefits from the organization of public power. Nevertheless, removal of protection and direct and indirect subsidies had negative consequences in the short-term for most forms of productive private enterprise in industry and agriculture below the level of the transnational capitalist elite. In this context, the maintenance of some of the political channels for wealth accumulation (primarily at the expense of the powerless) was a necessary feature of the neoliberal transition.

Mere activism in the PRI brings tangible economic benefits, and these were substantial in the case of the political "promotores" mentioned earlier. Despite Salinas's much publicized move against "La Quina," boss of the petroleum workers' union, the leaderships of the CNC and CTM organizations in Michoacán displayed no signs of modifying their behavior with regard to venality, and received official sanction for the coercion of dissent. Mill workers in the sugar town of Santa Clara, for example, asserted that the General Secretary of their CTM union had not only succeeded in securing re-election in a fraudulent manner, but had been able to exploit the restructuring process associated with privatization to his personal advantage, by conspiring with management to lay off younger employees in place of the more experienced workers formally included in the redundancy package, pocketing the surplus from the redundancy payments paid by the company. Yet as workers scrambled to save their jobs as individuals, the value of patronage rapidly seemed to outweigh the virtues of union democratization. Sacrifice of a few of the more outrageous bosses had a largely symbolic value, although the fall of "La Quina" rather symptomatically had a devastating impact on the economic life of his home region.

The relationship between political participation in the PRI and personal economic advancement has provided an important incentive to political loyalism, and an avenue of social ascent to potential elements of opposition whose paths would otherwise be blocked in a political economy dominated by market relations. At the root of the apparent "depoliticization" of the Mexican masses and the congenital distrust which members of popular organizations display towards their own leaders is an acute understanding of how politics works in practice. Here it should be stressed that representatives of the regime generally make active efforts to suborn leaders of popular movements. Furthermore, one of the PRI's more subtle tactics in coping with popular unrest has been to use *agents provocateurs* masquerading as popular leaders to trap the unwary into situations in which they can be repressed. The regime has even financed spurious "radical" organizations. Popular suspicions are thus grounded in the knowledge that appearances can be deceptive, and that leaders can have hidden agendas and covert relations with the enemy.

Yet these are not the only problems popular movements face. Even when they succeed in wresting resources from the control of members of the local economic elite, the social power and political influence of their opponents may not be seriously diminished. *Caciques* can fight back by financing another group of equally needy people to press for a share in what the original movement has won, exploiting the resulting dissension to their own advantage. They may also deploy their economic power to destroy the solidarity of the original group by offering work or other patronage to some of its members. The destabilization of popular movements therefore frequently reflects active tactics of intervention by the holders of political and economic power, effected through "dirty tricks" and clientalism. The "realism" of the poor is based not only on the exigencies of their poverty, but on hard and disillusioning collective experience.

Clearly, "realism" is not sufficient to eliminate popular struggles, and recognition of realism as a limiting factor should not blind us to the fact that, as I have argued elsewhere (Gledhill, 1994: 113), the Mexican masses do maintain their own counter-hegemonic visions. They manifest both their antagonism to the political class and their realism in their celebration of the martyred popular heroes of the revolution, true representatives of the people by virtue of their betrayal and murder (Powell, in press). Such disparate figures as Madrazo, a PRI reformer, and Clouthier, a *panista*, fit comfortably into this "logic of betrayal" as far as Michoacán's peasants are concerned. What reduced the potency of the popular "political imaginary" of the Mexican revolution was the fact that the state gave it limited recognition, disposing popular movements to accept the logic of realism, and to pursue their goals through alliances with "progressive" factions of the political class and by petitioning the state to concede rights to them under the law.

The more exclusionary stance of neoliberalism threatened the effective management of movements articulating counter-hegemonic positions, but the Salinas regime adopted specific strategies to fragment the bases of support of the PRD opposition. By a subtle politics of "concertación," discussed in more detail in the last section of this chapter, it persuaded the leaderships of a number of key movements that a qualified accommodation with the government was preferable to insistence on a change of governing party. It is, however, also essential not to lose sight of the role of other factors in the survival of the regime, and in particular, of the role of violence.

The Political Value of the Inevitability of Violence

The Mexican military have not seized control of the government since the revolution. This is not to say, however, that the military do not fulfil functions of internal political control, or that military interests have no voice in the inner deliberations of the elite. The possibility of contradictions emerging between the civilian authorities and the military where the army's dignity is undermined by political interference became apparent in the wake of the Chiapas uprising. Yet despite the army's initial humiliation by the public questioning of its normal impunity in Chiapas, it has not ceased to violate the human rights of indigenous *chiapanecos,* and may well have received new guarantees as it supported Interior Ministry agents in a campaign to clear the conflict zone of foreigners in June and July of 1994. Impunity was certainly the norm in Michoacán through the Salinas sexennial.

The army was used extensively after April 1990 in operations to dislodge *perredistas* from the town halls occupied after the disputed gubernatorial and municipal elections of 1989. Troops were also dispatched to Los Reyes just before the 1991 congressional elections to ensure that there was no popular reaction to a bodged theft of voting cards from the offices of the Electoral Commission, which appeared to have been organized by the former municipal secretary of the PRI. Deployment of military power is, however, generally of lower intensity. Military checkpoints set up periodically on highways serve to remind the population of the power of the state. There is a rather thin dividing line between "legitimate" social pacification action on the part of the military and their involvement in illegal actions. Other routine contexts of military deployment are campaigns against drug cultivation and possession of arms. These not only serve as convenient pretexts for politically motivated repression, but also lend themselves to practices of extortion. Many abuses are, however, simply tacitly legitimized perks of the kind allowed to all who perform services which maintain the structures of social and political power.

The military are not, however, the main agency of repression at local level. This role is fulfilled by the state and federal judicial police, equipped with heavy caliber weapons. Although they normally operate in small teams, they can be massed for major operations, and their formal role, as agents of law enforcement and criminal investigation, provides them with extensive powers. The effectiveness of the *policía judicial* lies in their capacity to create a climate of fear, which is productive for power holders in a number of different domains and is premised on public perception that they are not subject to any effective legal restraint.

In 1991, the mother of a girl murdered in Jacona managed to remember the name of a former boyfriend, who was promptly accused of the crime and imprisoned, in the absence of any evidence against him. Public protest was answered by threats of violence against the children of some of the protestors. This typifies the *modus operandi* of the judicial police. Despite endless official promises of reform, the force in Michoacán continues to use beatings and torture to extract confessions for even minor crimes, but the functioning of the judicial system is not arbitrary. It is marked by a routinized social discrimination against the poor—in particular, members of the indigenous population—and habitual use of monetary payments to escape justice on the part of offenders of greater economic means and political influence. Yet this problem pales into relative insignificance in comparison with the fact that those who attempt to take a stand in defence of justice are routinely threatened with violence.

In more remote communities, a policy of shooting first on the part of the police makes self-defense with the gun the preferred option. Since the police command such fire-power, it is best to defend oneself by stealth, ambushing the patrol before it reaches the community. The "untouchability" of the police creates a self-legitimating cycle of violence in which the public are drawn into the patterns of behavior which provide the pretext for police violence against them. The cycle is reinforced by the tendency of law enforcement officers to exploit their repressive power to commit acts of robbery, a practice which is often a systematic plunder of the local population organized on a profit-sharing basis between the judges and the agents.

The perception that the rule of law remains an illusion is not restricted to the provinces or the countryside. Rural areas are, however, zones of heightened anxiety. The population at large see the impunity of the judicial police as derived from their political functions, although they also act as agents of private class power, hired privately for their services in contexts such as land disputes, and sometimes as legalized assassins. Their directly political role as agents of the national state was most clearly demonstrated by the campaign against the PRD in 1990, during which both elected and (fraudulently) defeated *perredista* candidates were seized in their homes by the judicial police, and subjected to torture in the course of their transfer to Morelia and on to Mexico City.

The case of Salomón Mendoza Barajas, elected PRD mayor of Aguililla, attracted most public (and international) attention, because the National Human Rights Commission (CNDH) eventually secured his release from prison on grounds of false conviction.[3] Yet Aguililla was only one of a series of cases, and it is difficult to see the eventual recognition of injustice in Aguililla as more than a cynical political gesture towards international public opinion after the benefits of repression had been reaped. Since the CNDH remains dependent on the Interior Ministry (Secretaría de Gobernación), which is also responsible for "internal security," its role as an enforcer of the rule of law is compromised, but even giving full credit to the efforts of its members to assert their impartiality, the most significant conclusion to be drawn from both Michoacán and Chiapas is that its capacity to control the use of repressive power is limited.

According to Salomón Mendoza's testimony, he was arrested after going to the head of the invading force of federal *policías judiciales* to complain about the theft of a pick-up by the agents. He was informed that his presenting himself had saved the police the trouble of finding him, since: "We have orders to 'darle a la madre' and do not know whether you will live or die." A parallel experience was related to me by the *perredista* candidate for municipal president in Chavinda. He, like Salomón, required hospital treatment for intestinal injuries received during interrogation prior to his three months of imprisonment in Mexico City. Such systematic repression was clearly designed to convince the population that the PRI still possessed the means to wipe out dissidence by a violence against which there was no defence. The message was, however, reinforced by other tactics.

Sixty-eight *perredista* militants were assassinated in Michoacán between November 1988 and May 1994, a quarter of the national total. Many of those killed have been elected officials, and the patent ludicrousness of the official versions of these incidents suggests that the object of the exercise is that the public should see them as lies, and be convinced that the impunity of the regime and its servants is absolute. A typical example is provided by the events of 5th August, 1990, in the community of Churumuco (*Guía*, 9th September, 1990). The *perredista* mayor, treasurer and other officials were ambushed by a group of gunmen equipped with high-power automatic weapons of the kind normally carried by the judicial police and the military. The treasurer's wife was killed, but the municipal police succeeded in detaining the assassins, who came from Apatzingán and Guerrero. On interrogation, they stated that they had been paid seven million pesos by the *priísta* former

---

3 I should stress, however, that not all of those arrested in Aguililla were released with him, despite the fact that the CNDH declared all the accused to be innocent. Neither the police responsible for the torture nor the senior members of the government responsible both for the arrests and the subsequent dissemination of false evidence of involvement in the drugs trade against the accused were brought to book for their actions. Ironically, the most senior government legal officer involved, Enrique Alvarez del Castillo, was himself subsequently accused in the United States of involvement in the Guadalajara drug cartel and complicity in the murder of Drug Enforcement Administration agent Enrique Camarena.

police chief to carry out the crime. After they were removed to Morelia, the official version was changed, to attribute the attack to personal grudges between the disparate band of gunmen and their victims. Still more terrifyingly, stories of massacres of the populations of small *ranchos* by the judicial police began to circulate throughout the countryside in 1990 and 1991, reinforcing the normal climate of doubt which the habitual practices of law enforcement impose on the minds of the citizenry.

State terror raised to the intensity which Hobbes regarded as a justification for the citizenry's revolt against its government has been experienced by certain segments of Central American society in recent decades. Yet even where it is pursued with the utmost, genocidal, ruthlessness, as in the case of Guatemala, such violence can be counter-productive, and needs support from other technologies of and strategies of power if it is to promote fragmentation of resistance and submission (Wilson, 1993: 131–3). Nevertheless, it is important to see that the role of violence in the social pacification of rural Mexico is not simply that of a tactic of last resort in critical moments when other system-sustaining mechanisms have broken down. Violence is subtly interwoven into the fabric of everyday existence, as a series of practices which intrude into the lives of most families at some time. The diffuse but pervasive threat of arbitrariness and violence is present in the mind of all those considering how far to commit themselves to an oppositional cause.

Take, for example, the case of a young woman primary school teacher who was physically beaten in front of her class by the judicial police before being hauled off to jail. The official pretext for the intervention of the police was a matter relating to a property, not her political militancy in the PRD. The assault was, of course, grossly illegal, but the protesting parents of the terrified children were under no illusion that pressing the issue would redound on them. The officers responsible might be reprimanded and transferred, but they would be replaced by persons of the same vocation. Such tactics do sometimes provoke an increase in militancy on the part of a larger group in the short-term. Yet the absence of legality as a pervasive fact of life disposes people towards accepting limited gains and making compromises. For any individual, the question is one of deciding how much risk to take, and how far the group can contain the risks implicit in any particular form of conflict with the power structure. Leaders expect to be victims of police action, but they tread a fine line in evaluating the extent of the risks.

There are, however, other dimensions to social violence in rural Mexico. One type of violence is associated with disputes over the control and ownership of resources, although the prospect of resolving such disputes by the killing of a rival claimant is not unrelated to the official justice system: if municipal legal officials can be suborned in advance, the risks involved in recourse to violence are greatly reduced, though not eliminated, since there can be no guarantee that kinsmen of the deceased party will not seek revenge, even if the perpetrator of the crime is absolved by the law. It may be possible, however, to relate other types of violence in social relations to the environment created by the historical relationships between violence and power in Mexico. The image of power stemming from the barrel of a gun is central not only to public law enforcement but to private social power—the "white guards" of landlords and hired guns of political bosses. This helps to perpetuate the valorization of carrying arms on the part of those who have the economic means to afford the ammunition, whilst the systems of justice and law enforcement serve neither to encourage recourse to legal channels nor to inhibit resort to violence. Not only can judges and policemen be bought off, but their lack of predictability discourages witnesses from speaking out.

Community pressure often forces the perpetrators of violence (and sometimes their kin as well) to move elsewhere. Yet since the consequences of violent action vary according to the social position and networks of both perpetrators and victims, it often transpires that legal punishment is meted out only to a weaker party who has taken revenge for an unpunished crime. Everyday social violence often appears to be a product of the *machismo* complex, sometimes taking almost comic, but still potentially tragic, forms, as when a young man reacts aggressively to a kiss blown to his girlfriend by an artist from the big city at a concert. As I suggest in Chapter Six, phenomena such as domestic violence towards women are related to more general problems of the construction of maleness in relation to the realities of social power and powerlessness.

I am arguing, then, that what appear to be qualitatively distinct types of social violence are best analyzed as products of the larger scheme of power relations. This line of reasoning might be extended to embrace the figure of the *Judicial* himself. Fearful of reprisals and called upon to commit acts which violate moral principles, the *Judicial* is drawn into a collective ethos in which the violation of normal morality becomes what is appropriate to an agency charged with the regulation and purging of society's enemies. Women and children become suitable objects of punishment. Degradation, even, on occasion, mutilation, of the victims, serves to expel them from the ordinary world of persons with rights, and transforms them, culpable or not, into a condition appropriate to culpability.

Violence is a background feature of social life. Better-off members of the community often feel they have less to fear, and its poorest members tend to be more preoccupied with their economic difficulties on a day-to-day basis. Certain places achieve a reputation for being violent in the eyes of people in other places, sometimes as a result of historical experience, but partly because they are perceived as different kinds of communities in social terms. It is not uncommon to find that these perceptions are mutual: both populations construct themselves as pacific in relation to the violent other. Yet the fact that violence is to some extent a construction, and mainly kept in the background, does not justify its neglect as a central part of the political condition.

At election time, people routinely expect to see greater activity by the *judicial* and the army. Many electors remain unconvinced that their vote is secret and that exercising their democratic rights might not involve personal danger. The pervasive possibility of repressive violence is a disincentive towards even passive support for dissident social and political movements, and this makes many people suspicious of democratic politics. "Political parties" are seen as "stirring up trouble." They create confrontations which lead to an increase in policing activity, which may then prejudice those who are unconnected with the conflicts in question. The PRI has been adept at manipulating these anxieties to its own advantage. Its propaganda often stresses that voting for the official party is a means of securing social peace. The message is reinforced by its ambiguity: it can be read as an implicit threat that state violence will be deployed. The best way to cope with the repressive power infrastructure is to keep it out of one's life as much as possible, particularly where dissidence is unlikely to bring any immediate material benefit, let alone prospects of fundamental change. Even without conscious manipulation, the "defects" of the justice system and the capillary quality of the threat of violence can be productive for the regime.

This proved an enormous resource for the ruling party after 1988. The greatest error the PRD made was to assume that the government of Salinas would be permanently debilitated by the circumstances of the 1988 election: this not only underestimated the informal and institutionalized power resources at the disposal of the regime, but of the way those resources would be revitalized by the mere fact that the opposition failed to prevent Salinas becoming President.

Repression and manipulation of popular fears related to the absence of the rule of law is thus not the only factor to consider in seeking to explain the declining strength of the PRD opposition after 1988. Some of the other issues are of wider significance, because they are equally germane to the role of popular social movements, which are often seen as more promising candidates for promoting democratization and social justice in Mexico than political parties. It is worth reviewing them in conclusion to this chapter because they are also relevant to understanding why people may abandon collective solutions to their problems through social struggle and political activism, in favor of what appear to be more "individualistic" solutions like international migration.

The PRD and the Social and Political Roots of Disillusion

Mestizo and indigenous peasants who have affiliated to the UCEZ usually begin an account of their relationship with the organization by observing that its leader, Efrén Capiz, is a *licenciado* who does not charge them for his services. This highlights the most obvious reality facing poor people who attempt to struggle for resources through legal channels which will secure the recognition of their claims by the state. Negotiating terms with the state demands the services of educated mediators with appropriate skills. Even if the *licenciado* does not charge, maintaining legal claims involves expenses of other kinds: land claimants, for example, have sometimes told me that the level of *cooperaciones* required to maintain their juridical claim exceeds the economic value of harvests obtained from sowing the land. Although they may still be disposed to view the expenditure as a long-term investment, which will eventually no longer be necessary once the question of title has been resolved, the more problems they experience in meeting basic living costs, the less attractive such investments seem. The solidarity of individuals begins to be threatened, even if there are no external forces acting to disarticulate the movement and sow doubt and dissension in the ways which I discussed earlier.

This suggests that rural social movements have a built-in tendency to demobilize, as the initial intensity of the struggle and confrontation with power holders gives way to a phase of "normal politics" in which state agencies keep the possibility of total fulfillment of demands open but delay the moment of definitive settlement indefinitely. Such a strategy feeds on people's tacit acceptance that neither the political regime nor the basic balance of class power in society can be overthrown. Only in extraordinary moments, such as July 1988, does the prospect of achieving radical change in the systemic organization of society seem thinkable as a possibility. Even then, it is clear that many who voted for Cuauhtémoc Cárdenas doubted whether his victory would really lead to a fundamental transformation in the practices of power. It can, of course, be questioned whether it is reasonable to expect a maximalist stance from members of social movements pursuing concrete and immediate social objectives, such as land rights and urban services. Hellman has argued that social movements cannot achieve major transformations of the social and, in particular, political system: this, she contends, is more properly the task of political parties, which bear "the burden of theorizing and organizing to promote broad societal change and the expansion of institutionalized forms of democratic expression" (Hellman, 1994: 139).

One "social movement" which has achieved local political power and gone beyond "bread and butter issues" is the Coalition of Workers, Peasants and Students of the Isthmus (COCEI), which governs Juchitán in Oaxaca. COCEI's success is based on a particularly effective kind of "postmodern" identity politics. Its promoters successfully articulated a "reinvented" Zapotec cultural tradition to the popular culture of the movement's base, maintaining popular mobilization on economic issues within a framework in which "ethnicity" became a political identity (Campbell, 1993). At the same time as they developed a language for communicating effectively with their base, they proved equally adept at speaking the language of national politics, combining "public militancy with public and private negotiation" (Rubin, 1994: 58).

COCEI is unusual because it has secured recognition and guarantees of respect for its autonomy from the government which are not entirely empty. The first COCEI administration of Juchitán was ended by a military occupation in 1983, but the organization returned successfully to the electoral arena after what Rubin argues was a relatively mild episode of repression. This seems to reflect historical particularities of the relationship between Juchitán and the national regime, whose past backing for anti-caciqual struggles created a space in which elements of the local middle class and elite were not antagonistic to the COCEI project (Rubin, op.cit.: 61). Rubin also suggests that COCEI's leadership skillfully manipulated the center's fantasy images of the indigenous population as "violent" and "explosive," allowing the threat inherent in such images to "alternately surface and disappear." Independent regional social movements can negotiate with the state most successfully when they remain on the ambiguous border between violence and non-violence (Rubin, op.cit.: 58–59).

From an internal perspective, the COCEI reveals familiar tensions between coexisting political styles, *continuismo*, authoritarianism and male domination in leadership, on the one hand, and respect for difference and openings for female activism, on the other (Rubin: ibid.). Leaders have been accused of hidden compromises with the PRI and personal corruption (Haber, 1993: 247–8). The continuing strength of the COCEI reflects its capacity to live with these contradiction and perhaps work towards their resolution, but it also reflects the movement's regional character. COCEI does not need to articulate the national strategy required of a mass political party.

Some other social movements, like the Committee of Popular Defense (CDP) in Durango, have found *convenios de concertación* (collaboration agreements) with the Salinas government a preferable option to continuing commitment to the PRD as a means of securing some degree of local political influence (Haber, 1993). As Harvey has pointed out, *concertación* appears to offer a new "terrain of negotiations" which competes with traditional corporatist arrangements, but it is a strategy which has been applied in a selective manner, alongside repression, may well serve to depoliticize the demands of popular movements, and contributes to the concentration of presidential power (Harvey 1993: 17–18).

It could be argued that the creation of regional spaces of political independence, even if it is a limited and qualified independence, can make a positive and cumulative contribution to strengthening democratization in the long-term. It could permit a greater number of popular voices to find ways of expressing themselves, and even small achievements may enable citizens to feel that political activity is both viable and meaningful in its consequences. It might be doubted whether regional movements in their severalty would have a significant aggregate effect on the evolution of national policy simply by forcing the government to engage in a dialogue. Yet the notion that social movements can contribute to transformations in civic consciousness and popular feelings of empowerment is not *a priori* absurd, even if one takes the view that Salinas's interest in *concertación* is largely motivated by a desire to fragment popular movements and remodel systems of political control. These arguments do, however, have something of the quality of James Scott's justification for his claim that "everyday acts of resistance" have substantial cumulative system-transforming capacities (Scott, 1990; Gutman, 1993): the case is difficult to prove and the overall impact of positive developments on the structures of class and political domination may not be great. We should also recognize that voices from below will continue to be mediated through their leaderships, with all that entails in the Mexican life-world. On balance, Hellman's doubts about the transformative potential of social movements do not seem entirely misplaced.

Yet on her own criteria, the principal political party alternative, the PRD, could itself be judged a failure. An uncomfortable coalition of socialists, social democrats and PRI dissidents, its history has been dogged by factional struggle at the top. The ideological vision of the PRD failed to emerge with total clarity in the period 1988 to 1994, and Cárdenas had difficulty dispelling the charge that he was "yesterday's man," advocating a return to the old ways of statism. His attempt to bolster his 1994 campaign by associating himself with the cause, if not the methods, of the Chiapas rebels fell somewhat flat in the face of subcomandante Marcos's public dismissal of the PRD as "repeating within itself all the vices which poisoned from birth the force now in power ... palace intrigues, agreements made by cliques, lies and the worst manner of settling accounts, betrayal" (*Latin American Weekly Report*, 94-20: 230).

On the other hand, it seems necessary to acknowledge the practical difficulties the PRD faced in consolidating itself under Salinas. Where the PRD gained power at the local level, the PRI's retention of the levers of state and federal power presented local leaderships with a difficult choice, particularly after PRONASOL came into the picture. In order to satisfy their followers, it was necessary to negotiate with *priísta* authorities for resources. While the national leadership maintained a position that there could be no negotiation with "illegitimate" authorities, leaders on the ground were faced with real dilemmas, since they were often already in difficulties because of accusations that they were favoring their particular electoral clienteles, especially indigenous communities. Where they opted for negotiation, this tended to trigger factional splits within the local party. Although much of the negotiation proved futile because of the exclusionary tactics adopted by the PRI towards the Left opposition, its mere existence excited the suspicious cast of popular political culture, which the PRI could exploit in its own "black propaganda," as I noted earlier. Faced with the contradictions of trying to get things done and maintaining political leverage, *perredista* politicians were eventually drawn to resort to "traditional" methods, "dragging" supporters to rallies and reviving clientalistic practices. In Michoacán, the PRD state leadership's practice of "fingering" candidates to be imposed on local parties (*dedazo*) had become a major point of contention by the end of the sexennial.

All this was despite some genuine attempts to foster the participation of ordinary members in the political life of the party. On the basis of my observations in the field, these tended to founder on the kinds of problems which Bourdieu (1991) has identified as the root causes of the tendencies towards "professionalization" of political representation and the "bureaucratization" of mass parties. Poor members could neither afford to meet the expenses of participation nor, in many cases, felt themselves to be equipped for such roles, preferring to elect as their representatives the better educated members who were more willing to make economic sacrifices, and had more time free from the daily struggle to get by.

Some of the problems experienced by the PRD in maintaining mobilization of its supporters can be illustrated by the history of an individual from the sugar town of Santa Clara. Jaime was a sympathizer of the PRD, in which kinsmen also played prominent roles, but also a member of the mill workers' union, constitutionally a *priísta* organization. When I first met him, he was an active participant in the PRD-led campaign to depose the union boss which I mentioned earlier. The campaign's failure provoked little surprise, although Jaime and his friends expressed appropriate indignation. More significantly, however, Jaime subsequently told me that he had not wished to pursue defense of his vote beyond that point, since two years ago he had a problem at work, and the union leader had aided him in an active and correct way: his "personhood" realized, he felt obligated and thus constrained.

Jaime also participated in a UCEZ-sponsored group of *comuneros* fighting to retain control of some land on the upland periphery of the town, illegally sold to ranchers from the neighboring community of Tocumbo by the *ejido* authorities, and won back in a bitter and violent dispute. Jaime expressed hostility towards the cattlemen, whom he described as *caciques*, and was friendly with several families of impoverished cane cutters resident in the socially downgraded high *barrio* of the community. Yet his commitment to the *agrarista* group showed signs of strain: he complained about the costs of maintaining the judicial claim for the land, and that *compañeros* better off than himself did not pay their proper share. His discourse on this question revealed the contradictions arising from social differentiation in a community divided between landholders, mill workers and the completely landless, with some individuals having land plus a job, some having more secure jobs than others, and some having virtually nothing except a wage which had been static in money terms for several years.

Jaime doubted whether true solidarity was possible between people who were not equal. He is a person very critical of the regime, well informed about the practice of politics at both local and national level. Nevertheless, he proved susceptible to one aspect of PRI propaganda, despite his generally negative attitude towards the party itself: that was when the PRI began to denounce Cuauhtémoc for "lack of patriotism" for criticizing his country abroad. When I last saw him, in December 1992, he told me that he had agreed to act as a scrutineer for the PRI in the municipal elections. The mill was planning further reductions of the workforce, and this may well have influenced Jaime's decision to draw closer towards conformity, but it was also consistent with a stance of resignation to the inevitable corruption of all political life and a growing feeling that the PRD did not represent anything truly distinct.

This example illustrates two faces of popular disillusion: firstly, a political disillusion, a product of political practices and the limited gains from so many social struggles, and secondly, a social disillusion, rooted in the "individualization" and culture of envy produced by social change (and cynically exploited by the holders of power). It might also be argued, however, that the PRD's problems in maintaining the active mobilization of its base simply reflected the way it was a creation of actors who were already "políticos," and was dominated by former *priístas* who lacked a class perspective on politics, although leftist dissidents within the party also accused Cárdenas of failing to restrain popular mobilizations likely to lead to violence for reasons of personal ambition which were premised on an authoritarian and caudillistic outlook (Carr, 1993: 92–3). It was, however, also difficult for the PRD, as an aspirant national party, to articulate a traditional class-based perspective, because it was a Center-Left party built on alliance between segments of different classes (Gledhill, 1991; 1993). At the same time, its popular base was afflicted by contradictions arising from non-class divisions. The fact that the PRD won power in some *municipios* on the basis of the indigenous vote was frequently exploited by its *priísta* opponents. Ethnic divisions are not necessarily insuperable, as shown by the success of the UCEZ in getting indigenous and *mestizo* groups to display practical solidarity. They are, after all, a construction, born of the "deindianization" of the Mexican masses under colonial conditions (Bonfil, 1990). They have, however, become deeply sedimented in social practice: even committed *mestizo* radicals within the UCEZ may still refer to their indigenous allies down the road as "naturales" or "inditos," and continue to valorize their own relative "whiteness." Such fragmentation tends to reassert itself in the long periods of "normal" struggle for defense of gains, along with individual recourse to the patronage relations which can offer immediate solutions to practical problems. Nevertheless, the exclusionary and selective nature of patronage under neoliberal regimes means that such solutions may no longer be available to those who are most disadvantaged by their policies, and it is clear that the core of the continuing support for the PRD does come from the subaltern classes. This may be significant for the future course of Left opposition in Mexico, as I will argue in the final chapter of this book.

In this chapter, I have argued that the political triumph of *Salinismo* was partly an illusion, but that the regime's strategies articulated with diffuse and capillary forms of power in a way which promoted popular disillusion with the prospects for political reform in Mexico. This may have contributed, along with the more evident social consequences of neoliberal economics, to the forces fostering a continuing growth of international migration after 1988, the subject of the next chapter.

4

The Transnationalization of Regional Societies: Capital, Class and International Migration

This chapter sets the scene for the more detailed analysis of ethnographic data which follows, by offering a broad discussion of the impact of transnational processes on Mexican rural society. In the case of rural Michoacán, the most evident facet of transnationalization is international migration, but one of my objectives here is to provide a preliminary justification for extending the discussion beyond the traditional problematics of the migration literature. In my view, migration as such should be treated as simply one dimension of the transnational class relations produced by the economic, cultural and political restructuring of the global space of capitalist accumulation.

I will, however, take the migration literature as a point of departure. It seems eminently reasonable to assume that the movement of people across international boundaries in search of work must be related to limitations in the economic opportunities available to them at home. Such a view seems to be reinforced by the evidence on change in both the extent and social composition of international migration during the crisis of the Eighties (Cornelius, 1990). Cornelius argues, however, that the Eighties marked a distinctive phase in the history of Mexican migration because this was actually the first time in that history that a direct link could be established between economic crisis and international migration. He suggests that earlier migratory processes in the main represented a search for "social mobility," whereas falling employment and real incomes in both the urban and rural economies in the Eighties forced people to turn to the North as "authentic economic refugees" (Cornelius, op.cit.: 114). Although I will criticize this distinction later on, it is true that research on migration from Mexico to the United States before the 1980s demonstrated conclusively that no simple correlations could be established between economic conditions, on the one hand, and the scale and social composition of the migratory movement between particular regions of Mexico and the North, on the other (Durand and Massey, 1992). Even in the Eighties, international migration was not the predominant response in all regions, and participation in international migration continued to show some patterns of social selectivity within regional societies. Nor have the factors determining migration patterns ever been purely economic. Political factors on both sides of the frontier, and the social organization of migratory networks by the migrants themselves, have played an important role in determining the extent and nature of participation of Mexicans in U.S. labor markets (Cross and Sandos, 1981; Massey et al, 1987; Gledhill, 1991; Wilson, 1993).

The importance of kinship and friendship networks in influencing where people go, and which members of the Mexican population participate in migration, does not, of course, allow us to discount the role of macroeconomic factors in determining why migration happens in the first place. Even so, the impact of the uneven development which these factors produce is experienced by people in different ways within particular local settings, and determines social behavior through a process of interpretation by the actors which makes migration a meaningful process (Wilson, op.cit.: 119). As I pointed out earlier, migrant behavior reflects the formulation of expectations about the entire quality of life and not simply relative wage levels. The fact that migration is a socially organized process also suggests that it may be unwise to regard it as a purely "individual" solution to problems of resource scarcity, poverty or restricted social mobility. As I will demonstrate later in my analysis, international migration may be associated with certain kinds of behavior which might be labelled "individualistic" and cause conflicts over personal obligations to others within migrant communities. Yet it may also reinforce or even create new forms of social solidarity and collective identities (Kearney, 1986). Furthermore, both tendencies may be present simultaneously in a dialectical tension within migrant communities. These observations suggest that there is some value in maintaining a broader perspective on the political economy of migration and at the same time avoiding an economistic account of the social processes associated with it.

International migration is also evidently a highly politicized issue within metropolitan countries today. As one of the leading Mexican students of international migration, Jorge Bustamante, has tirelessly stressed, official American and Mexican conceptualizations of what is perceived as one of the major "policy issues" in international migration, the problem of "undocumented migrants," are radically distinct. As far as Bustamante is concerned, there is a consensus within the "scientific community" that undocumented migration results from "the interaction between a demand for cheap labor from the United States and a supply of it within Mexico" (Bustamante, 1988: 109) . The official American view remains, however, that undocumented migration is a problem of "criminal behavior," a political echo of a widespread public view of undocumented migration as:

> a silent invasion, a national threat, the cause of a variety of public calamities such as loss of control of U.S. borders, a burden for U.S. taxpayers because of illegal aliens'

abuse of welfare and other public benefits, a cause of unemployment, even a cause of drug traffic (Bustamante, op.cit.: 109–10).

For most liberal academics outside Mexico, an appropriate response to these popular constructions of the Mexican migrant within U.S. society is to demonstrate "scientifically" that they are false, and to hope that the intensity of public passion on the subject of undocumented migration is related to the economic cycle. The problem with such a discussion is that it fails to address the issue of why Anglos are prone to such constructions, and what this signifies for the evolving relationship between Mexico and the United States. It is certainly not adequate to argue that because hysteria about Mexicans is nothing new historically in the United States, no significant social consequences follow from it in a changing situation. I will discuss these issues in more depth in Chapter Seven, but taking up Bustamante's suggestion that political economy is a preferred starting point for analysis will rapidly demonstrate the limitations of abstracting labor market conditions from their social and political context.

The Political Economy of Transnational Class Relations

The role of transnational companies (TNCs) is one of the most obvious factors in the internationalization of the global economy, and the investment strategies of such companies have an obvious impact on labor markets worldwide. The global social impact of TNCs is, however, much broader than this, since their activities have cultural-ideological and organizational consequences. Leslie Sklair, for example, has argued that TNCs are engaged in a veritable global hegemonic project in the realm of culture, focused on the implantation of the "culture-ideology of consumerism" (Sklair, 1991: 72–3). In Sklair's view, the local agents of this transformation are an "international managerial bourgeoisie" which encompasses senior state functionaries, politicians and members of the learned professions as well as entrepreneurial elites and managers of firms (op.cit.: 62). Direct ownership and control of means of production is not, he suggests, the exclusive criterion for "serving the global interests of capital" in the contemporary world order (ibid.). In the light of the consensus achieved among political technocrats, business managers and some intellectuals in Mexico on the current paradigm of "modernization," such a view does not seem entirely misplaced. Yet questions of ownership and control remain of some significance.

Privatization of state-owned assets has concentrated economic power over key sectors of the Mexican economy in the hands of a relatively small circle of investors, organized into groups which dominate the export-orientated branches of the economy and also operate businesses in the United States. The character of this bourgeoisie is clearly transnational in Sklair's sense, but its operations take place within a framework of transnational class relations in a less obvious sense. Petras and Morley (1990) have argued that the external debt crisis in Latin America should be viewed not as a demonstration of the thriftlessness and irresponsibility of overblown states detached from civil society, but as a class process. The formation of the debt was a cyclical process which began with the investment of financial capital abroad by the local bourgeoisie when economic conditions at home were unfavorable: faced with shortage of investment capital at home, Latin American states turned to foreign banks for loans, which were then transferred back, directly or indirectly, to entrepreneurs within Latin America on favorable terms, whilst the debt was guaranteed by government. This process established a transnational class relationship mediated by the state, in which the cost of debt repayment was transferred to the national subaltern classes in the form of the "austerity" programs which accompanied the renewal of crisis.

The small but powerful group of transnational owners of capital which develops within this relationship is in fact a beneficiary of crisis. When local conditions do not favor investment in production, returns on capital can still be maximized through investment in international financial circuits. This group is also the prime beneficiary of government loans and foreign investment in those sectors of the economy with guaranteed profitability. Crisis reduces the real value of capital goods within the national economy. When the upturn comes, repatriated capital can acquire physical capital goods at relatively low cost. The privatization of public assets represents a particularly attractive variant of a more general principle, particularly when, as in Mexico, it is accompanied by tax incentives to repatriate capital. Thus, Petras and Morley argue, "international financing is the other side of the coin to the internationalization of production" in the form of *maquiladoras* and large scale agro-export enterprises (op.cit.: 198). No distinction should be made here between speculative capitalism operating on financial markets and profiting from changes in the value of "fictitious capital," on the one hand, and capital orientated to production, on the other, because the transnational capitalist participates in both types of accumulation. The social cost of this form of accumulation for the masses, crisis and austerity, is highly beneficial to the transnational capitalist class, because it leads to another restructuring of the local accumulation process, in itself a means of accumulation.

This manifestation of the transnational quality of the class relationships involved in the modern capitalist accumulation process is one of a series of ways in which we might distinguish the "post-colonial" phase of development of the world economy from its predecessors. Michael Kearney has, in fact, suggested that there is an organizational counterpart to the transnational corporation among one segment of the working classes of the global economy, the "transnational communities" formed by the migration of workers from peripheral to metropolitan countries (Kearney, 1991: 58; see also Rouse, 1991).

His argument runs as follows. The nation-state, a condition for the development of capitalist production, developed as the product of both competition between expanding European powers and the differentiation of the world's peoples into "developed," "underdeveloped" and "de-developed" regions (Kearney, 1991: 53). The United States did not, however, need to subject movement across its Southwestern frontier before the Great Depression to the same controls as were introduced to control entry from Europe and Asia, because the military conquest of Mexican territory had already given the southern border a categorical absoluteness: through the exercise of military power, Mexicans had been definitively "othered" and Mexico defined as a "periphery" (Kearney, op.cit.: 54). It is true that there was a considerable amount of movement of colonized people between different regions of the capitalist world economy even in the colonial period (Wolf, 1982). Yet even the position of white settlers within the colonial order was defined as inferior through the distinction between "mother country" and colonies (Anderson, 1991: 93). Thus Kearney seems correct to argue that the essence of the colonial situation was that it involved:

> the spatial separation of peripheral production and extraction of value and knowledge as raw materials from their consumption and transformation in metropoles such that they could be reinvested in the colonial project (ibid.).

As Kearney points out, it was this separation, effected through the construction of nation-states and political nationalism (Gledhill, 1994: 20), that underlay the clear categorical distinction between "self" and "other" on which classical anthropology itself was premised. The "End of Empire" in the formal sense not only brought an end to the previous system of political classification of the world into metropoles and colonies, but coincided with the long-term result of capitalist restructuring of the peripheries, a labor surplus in peripheral zones which flowed towards the centers as migrants and guest workers (Kearney, op.cit.: 57).

In this phase, the national state continues to seek to exercise its defining power over "domestic" society for the reasons mentioned in the previous chapter, and one of the sites at which it does this most conspicuously is the border, where the state supposedly dictates the terms under which outsiders enter national space. Yet as is graphically demonstrated by the studies of Jorge Bustamante and his team of the flow of undocumented migrants across Zapata Canyon, Tijuana, located between Colonia Libertad and San Isidro in San Diego County,[1] the de facto policy of the U.S. government remains one of regulating the flow of "undocumented migrants" rather than closing the border to unwanted guests. This is despite the passage of the Immigration Reform and Control Act (IRCA) of 1986, more popularly known as the Simpson-Rodino law after its sponsors in the U.S. legislature (Bustamante, 1988; 1992).

---

[1] Daily observations of the flow of migrants in Tijuana have been complemented by weekend observations at Mexicali, Nogales, Ciudad Juárez, Nuevo Laredo and Matamoros since 1987 (Bustamante, 1992: 12).

As a means of articulating core and periphery, transnational labor migration separates the sites of production and social reproduction between national units (Kearney, op.cit.: 59). This is again not a new phenomenon, and in the case of Mexican migration, might be said to be less relevant today than it was during the period of the *bracero* labor contract system, which ended in 1964.[2] As we will see, more recent migration has been marked by increasing family migration and tendencies towards more permanent residence in the North. Nevertheless, because migrants are still excluded from full "personhood" in the United States, they are still consigned to a "betwixt and between" kind of existence in a structural borderland between two national societies. As Kearney argues, this has important consequences because of the way migrants are drawn to reconstitute their identities outside the control of nation-states.

Kearney's primary example of a "transnational migrant community" is the Mixtec migrants from Oaxaca, whose peregrinations into the U.S. labor market were mediated historically by a period of migrant farm work in Northern Mexico (Kearney, 1986). Their collective experience of particularly oppressive labor conditions and racist stigmatization within their own country laid the ground for their subsequent response to the role of stigmatized "alien" in the United States, which was one of developing a strong "ethnic" consciousness. As Kearney demonstrates, this is at first sight paradoxical, since the villages of the eroded countryside of the Mixtec region had not possessed a cohesive collective identity in the Mexican colonial past. Their social interaction with the colonizing "Other" was limited, and endemic conflict between villages privileged local identities. Yet it is entirely understandable in a people who lack the resources to sustain themselves in their "homeland," and are effectively denied participation in both of the two national identities which are hegemonic in the spaces between which they move. Kearney argues that ethnic consciousness is "the supremely appropriate form for collective identity to take" for those who exist on the borderlands, because it is a way of reconstructing their existence as a subaltern other which is meaningful to both the migrants and those who mark them (Kearney, 1991: 62–63). In the case of the Mixtecs, this self-differentiation is a means of realizing grassroots organizations in both Mexico and the United States, organizations which allow them to defend themselves "as workers, migrants and 'aliens'" (op.cit.: 63).

Mixtecs are not the only migrants who have organized themselves in transnational space, which has now been compressed by air travel and immediate communication by telephone. Mestizo migrants from Michoacán in California have sometimes shown an interest in "identity politics" beyond the formation of recreational associations which may also provide an infrastructure of mutual help,

---

2 I have discussed the historical evolution of international migration from Michoacán from the 1920s to the start of the 1980s in some depth elsewhere (Gledhill, 1991: Chapter Eight), and refer the reader to that work for a more detailed analysis.

and at a more mundane level, many rural communities possess social facilities such as children's playgrounds financed by emigrant groups. Emigrant members of indigenous communities may also play a significant role in community life in their homelands, although I give examples in Chapter Eight of emigrants losing interest in supporting "traditional" community rituals. It may, however, be unwise to push the analogy between the migrant "transnational community" and the transnational corporation too far, because of the differences in power between the two kinds of organizations, and it cannot be assumed that the transnational community is a wholly positive phenomenon in all contexts.

It is true that attempts on the part of migrant workers to defend their individual and collective social dignity through organization, and their conversion of "ethnicity" into symbolic capital, creates problems for the national projects of both "home" and metropolitan states. These developments can be seen as resistances to forms of power which remain significant for the capitalist regulation process, as well as potential threats to the integrity of national power, although it is important to see that they are in part *reactive* responses to circumstances of marginalization and exclusion. The potentially destructive consequences of transnationalization are especially evident where emigrant communities provide the logistical base for separatist movements, and this is only one of the contradictory results of a global capitalism which makes political borders open to the flow of commodities, people and media images (Appadurai, 1990; Gledhill, 1994: 157–60).

As far as power differentials are concerned, the border remains a space of discipline as well as resistance. As Kearney himself notes, contemporary processes of border surveillance are crucially important for maintaining the disadvantaged class position of workers from the South as workers (Kearney, op.cit.: 61). The Border Patrol fails, like the prison in Foucault's famous study (Foucault, 1979), to fulfil its official program (excluding people), but thereby fulfills another function which is very positive for some sectors of capital, the creation of "undocumented workers." The Mexican migrant population in the United States is not socially or economically homogeneous, and neither individuals nor different segments within that population necessarily display solidarity, as we will see. Attempts by migrants to defend their human value may simply reinforce the effect of a growing public presence of laborers rejected as persons within metropolitan societies, strengthening demands for the state to intervene to defend the hegemonic identities which define the superior status and privileges of "natives" (and not necessarily simply of white "natives," as I will demonstrate in Chapter Seven). I suggested in the last chapter that ethnic identity politics within Mexico is in danger of foundering on the principle that it cannot articulate an alternative hegemony. This problem is even more acute in metropolitan societies. The U.S.-sponsored diffusion of neoliberal economic regimes in the South seems set continue the processes of rural displacement which begun with earlier phases of the capitalization of agriculture, and was reinforced by U.S. support for military "counter-insurgency" in Central America during the Reagan-Bush years (Hamilton and Stoltz Chinchilla, 1991). In consequence, Latinos in the United States may find it harder, at least in the medium-term, to overcome the exclusionary consequences of the fact that, to use Kearney's words, "imperial projects to differentiate the colonized Other promote indigestible differences within the colonizing self" (Kearney, op.cit.: 69).

The formation of transnational communities is a global phenomenon produced by the uneven development of capitalism and successive restructurings of the capitalist accumulation process. There is, however, also a more specific relationship between the transformation of rural Mexico and the transformation of rural America, although this relationship has tended to be ignored because analysts have emphasized the growth of migration from the Mexican countryside to urban destinations in the United States. By the early 1980s, approximately 90% of the farm labor force for California agribusiness was of Mexican origin or descent (Palerm, 1991: 14). In the 1990s, Mexicans have been materializing in less familiar places, picking mushrooms in Pennsylvania, dressing chickens in Atlanta, Georgia, and packing meat in towns on the High Plains, as agroindustries which remain labor-intensive despite mechanization seek to cut costs by displacing established local workforces in favor of immigrant minorities (Stull, 1993). As Palerm and Urquiola (1993) point out, in an analysis of the relationship between the evolution of capitalist farms in California and peasant farms in the Valle de Santiago region of the Bajío, the relationship is a systemic one, which dates back to the 1940s but has undergone progressive transformation.

Developments in the Bajío resemble those I have described for the western zone of Michoacán (Gledhill, 1991). The official agricultural policies of the Díaz Ordaz and Echeverría periods deepened the integration of local farmers into a transnational system of agricultural production—as consumers of industrialized farm inputs as well as producers—and this process also reinforced involvement of *ejidatario* households in international migration, for reasons explored in more depth in the next section. Even well-to-do *ejidatario* families in the Bajío were drawn into international migration, because the replacement of their capital stock in the form of tractors and pumps required a dollar income (Palerm and Urquiola, op.cit.: 345). During the crisis of the Eighties, population boomed in the Valle de Santiago, as high fertility coincided with return migration from devastated Mexican cities and commuter migrants to Bajío industrial centers lost their jobs. Bajío farms were unable to absorb the growing labor surplus, and U.S. migration both intensified and changed. Individuals stayed for longer periods in the North, more spouses accompanied husbands and true binational households were established (ibid.). At the same time, people displaced from urban jobs and rural professionals were drawn into the migrant stream in significant numbers.

As I will show in the next chapter, similar tendencies were manifest in the Ciénega de Chapala. Escobar notes that one of the effects of unrestricted rice imports was to drive once prosperous (and fully technologically modernized) rice farmers from Colima back into the migrant process, along with manual workers from Guadalajara and lower middle-class urban professionals who saw little future even in turning to small business within the country (Escobar, 1993: 76–77). Nevertheless, the overall picture on the changing social composition of international migration is complex. As I noted earlier, the Eighties' crisis brought into the flow many relatively uneducated urban migrants and people from more marginal rural areas who had previously moved internally. Bustamante's studies of undocumented cross-border movements separate migrants of rural and urban origin (Bustamante, 1992). His results for 1988 to 1990 suggest, for example, that differences in the educational levels attained by the two groups have tended to decrease, those of urban migrants falling, and those of rural migrants increasing slightly (op.cit.: 16). This is consistent with the notion that the advantages of urban residence in Mexico were reduced with impoverishment, but Bustamante's data also suggested that rural migrants with the lowest incomes were having to meet higher costs in order to get to the United States than urban migrants, and faced a higher risk of suffering extortion on the part of the Mexican police in the frontier zone (op.cit.: 15–16).

The transnationalization of labor markets may therefore reproduce existing social inequities, but the issue I wish to stress at this stage of the argument is the role of the *ejido* in the transnationalization process, defined in Kearney's terms as a division of the sites of production and social reproduction. Palerm and Urquiola argue that the *ejido* farm of the Eighties continued to perform an essential social reproductive function in regions with high levels of international migration, holding the extended family together, maintaining those left behind, and enabling those who were now absent for an extended period to survive on what were absolutely low wages in U.S. terms (op.cit.: 347). At the same time:

> *Modernized* but cash-starved *and overpopulated* peasant/ejido farms continue to provide labor hungry California agribusiness with a steady, reliable and growing supply of immigrant and migrant workers, giving agricultural entrepreneurs *the confidence needed to intensify farming operations* to produce a cornucopia of goods which are devoured avidly by national and international markets (ibid., emphasis added).

The irony of this situation is that Mexican governments pursued rural policies which provided California agribusiness with the kind of labor force they required to sustain a shift out of low-value field crops and dairy farming towards high-value fruit and vegetable crops (Palerm, 1991). Despite mechanization, growing world surpluses—in part the product of international transfer of U.S. technology—and spiralling costs of production set in train by the oil crisis, made field crop production and dairying unprofitable. The period 1975 to the present saw a massive switch towards fruit and vegetable products, which were not merely labor intensive but augmented the demand for workers who remained year round in the region and possessed specific skills (Palerm, op.cit.: 78–80). As Palerm has shown, this shift was accompanied by an increasing domination of corporate over owner operated farms and, through the 1980s, by the growth of Mexican-dominated rural enclaves which have become sites of poverty and social problems as significant as those of the inner cities.

Migration is often represented as a flight from rural poverty. Yet transnational class processes are creating new forms of rural poverty in the midst of relative affluence in metropolitan countries. There is much more to be said about the political processes which underlie Mexican poverty in the United States, and about the conflicts recent changes in patterns of international migration have induced within the migrant population itself. In the light of such perspectives, it is less responsible than ever to adopt a complacent attitude towards international migration as a "safety-valve" which might help resolve the new problems posed for Mexican society by neoliberalism. At this stage of the analysis, however, it is more important to look at what determines the differential involvement of different regions and communities in the international migration process.

Economic Factors in Differential Patterns of U.S. Migration

Although Michoacán is one of the principle "sending regions" for Mexican migrants to the United States historically, and had rates of participation in excess of 15% of the economically active population in some zones at the start of the Eighties, patterns were not uniform. The eastern and north-eastern parts of the state, in particular, remained relatively uninvolved in transnational movement. In an analysis based on the 1980 population census data,[3] Gustavo López and Sergio Zendejas offered an hypothesis of this variation in terms of differences in local agricultural regimes. They suggested that:

> The development of profitable commercial crops at the expense of the cultivation of basic grains, together with the development of pig-raising and the production of balanced feedstuffs, produced an increase in international emigration, principally for two reasons: firstly, the increase in living standards, or at least, in the short-term, of household income, made it possible for a larger number of families to meet the costs necessary to send one of its members "to the North"; secondly, some of these commercial crops reduced the possibilities of employment in agriculture because of their high levels of mechanization, as in the case of sorghum (López and Zendejas, 1988: 58, my translation).

The first element of their explanation for differential migration rates suggests that participation in international migration is, other things being equal, positively

---

[3] The Mexican decennial population census is subject to a number of failings, but presents particular difficulties from the point-of-view of studying international migration. López and Zendejas adopt a specific methodology designed to cope with the census's defects, though they admit that their results can only be in the nature of an approximation.

related to living standards and peasant income, since it is an economic strategy with a significant element of cost. This argument is consistent with my own research on the social selectivity of international migration from the Ciénega de Chapala (Gledhill 1991), which indicated that *ejidatarios* and their children participated more extensively in international migration, up to the early 1980s, than persons from completely landless families. This was not, however, necessarily because their incomes were substantially higher than those of landless *jornaleros*, but because they were in a better position to raise a loan to embark on a migrant journey. The same reasoning applies with even greater force to entry into the legalization programs established under the IRCA, which, as I will show in the next chapter, resulted in an increase in the number of migrants, but with a significant socially selective effect. This reflected the investment required on the part of those who did not, in reality, meet the conditions of the law for legalization, but were able to enter the program by buying spurious documentation.

It cannot therefore be assumed that declining peasant living standards and reduced local employment opportunities automatically produce a massive increase in migration to the North, since greater poverty makes international migration more problematic. This argument is reinforced by the evidence already cited from Bustamante on the relatively high and rising costs of undocumented migration for rural people at the start of the Nineties. When, however, very poor people do go to the North as undocumented workers, the costs of movement to and fro should encourage longer periods without return, which was, as we will see, the pattern observed in this period in the Ciénega de Chapala communities.

The second element of the López and Zendejas hypothesis, the role of technological change, suggests a direct relationship between local employment opportunities in agriculture and international migration, although deficiencies in local demand for agricultural labor in themselves do not suggest anything more than greater pressure on the population to migrate somewhere, which could be to regional or metropolitan urban centers rather than the North. The Ciénega de Chapala, Bajío Michoacano, and the *municipios* to the south-east of the state, Aguililla, Coalcomán, Chinicuila, Coahuayana and Tepalcatepec, are the zones where the impact of this type of agricultural transformation has been greatest, and they are indeed the zones characterized by the highest rates of emigration to the North (López and Zendejas, op. cit: 59). The "development" of these regions never left enough income in the hands of the peasant producers to make dedication of the entire family labor force to agriculture either viable or more attractive than investment in intensified migration (op.cit.: 62).

Regions with low rates of international migration, like Zitácuaro, were characterized by the predominance of rain-fed cultivation of basic grains. Tuxpan was a major meat and dairy producing zone, but imported most of its forage: 80% of the land was sown in maize, alfalfa being the only significant forage crop (ibid.). *Municipios* in this zone were close to the labor markets of Toluca and Mexico City, facilitating internal migration and increasing its advantages relative to more costly and risky international migration. The same argument was made about the *municipios* close to Morelia (Trigueros and Rodríguez, 1988). Other relationships between urban centers and rural zones which may influence rates of migration include the existence of rural craft industries and use of former agricultural land for brick and tile making for the construction industry, the latter particularly notable in the case of Chilchota in the Cañada de los Once Pueblos near Zamora (Ramírez, 1986).

The Cañada sub-region also demonstrates the importance of social selectivity in the determination of migration patterns. Its indigenous population had a relatively low rate of international migration in comparison with that of nearby *mestizo* communities. Both men and women from the indigenous communities dedicated themselves to the most socially demeaning and heaviest work in brick-making, as well as to agricultural day-laboring in the commercial agriculture of the Valley of Tangancicuaro.

The social stratification of labor markets is an important complicating factor in discussing the impact of crisis on peasant economy. It is not uncommon to find that landless sons of *ejidatarios* migrate to the United States, while members of poorer communities work as *jornaleros* in local agriculture. Nevertheless, there are significant variations in labor systems, even between neighboring communities. In the Santa Clara-Los Reyes zone of Michoacán, for example, landless residents work in the cane cut in the community of Santa Clara, whereas in other local communities most of the labor for the *zafra* is imported—from the Nahuatl-speaking villages in the Río Balsas zone of Guerrero to which I referred earlier in the case of the *ejido* of Los Limones in 1991. These differences can be related to micro-variations between local agrarian communities which are not evident in *municipio*-level figures, such as differences in degrees of land concentration and the average size and quality of land-holdings between *ejidos*, possession of pasture lands susceptible to cultivation or use as orchards for fruit trees or avocados, and in some cases, the possession of private as well as ejidal land. They are also, however, related to the differences in the extent to which the poorer members of different communities see work in the United States as a preferable option, which is often a function of the community's particular long-term pattern of involvement with the North.

In the case of the western Ciénega de Chapala, where land is almost entirely ejidal in the irrigated plain, save for a few private properties on the outskirts of Jiquilpan and Sahuayo, most *ejidatarios* possess a four hectare parcela, though some also cultivate a small rain-fed maize plot (*ecuaro*) on the now eroded slopes of the surrounding hills and milk a couple of cows. They cannot, however, cultivate avocados or peaches, and suffer from problems of limited water supplies and increasing water costs. The main source of off-farm work for those with limited education has been public sector employment as a manual laborer. Little work outside agriculture is available in the local towns, and what there is pays low rates even in comparison with agricultural work in the region. In the Los Reyes area, with its two sugar mills and urban employments deriving from the multiplier effects of the sugar industry and avocado cultivation, with its packing plants, local labor markets were more diversified, and even agricultural day-rates were higher in the avocado orchards than in the fields of the Ciénega. On the periphery of the sugar fields, a considerable amount of land remains available for subsistence cultivation and cattle-raising, and, as I noted in the previous chapter, in the case of Santa Clara, where around 50% of the workers in the sugar mill are also *ejidatarios*, landless families fought a successful battle to sow maize as *comuneros* on land disputed with cattlemen. Though these families lived at a considerably lower level of affluence than other residents of their community, they continued to sustain themselves primarily by working in local agriculture at the start of the Nineties, arguing that the U.S. option had become less viable as its costs increased and work became scarcer, particularly for those who had not secured legalization.

Most of these *jornaleros* had been to the North at some time in their lives, and some had stayed there for a year or two without returning, but the real and continuing deterioration in their incomes provoked by the crisis of the sugar industry[4] had not, as yet, pushed them into the position of Cornelius's "economic refugees." They perceived the cost-benefit ratio of undocumented migration under current conditions as adverse relative to the alternative of sowing maize and working as *jornaleros*.

This example suggests that the IRCA proved something of a watershed in the history of migration from some communities, since Santa Clara is not a community lacking a migrant tradition. Some landless people had committed themselves to a career of undocumented migration during the Seventies, and legalized under the IRCA. Many *ejidatario* families, including some of those which had most land, also had one or more sons who had made permanent careers in the North. This pattern, characteristic of all the irrigated ejidos of the Los Reyes area, corresponds to López and Zendejas's notion of relatively better-off families making an "investment" in the North by financing a son to go. This region has not, historically, been one of acute land shortage, as I pointed out in the last chapter. What has been lacking has been sufficient income from local farming and agricultural labor to ensure the future of the whole of a next generation of ten or more children.

Mestizo communities on the rain-fed periphery of the irrigated *ejidos* are, however, poor in agricultural resources, and embarked early on seasonal interna-

---

[4] Cane cutters had seen their real earnings diminished not only by the slow growth of their money wages relative to consumer price inflation, but also by insistence on the part of the new private owners of the mills on delivery of cleaner cane. This reduced the number of tons an individual could cut in a day. Some non-cash payments cane cutters had traditionally received were eliminated, including the traditional bag of sugar at the end of the *zafra*. The non-delivery of *dispensas* of foodstuffs which formed part of the payments stipulated in the sugar decrees in the later stages of the *zafra* of 1990–1991 was particularly offensive to the cutters, who identified with the PRD: the items in question were subsequently distributed as political largess by the *priísta* leaders of the CNC Unión de Cañeros just before the elections of August 1991.

tional migration as a generalized strategy. Such communities may, ironically, have achieved some of the highest levels of integration into the U.S. labor market, since people from these communities, notwithstanding their initial poverty, have had the greatest number of opportunities to benefit from amnesty programs and other processes promoting legal emigration. In the rain-fed region behind the village of Guaracha, there are notable cases such as Jaripo, a community not incorporated into the ex-*hacienda* of Guaracha, which retained some private land, concentrated in a few hands (Fonseca, 1988). A majority of Jaripeños worked as seasonal migrants in the *Tierra Caliente* or as free peons on the *hacienda*, but a few participated in the early phase of migration from the Ciénega to Chicago in the period before 1929, and subsequently became active participants in the agrarian struggles of the Cárdenas period (Gledhill, 1991). The main entry of the community into the U.S. labor market was, however, the result of the patronage of an official born in the community, who enabled his *paisanos* to participate massively in the *bracero* program and achieve a high level of legalization through emigration by the time the contract system ended.

Fonseca argues that participation in the *bracero* phase was common to all sectors of the community, *ejidatarios*, *jornaleros* and sharecroppers working private land. By the 1950s, Jaripo migration was establishing its own social network focused on San Joaquín County and the farm town of Stockton, through the formation of personal links with foremen, ranchers and the employees of the office of the Stockton Farmers' Association. In the period 1960–61, Jaripo migration became emigration, at the suggestion of the *licenciado*. Individual migration then turned into family migration, as *emigrado* men sought residence permits for members of their families. Migration focused definitively on Stockton, where the migrants were able to live with their wives and children throughout the season in a camp for seasonal workers, which offered school and child-care facilities and a laundry. This enabled women to participate in work in the fields (Fonseca, op.cit.: 369). From 1974 onwards, there was a shift away from the camp towards rental of houses within the City of Stockton, in particular the Sierra Vista suburb on the south of the city, and this change was associated with tendencies towards longer stays of one or two years in the North. Fonseca suggests that the tendency to stay longer was the result of the several factors. The new residential area created problems of robbery, crime and damage to houses and possessions during absence, children could not readily be taken out of school in the North, and earnings did not always cover travel expenses plus the social prestige expenditures migrants incurred in Jaripo itself. The latter were more individual and conspicuous than collective, although *cooperaciones* (contributions) were expected towards the cost of the *fiesta* of the peregrinations of the Virgin, and *norteños* were expected to be lavish in meeting other obligations in social ritual, such as those of godparents.

By the Nineties, the smaller *ranchos* around Jaripo manifested the effects of a long-established emigrant tradition. The younger generation were now predominantly legal residents of the United States, mostly dedicated to factory work, and as the local region came to offer them less and less, entire communities were left deserted for a good part of the year, if not the whole of it.

López and Zendejas themselves concede that recent processes of agricultural transformation cannot explain the whole of the pattern of variation within the state, since migrant traditions and social networks arising from them have deeper historical roots. They suggest that "cultural traditions," and the transformation of the migrant journey into a *rite de passage* for young men, play a role in determining the behavior of local communities and individuals which is independent of their economic circumstances. The same argument has been made by other comparative studies, in particular Massey et al (1987), which is based on case studies of urban as well as rural places of origin. The contention that a "migrant tradition" as a cultural phenomenon tends to shape international migration in a relatively autonomous way certainly has some element of truth, but it is worth bearing in mind that some young people who report that they went to the North as a kind of "adventure" to prove themselves often also seem to be reacting to tensions which have developed within the family unit, particularly with their fathers, and are seeking a way of freeing themselves from irksome obligations and achieving greater economic and social autonomy. Communities with established historical traditions of international migration also enjoy substantial pragmatic advantages: the social networks which migrant communities establish as they form regular contacts with employers and labor contractors in the North, and the colonies of relatively permanent residents they create, are extremely important for reducing some of the uncertainties, if not the economic costs, of migration.

Variation in the Social Organization of Migration

Migrant social networks take different forms. Some communities orientate their migration towards particular regions where a son of the village has become established as a labor contractor. In some cases the contractor is simply the foreman of a ranch, who finds his *paisanos* work either with his own employer or somewhere else in the locality, but he is more generally a *raidero*, a person whom employers contact to recruit workers, but who is paid by the workers themselves. Under the IRCA provisions, which impose sanctions against employers who knowingly hire undocumented workers, the role of the contractors as sources of documentation became exceptionally important and lucrative, as we will see in the next chapter, but the original essence of the role was that of freeing the migrants themselves from the necessity of seeking out work. The *contratista* presents himself to the worker as the owner of a vehicle who knows where work is, and the latter pays him for the "ride" to work. To this service, which is profitable in itself, is generally added the supply of a false national insurance card ("seguro chueco") and food. At the end of the Eighties, each part of the service was charged at $3, and a man who worked with a *contratista* in Stockton or Merced could expect to earn $21 a day net, after the deduction of almost a third of his earnings by the intermediary.

There is no doubt that the charges are inflated in relation to the costs of supplying the services in question: agricultural migrants in the San Francisco region who found their own work would have between $1 and $1.50 deducted for transport provided by their employer, for example. The *contratista* system evolved to service the needs of a mass of undocumented migrant farm workers who were prepared to pay a high price for being guaranteed some work for the day, although the *contratistas* could not do more than allocate what work was actually on offer. Established migrants who had begun with the community contractors could subsequently form their own personal networks, often with people with different origins in the home country. As time went by, they might move to new regions and work with a regular employer. Even communities which remain heavily orientated towards seasonal farm work with the contractors, as is the case in Cerrito Cotijaran, discussed in the next chapter, contain some individuals who have established personal networks.

In some cases, particularistic relationships with contractors may be perceived as excessively exploitative, as happened in the case of the sons of an *emigrado*[5] migrant construction worker from Guaracha. The father had formed a small company in San Francisco with his older brother. The sons felt that their father and uncle were deducting too much from their pay for board and lodging in a house they had bought for their workers, and left them to seek work independently in the agricultural sector. Whether people work with contractors or not is, however, also influenced, at least initially, by whether they have the cash reserves needed to seek out work independently. Those who have legalized have a greater amount of flexibility, since they can claim unemployment benefit. Nevertheless, as the data from Guaracha presented in the next chapter will demonstrate, migrants who secured legalization and chose to work in the San Francisco region, where contractors are only significant in the construction sector, have drawn a number of undocumented kinsmen and friends after them.

The establishment of colonies of migrants in certain locations plays an important role in facilitating the entry of new persons into the network, whether the migrants are permanently resident or simply annual returnees who rent a house. At the very least, the new arrival can expect a bed and meal for a few days, and some advice about the work available. The existence of colonies can, however, have more substantial effects, including the sharing out of migratory and social security documents among different individuals. In some cases, permanent residents of the United States have crossed the frontier to deliver the work permit of a newly arrived kinsmen to an undocumented brother, who then entered with his sibling's papers.

---

[5] The local term "emigrado" may refer to both legally resident aliens and persons who are naturalized U.S. citizens, though the former are much more common among the populations I am describing.

At the opposite end of the social spectrum of migrant communities, residents of one indigenous community in the Meseta Tarasca,[6] generally too poor to pay *coyotes* for passage across the border, have adopted the strategy of arriving in Tijuana and telephoning their kinsmen or *paisanos* resident in the North to alert them of their impending arrival. They then simply launch themselves across the frontier. If they are captured by the border patrol, they try again for as long as it takes, while their kin wait at an agreed point at the other side until they have success, and take them off to a house in which they can stay until they find work. Deportation is at best a disagreeable experience, and may be a dangerous one, given the propensity of the Mexican police to victimize the most vulnerable of their countrymen. The Indians are already accustomed to victimization at home, and may therefore be more hardened to cope with the experience than some *mestizos*, but the basis for this form of behavior is the additional confidence gained from knowing that there is someone in whom they can trust waiting on the other side.

The existence of a long-established migrant tradition is a significant factor in enabling poorer members of a given community to access U.S. labor markets, and past history also influences the specific ways in which different communities are incorporated into the U.S. labor market (Durand and Massey, 1992: 33–34). Yet it is not a prerequisite. There seems to be an emergent pattern of young people from indigenous communities with low rates of migration in the past to turn to international migration, perhaps in part as a reaction against the willingness of the older generation to accept social marginality and in response to new expectations created by the diffusion of mass media. In some cases, there may be a mediating agents in the development of migration, such as the influence of emigrant *mestizo* labor brokers from the *cabecera municipal,* or even the arrival in the community of *gringos* trading in indigenous arts and crafts. Yet the entry of many such communities into the international migrant circuit is also the product of systematic economic and social change. Traditional agricultural systems are in accelerating decline due to deforestation, soil erosion and the depredations of local cattle ranchers, and there is also a diminishing economic return from internal agricultural labor migration circuits, which have always entailed suffering bad working and living conditions and social discrimination. The greater Spanish language competence of the young is also an important factor in making international migration more feasible. A significant proportion of the new indigenous migrants are women, who can find work both in agriculture and domestic service.

Michoacán's indigenous population in fact has a much greater time depth of historical involvement in the North than the indigenous communities of Oaxaca. Nevertheless, many communities were not involved in the earlier movements, early indigenous migrants tended to come from the village elites, and the variability of migration rates was heavily influenced by particular local histories of loss of

---

[6] I am indebted to Andrew Roth for describing this case to me.

economic resources to *mestizo* interlopers and the intensity of local violence in the period of revolution and land reform (Gledhill, 1991). The lesson to be drawn from more recent developments in the indigenous communities, in Michoacán and in other areas, is, however, that whilst past history undoubtedly facilitates current migration, and, through its impact on access to legalization, has played an important role in enhancing the social differentiation of the migrant population, it has, to date, been possible to establish new networks more or less *de novo*, where factors impelling movement to the North have been strong.

Much of the social process which produces a network seems to be idiosyncratic, a fortuitous relationship of patronage, or the good fortune of an individual who achieves a position in the North on a farm, in a factory or as a contractor which provides a bridge for others. Even the factors which might have impelled that individual towards the North may not be directly related to economic conditions: direct or indirect involvement in violent death, for example, may also be a significant factor in promoting the movement of individuals and families. Yet it seems necessary to look beneath these idiosyncracies towards more structural explanations, in which political economy should figure prominently, though not to the total exclusion of other, equally structural, perspectives. This brings me back to Cornelius's argument that the historical social selectivity of international migration from the "traditional" sending regions in western Mexico demonstrates that the motive for past migration was one of aspiration for "social mobility," a "target" migration orientated to the acquisition of money savings:

> In the traditional sending states such as Jalisco and Michoacán—whose economies have not grown but equally have not contracted during the crisis—the larger part of the families send migrant workers to the United States not as a requirement of economic survival but in order to improve their economic perspectives and conditions of life, to accumulate capital for very diverse ends, from the construction of a house or its repair, to the acquisition of durable consumer goods and the opening of a small business (Cornelius, 1990: 114, my translation).

Even allowing the validity of this assessment of the relative impact of crisis on states such as Michoacán—which seems debatable—and also allowing for the social heterogeneity of the migrant population within and between different sub-regions of the state—which is undeniable—the thinking underlying the distinction Cornelius makes here between "economic refugees" and other kinds of migrants seems flawed.

It is true that some long-term migrants from western Mexico have been able to invest in land and set up small, and in a few cases, not so small businesses. Shops and small owner-operated mechanical workshops are typical. It is also true that some have built splendid two-storied houses in their communities of origin. Yet these are not universal patterns, even for people who have been going to the North for many years. It would be difficult to describe the modest homes in which many migrants live as either capital investments or conspicuous consumption. Poorer migrant families in some communities can be found living in cardboard shacks which can be destroyed by a hailstorm. Both of the extremes of housing quality and other aspects of lifestyle reflect differences in labor market position in the United States, and they also often reflect differences in the initial local socio-economic status of the migrants and their households of origin. Many young couples will never build a palace in Mexico. Without migration, they would be forced to bring up their families in the already overcrowded dwellings of their parents. The psychological stresses such situations cause may even be a factor in individual decisions to migrate.

Nor is it difficult to see why people—and in particular women—regard their lives as enriched by the acquisition of a few "durable consumer goods." It may be true that the "old days" before the television were characterized by greater attention to family and collective *fiestas* and homemade, non-technified forms of entertainment, but it is as easy to romanticize this supposedly "more creative" past as it is to condemn the negative impact of modern mass communications. Men could drink and gamble, but most of a woman's life was devoted to housework and caring for children, with religion the major source of respite from these burdens. The real incomes obtained by the majority of Michoacán's *norteños* and lifestyles associated with them would be regarded as symptoms of poverty by most Anglo citizens of the United States rather than a basis for "capital investment." Most seasonal migrants of the 1960s and 1970s only earned enough to cover basic social reproductive expenditures, as the people themselves insist—with some irritation—when asked about "assets" they might have acquired with their earnings.

The term "economic refugees" used to characterize the "migrants of the crisis" also has its drawbacks. It has become entangled in metropolitan discourses on immigration control and asylum policy which seek to make a clear distinction between victims of diffuse class violence and those whose personal security is threatened directly, on grounds of political conscience. It obscures some of the crucial connections between poverty in Mexico and transnational economic restructuring. The contrasting concept of "seeking social mobility" is, however, too heavily loaded with ideological premises to serve any useful analytical purpose, other than reminding us that international migrants were not, by and large, traditionally the poorest members of rural society.

Rediagnosing the Crisis

An early draft of this chapter was written in a *colonia popular* in Los Reyes in 1991. Most of our neighbors were workers in the sugar mill of San Sebastian or self-employed craftsmen and owners of small workshops. Few if any of them would have shared Cornelius's relatively optimistic assessment of the impact of crisis on the state. With the sugar industry in continuing recession, fewer people had money, businesses lacked customers, and expectations about the future were ever more pessimistic. The dominant discourse was of going to the North as the only remaining resort, but this talk did not amount to all that much. People were also pessimistic about the prospects of finding work and earning enough to cover the cost of living "on the other side."

Disillusion about politics, democratization and the possibility of achieving a more just society also weighed heavily, as people discussed the amount of money the PRI was willing to pay for a vote in its favor in coming elections and the exaggerated promises of its candidates. There was also much expression of antagonism against the power of the United States and its project of global domination, in the aftermath of the Gulf War, and this was interestingly fairly pervasive amongst all sectors of local society. There is a certain irony in this anti-imperialist discourse. As figures like Henry Kissinger were publicly acknowledging on the cable TV channels I watched in Los Reyes, as an economic power, the U.S. was in trouble, its productive base in decline and its global economic hegemony eroded by the ever-increasing military spending mandated by the National Security State. From the Mexican standpoint, however, what seemed important was the ruthlessness this vastly more powerful neighbor displayed in pursuing its interests around the world, and the lessons which might be drawn from the events in the Gulf by a nation whose leaders claimed "there was no alternative" to allowing the *gringos* greater scope for investing in the national economy and controlling its resources. That, people thought, was the bottom line of neoliberal policies, but there were more immediate concerns.

White-collar workers in the mill complained that the new owners had extended their working day without a commensurate increase in pay. They also feared the reaction of the workers to new sackings threatened in the interests of modernization. This was a community which remained close-knit in many respects. The leader of the CNC cane-growers union reflected on the way that the comfortable middle class lifestyle of vacations and a new car every year which he enjoyed at the start of the 1980s was now out of reach. He expressed his doubts about the NAFTA and *Salinismo* without dissimulation, although he continued to go through the motions of performing his traditional political functions, trapped in the labyrinths of power. Crisis has many dimensions, but a central aspect of the continuing crisis of the early 1990s was that many people saw the essence of their problem as an absence of real options. For some, going to the United States did not really seem a practical option, but even for those who acquired legal status, it was often no more than the best of a bleak series of alternatives. Many had studied in the hope of going on to better things, but now saw their younger brothers leaving school early to join them in the North, without documents. Going to the North had now become part of the crisis and was itself in danger of becoming "in crisis" as numbers mounted across the border.

In order to develop this line of argument, I will now resort to the traditional anthropological tactic of using the detailed data provided by case studies. Since I wish to bring out the importance of certain historical factors, I will focus this exercise on two neighboring communities in the Ciénega de Chapala for which I have good longitudinal data, the villages of Cerrito Cotijaran and Guaracha (the official name of which is Emiliano Zapata). These two cases are, I believe, an adequate basis for drawing out the particular issues which I wish to discuss at this level of analysis, although it will be necessary to return to the larger regional picture, and to say more about the North itself, in order to complete my argument.

5

A Rush Through the Closing Door? The Impact of Simpson-Rodino on Two Rural Communities

Since I have published a detailed historical account of the two communities elsewhere (Gledhill, 1991), I will repeat only the bare essentials here. Guaracha, renamed Emiliano Zapata after land reform in 1936, is a community formed from the *peones acasillados* of one of the largest *haciendas* in western Mexico. It is in the municipio of Villamar, birthplace of the mother of Lázaro Cárdenas, which lies at a distance of fifteen kilometers from the town where the future president grew up, Jiquilpan de Juárez. Site of the *hacienda*'s Great House and sugar mill, Guaracha nestles at the foot of a mountain on the edge of the fertile plain of the Ciénega de Chapala. In 1990, the village had a resident population of some 3,700 souls and a majority of its 334 *ejidatarios* possessed irrigated land of high quality. Most *ejidatarios* received four hectares when the original collective *ejido* was parcellized in 1940, but 27% of the original parcelas were rain-fed (*temporal)* land. Those who received rain-fed land were assigned eight hectares, but two thirds of these plots are now irrigable.

Guaracha's *ejidatarios* were therefore relatively well-endowed with arable resources, but experienced difficulty in valorizing them. From the later 1940s to the era of statization, the region was dominated by rental of parcelas, primarily to an entrepreneur from the neighboring community of San Antonio Guaracha. His father had emigrated to the United States in 1918 and abandoned his Mexican wife, but continued to remit money, which served as the initial capital for the family's subsequent ascent. After the region was penetrated by commercial vegetable growers from the Bajío and Zamora in the later 1960s, the established agricultural regime of neolatifundist production of basic grains began to change, but the primary effect of the re-entry of the state into peasant agriculture was to favor the monocultivation of sorghum and safflower. These crops were susceptible to mechanization, and favored by peasants because of their lower costs. The era of statization brought some improvement in living standards, but inhibited the capitalization of the peasant farm. This was largely in consequence of the official policies pursued by BANRURAL, but the peasants' problems were exacerbated by the maladministration associated with state intervention, which further diminished the extent to which development resources actually reached the producers.

The development of the *neolatifundio* played an important role in local processes of social differentiation, which were then reinforced, in the 1970s, by patron-client ties between agrarian bureaucrats and peasant representatives. The peasant administrator of the neolatifundist in Guaracha converted himself into a community *cacique,* and eventually became an independent entrepreneur, renting land and owning agricultural machinery bought with private bank credit. He accumulated land titles by purchasing the rights of widows and persons who emigrated to the cities, and his second son has continued the tradition. Land values were originally very low and relatively stable, until the arrival of the commercial vegetable growers created competition between private renters, and peasant agriculture revived under state patronage. This allowed some migrants to acquire titles after a few trips to the United States as a *bracero*, and ejidal rights became commoditized quite early in the history of the community. A high rate of rural-urban emigration by the potential heirs of existing *ejidatarios* reinforced land concentration in the hands of a few wealthier families, so that the number of "real" *ejidatarios* is substantially less than the number of parcelas in the *ejido* might suggest.

Even in 1982, 11% of the *ejidatarios* controlled a quarter of the *ejido*'s land (Gledhill 1991: 304). Land concentration increased through the 1980s, as the prospects for small-scale farming seemed increasingly bleak. Historically, seasonal international migration acted to conserve peasant claims to the land, because migrants tended to rent their land rather than alienate it definitively, but as land values rose, it became increasingly difficult for ordinary migrants to buy themselves into the *ejido*. There have been land purchases by international migrants in recent years, but these individuals belong to a more affluent *emigrado* stratum of the migrant population. By 1990, control of land in the *ejido* was more concentrated than ever, temporarily through rental, or permanently through alienation of titles. Among the heterogeneous group of people who had the capital to continue farming were individuals who had enriched themselves in public service, and persons who had a salary from a non-agricultural occupation. Even before the amendment of Article 27, the *ejido* was drifting further and further from the ideals of agrarian reform under the weight of powerful forces of decomposition.

Cerrito Cotijaran: A Community of Poor Relations

Cerrito Cotijaran, with a resident population of just over 700 souls in 1990, presents a rather different picture. The community lies at the foot of the small hill from which it derives its name, at a distance of two kilometers from Guaracha. It is a daughter community of Guaracha, created by the *hacienda* administration in the 1920s in an attempt to thwart further claims for land restitution on the part of the *cabecera municipal*, Villamar. The original population of Cotijaran was recruited from the ranks of *hacienda* foreman (*mayordomos)* and their kin, persons whom the administration regarded as loyal to the system. As a rule, members of these families received substantially better treatment in the settlement of accounts on land which they farmed on a share-cropping basis for estate managers.

Many of the older men of Cotijaran still refused to participate in the land reform after the majority of Guaracheños had resigned themselves to the fact that the triumph of *Cardenismo* over their old master was irreversible. Nevertheless, some men and women of Cotijaran proved more realistic, including a number who had migrated to the United States in the years before the Great Depression. The community did secure an *ejido* of its own within two years of the original expropriation of Guaracha, since Cárdenas engineered the sale of the Guaracha sugar mill to the government, and the *hacendado* had no reason to retain any land. Cotijaran was assigned land in two of the old *hacienda* divisions (*potreros*), twenty plots plus a *parcela escolar* for instructing school children in farming in El Monte, shared with Guaracha, and seventeen in La Perla, bordering the *ejido* of Villamar. All were of three hectares. Lázaro Cárdenas was, however, determined that the community should benefit further from land reform. He offered it new lands outside Jiquilpan, in the *potrero* known as "La Beneficencia Pública," so named because it had been bequeathed by a rich and childless widow to alleviate the condition of the less fortunate of the region.

The decree signed by Avila Camacho to make a further *dotación* to Cotijaran was not executed because of the intervention of Cárdenas's younger brother Dámaso, now political boss of the region and head of a self-serving alliance of the old rich and new *cardenista* elite of Jiquilpan. This group included the regional leader of the CNC, one of a number of friends and lieutenants of Dámaso Cárdenas who had already appropriated the land that was to be given to the Cotijaran *ejido* as their own *pequeñas propiedades*. The community was therefore forced to embark on a struggle to regain its rights, somewhat hampered by the fact that its members' chief regional sectoral representative had a personal interest in thwarting their ambition.

The La Beneficencia affair turned the *campesinos* of Cotijaran into militant *agraristas*, but the fight to regain the land lasted nearly thirty years, and was only partially successful. Even after they turned to the newly formed Independent Peasant Central (CCI) for representation, they achieved only partial restitution of the land in Jiquilpan, and an exchange of the rest for land in La Palma, near Lake Chapala, which was of far inferior quality and thirty kilometers from their village. The final settlement was for forty-six hectares in La Beneficencia and an additional fifty-four in La Palma. For equity's sake, the land was divided up so that each new *ejidatario* received one and a quarter hectares in La Beneficencia and two hectares or so in La Palma, minor variations reflecting attempts to compensate for the high levels of saline infiltration in the latter *potrero*.

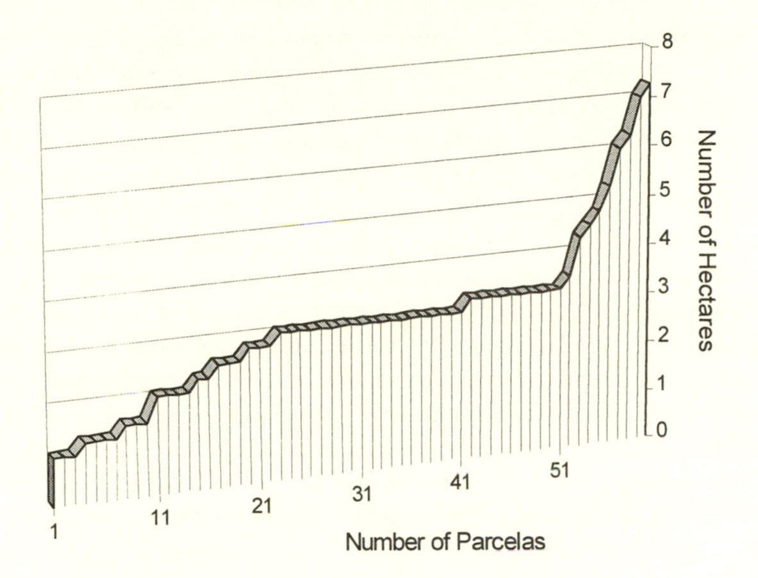

FIGURE 5.1 Distribution of *Ejido* Land Between 60 *Ejidatarios*, Cerrito Cotijaran, 1990

Patterns of land ownership in Cotijaran have been modified over time by inheritance, reassignment within families and sale of rights, but land concentration and rental is much less pronounced than in Guaracha. The pattern of land tenure, and low quality of part of the land, constrain commercial exploitation. Half of the *ejidatarios* only hold rights to a single piece of land, and the vast majority of the third who hold two do not have rights to more than 3.25 hectares in total. Indeed, as Figure 5.1 demonstrates, of the sixty persons with ejidal rights who belong to households resident in the village,[1] 35% hold rights to less than 3 hectares. Only 15% hold more than 4 hectares, two thirds of them persons with the good fortune

[1] One *ejidatario* has abandoned his (second) family and lives with another woman in Jiquilpan, though he has land in a *potrero* close to the village as well as in La Beneficencia. His case is excluded since he does not support his Cotijaran family. Also excluded is another *ejidatario* with two *parcelas* (bought from earlier holders), who lives in Tijuana with his wife's family. He began migrating to the U.S. in 1990, having previously worked in Mexico City, where he was brought up following the migration of his *ejidatario* father to the capital. He is unlikely to return, and was attempting to sell his land at the time of my fieldwork to a buyer from outside the community. This attracted considerable criticism, including that of his own mother, an *ejidataria* in her own right by inheritance of her late husband's land. Two other absentee *ejidatarios* are *emigrados* who play a leading role in channeling the community's migration to two specific regions of the United States. They do support families resident in the village and are therefore included.

to hold rights in three separate pieces of land. Four of the land holders in the figure are single women, and a further three are widows, all but one holding 3 hectares. Some members of the *ejido* rent their land, but some younger sons with their own land cultivate that of aging fathers, and some older men cultivate land of absent children and other kin. The community is certainly not "egalitarian," but differentiation within the *ejido* is not strongly linked to control over farming resources.

There are few comparatively "rich" *ejidatarios*. Those who are more affluent owe their advantages to patronage relations with state officials, help from a professional child, or, more commonly, factors related to migration. Even so, differentiation is less marked than in Guaracha. The community as a whole is markedly poorer, a situation which can be explained in terms of differences in educational attainment and migration patterns. One non-migrant *ejidatario* whose father benefitted from the patronage of a BANRURAL official was a major commercial grower of tomatoes at the start of the 1990s, working with the capital of a wholesale merchant from the Guadalajara *mercado de abastos*. Since the pattern of land holding within the Cotijaran *ejido* does not lend itself to large-scale rental to agricultural entrepreneurs, most of the land he rented was in the Guaracha *ejido*. Most of Cotijaran's own agriculture was dedicated to supplementing the contributions of migrant earnings to family subsistence.

Given the community's limited land base—and less than half of the existing land was available prior to the 1970s—it is not surprising that migration has played an important role in the reproduction of those families which have land. Beyond casual work as a mason and keeping a shop,[2] there are few local opportunities to work outside agriculture. Only six resident married men had any form of non-agricultural work outside the village in 1991. Two were school teachers, two truckers, one worked periodically as an agent of the judicial police, and the last worked in the Pepsi Cola factory in Sahuayo, along with another single man. The plant paid a mere 50,000 pesos per week in 1990, a rate lower than the agricultural wage, though it offered the advantage of being a wage earned throughout the year rather than for three or four months. Ninety per cent of the male holders of ejidal land had some past experience of U.S. migration, and only three men had no experience of any kind of migration. One of these, the agent of the Guadalajara merchant, is childless. His father is one of the most affluent members of the community. The other two are older men. One, aged 80 in 1990, looked after the land while his sons

---

[2] Two male heads of household work as masons. One is a migrant from Guanajuato who came to the community originally working for the company which built the village school. Five have shops, one a CONASUPO shop owned by a migrant from Mexico City with long experience of commerce, who also runs a billiard hall. Another of the shop-keepers, brother of one of the two leading *emigrado* farm workers of the community, and himself a long-term U.S. and internal farm worker migrant in the past, also operates a *tortillería*. His sons are all U.S. migrant, but not very affluent.

migrated. The other has brothers who were particularly committed migrants, and also has U.S. migrant children.

Forty-three per cent were past internal migrants, two former factory workers in Mexico City, but the majority seasonal agricultural workers. Two of these went to Zamora to work in the potatoes in the past,[3] but the main internal migrant activity of existing residents in this community historically was cane cutting, as might be expected given the traditions of the Guaracha *hacienda*. Most worked in the Los Reyes region, though some of older men went to Jalisco in the 1940s, when sugar cultivation was in relative decline in Los Reyes. A few ventured to Sinaloa and Veracruz in later decades. A majority of those who went to Los Reyes to cut cane took their families with them, and that region is the most prominent non-local source of spouses for people from Cotijaran.

One *ejidatario* spent twenty years working seasonally as foreman of a squad of cane cutters in the zone of the Santa Clara mill, going to the United States for another five to six month spell during the rest of the year. Internal migration within regional agriculture and international migration are not, therefore, mutually exclusive alternatives, but in Cotijaran, the latter has now become virtually the only form of migration practiced. Work in the United States is better paid, and cane cutting is considered a demeaning form of labor by the younger generation. In a sense, Cotijaran now occupies a higher position in the regional hierarchy of rural communities, since its people have abandoned what they consider an unremunerative and socially degrading survival strategy.

There are still some communities on the margins of the Ciénega de Chapala zone which supply labor for the *zafra*. The hills overlooking the plain conceal a number of impoverished *ranchos*, some of which even lack water supplies. People from these hamlets have survived by a combination of cattle-raising, work as *jornaleros* in local agriculture and migrant farm work within the region. Many of them preferred to work with local peasant *patrones*, and the role of their lack of the monetary resources needed to finance migration to more distant regions was, at least in the past, complemented by a certain social closure and lack of confidence in dealing with strangers. These marginalized *rancheros* are seen as a potentially dangerous, uncouth "Other" by members of the communities of the plain. The latter do continue to play a role in the local rural labor market: unmarried women from the *ejido* communities have long participated in local agricultural wage labor and in the plants of Zamoran agroindustry. The crisis of peasant agriculture increased participation in this form of work.

More significantly, however, poorer sections of the regional peasantry have tended to move into the occupational niches vacated by men now going to the North, as has also occurred in other regions, such as the Valley of Ecuandureo (Sergio

---

[3] One represents the surviving male member of a family whose other members settled permanently in Zamora, where work in commercial agriculture is available all year round.

Zendejas, personal communication). In this pattern of "agricultural development," then, the peasants resident in the more commercialized zones have benefitted from the process primarily in the form of being able to emigrate to seek work in the North, whilst deteriorating conditions in the more marginal agricultural and pastoral zones have forced their inhabitants, in increasing numbers, into a self-reproducing low wage regional agricultural labor market.

International migration is not, however, a new phenomenon in either Cotijaran or Guaracha, but dates back to the period before the Great Depression of 1929 (Gledhill, 1991: Chapter Eight). Both communities have solid migratory networks, and there is some overlap between them, since the villagers were kinsmen from the beginning and have continued to intermarry, despite the fact that the role of Cotijaran's founders in the *hacienda* period has left a legacy of tension, expressed symbolically in Guaracheño association of the Cerrito with witches. They therefore provide a good basis for comparative analysis from the point of view of evaluating the role of socio-economic differences between households in shaping current patterns of insertion into the U.S. labor market. The impact of these factors is not distorted by radically different histories of incorporation into the northern network. Since it is less complex, I will begin with the data from Cerrito Cotijaran.

International Migration from Cerrito Cotijaran

Defining "resident" households as those which possess a family home or reside with kin in a shared house lot, in the autumn of 1990, the community of Cerrito Cotijaran consisted of one hundred and twenty-eight households of married couples, seven households headed by widows, four headed by widowers, another four by single women, and three headed by women who were separated or divorced from their husbands. Not all of these families were in residence at the time of my census, and over half the married men spent at least part of the year in the United States. Eight households were headed by men who had migrated into the community in recent years.[4] Two of the men concerned are from Guaracha, but the rest come from different states, and only two of them brought wives from their place of origin, Guanajuato and Mexico City, respectively. Furthermore, the wife of the Mexico City in-migrant, a shop-keeper who decided to start a new life in the provinces, is from a Guaracha family which left the region in the previous generation. All but one of the non-Guaracheño in-migrants, who is a school-teacher from Guerrero, came to work in the region's agriculture or as laborers in public

4 Here I exclude from the list a migrant from Guanajuato who met his Cotijaran wife whilst both were working in the fields in Zamora. He abandoned her and their children for a new liaison which enabled him to obtain permanent resident alien status in the North.

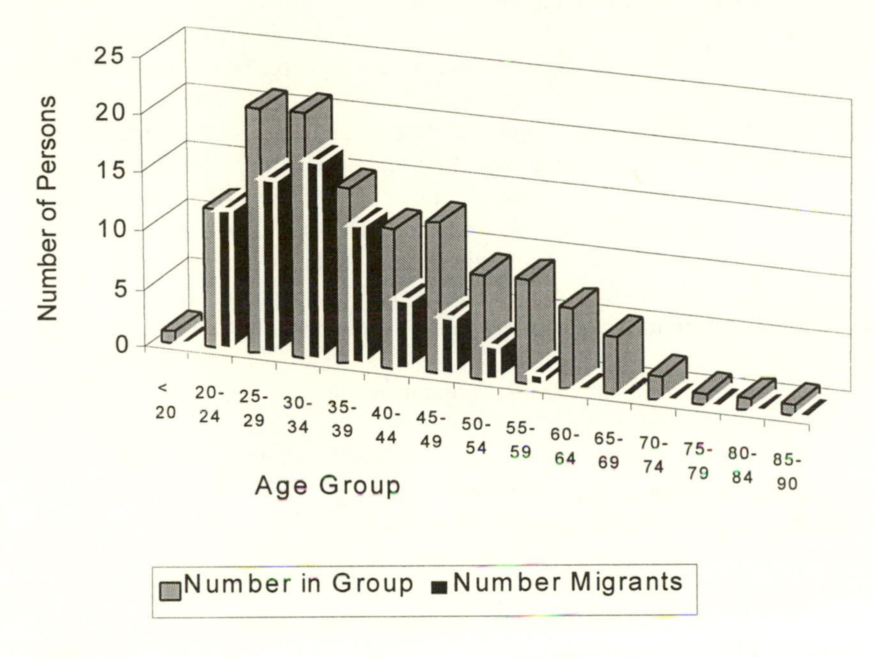

FIGURE 5.2 Resident and U.S. Migrant Household Heads by Age Group, Cerrito Cotijaran, 1990

works projects. They are not ranked among the community's better-off members. Two now have married sons resident in the village.

Removing the incomers, and grouping together siblings of parents in a previous, extinct, generation, analysis of the kinship relations between the remaining resident males reveals that the present male population represents thirty distinct families native to Cerrito Cotijaran. Twelve of these families are represented by only one person in the oldest living generation, the remainder being constituted by two or more siblings. A further eight families are represented by married women without any male siblings in the community. The majority of men born in Cotijaran in the older age groups are *ejidatarios*: only six of the thirty Cotijaran "grandfamilies" contain no *ejidatarios*, and two of these are represented by widows.[5] In the case of all but two of the *ejidatario* grandfamilies, all the resident male siblings of the oldest generation have *parcelas*. Four of them account for over a third of the total number of *ejidatarios,* because of the number of siblings of the older generation who are resident. The result of this pattern is a shortage of land available for the younger

[5] In another case, the entire family has returned from a long absence in Mexico City only recently. Most other returnees from Mexico have bought rights in the *ejido*.

generation. Apart from the in-migrants, landless men in Cotijaran are mostly sons and grandsons of existing *ejidatarios*. A number of the older landless men in the community are able to gain access to land by renting parcelas "a la cuarta" from some of the female title-holders without resident sons in the community.[6]

Yet as Figure 5.2 demonstrates, a high proportion of the resident married men aged below forty were U.S. migrants in 1990, and the U.S. migrants above that age were by no means all landless people. All three in the fifty to fifty-four age group were *ejidatarios*, two of them seasonal migrants. The smaller numbers of migrants found in the older generation reflect little apart from the fact that the role of going to the North has been taken over by children. This is a community which is, to an increasing extent, living from the livelihood its members can obtain outside the country.

Almost all male migrants from Cotijaran are farm workers. A mere three married, and two single, men of Cotijaran origin work in factories in Los Angeles. Even fewer work in the service sector: two married men and one single man. Another of the single migrants is in prison, following his conviction on a drugs-related murder charge. One resident married man who has now returned to agriculture spent a time working in a car repair workshop, and another tried construction, both working undocumented in Los Angeles. But Cotijaran migrants have yet to participate in the shift from agriculture to other sectors noted in the case of some other Michoacán migrant communities on any significant scale, and display a notably more homogeneous pattern of occupations in the North than their parent community, Guaracha (see Table 5.1, page 126).[7] Cotijaran migration also focuses on a comparatively small range of destinations in the United States in comparison with Guaracha migration, even as far as farm workers are concerned, as the maps on the pages which follow demonstrate (Figures 5.3 and 5.4). The basic role of Cotijaran in the transnational economy is to supply labor to U.S. agribusiness. Because of this, it is an ideal case for studying some of the effects of the IRCA, and provides interesting contrasts as well as parallels with the Guaracha case.

---

[6] Such rental is often from kin, though this does not seem to make such arrangements less prone to conflict, particularly in the recent years of poor harvests and money returns.

[7] In talking of a shift from agriculture to the manufacturing and service sectors as a recent development, it is worth stressing that migrants from this region of Michoacán before the Great Depression frequently worked in the manufacturing sector (Gledhill, 1991). People from the region who went to the North later on were able to draw on the support network provided by a previous generation of emigrants. Nevertheless, it would be wrong to talk of "history repeating itself." Early manufacturing work was generally in large-scale, "Fordist," plants, and the first generation found employment alongside other migrants from the Old World. Those who seek more permanent residence in the North today do so on different terms to the early pioneers, few of whom retain strong ties with their places of origin. Comparison of the Guaracha and Cotijaran cases suggests that the kind of migration pattern which evolved in the *bracero* period and the years following 1964 has a more important historical impact on contemporary patterns of variation.

FIGURE 5.3 Distribution of Cerrito Cotijaran Migrants by Destination in the United States, 1990

Key

- ■ Single migrant in location
- □ Less than five migrants in location
- ▩ More than five but less than ten migrants in location
- ▦ More than ten but less than twenty migrants in location
- ▧ More than one hundred migrants in location
- ● City without migrants from community

Note: males accompanied by wives or families are treated as a single case.

FIGURE 5.4 Distribution of Guaracha Migrants by Destination in the United States, 1990

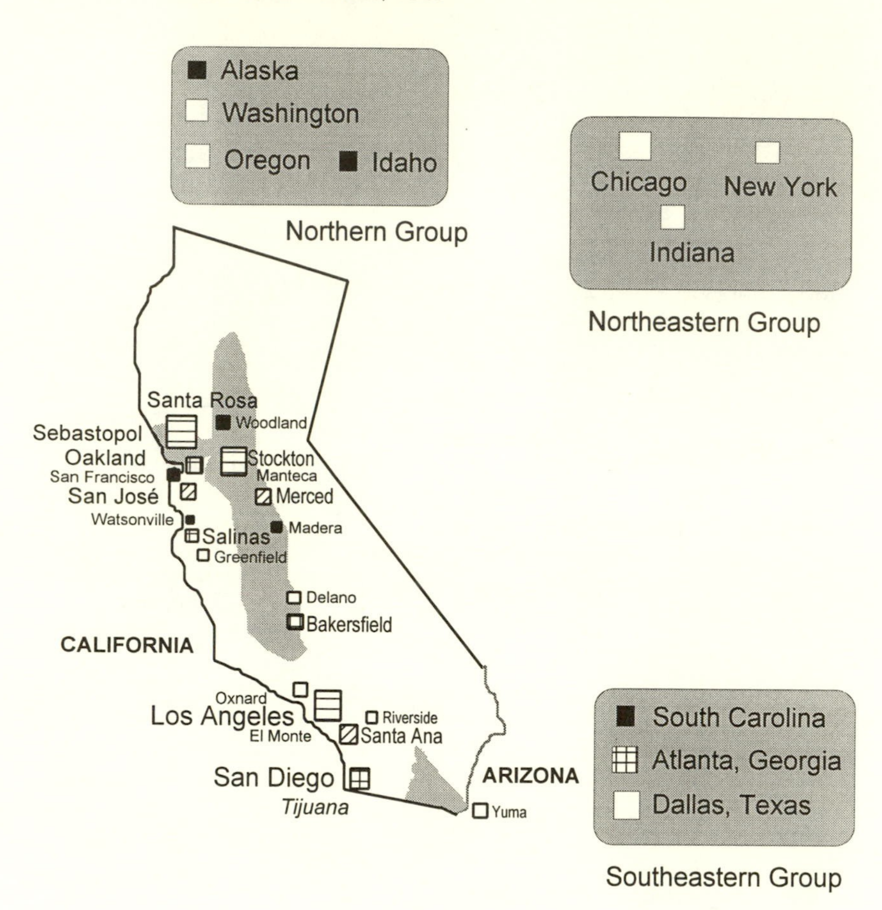

Key

- Single migrant in location
- Less than five migrants in location
- More than five but less than ten migrants in location
- More than ten but less than twenty migrants in location
- More than twenty but less than fifty migrants in location
- More than fifty migrants in location

Note: males accompanied by wives or families are treated as a single case.

The Formal Provisions of the Simpson-Rodino Act

Under the Immigration Reform and Control Act, two programs were introduced which permitted Mexican workers who had previously worked without documents in the United States to do so legally. Under the general amnesty program, legalization formally depended on five years continuous prior residence in the North and some knowledge of English, but less stringent requirements were applied to the second type of legalization scheme, the Special Agricultural Workers program.

The Amnesty Program

Undocumented migrants who could prove they entered the country before 1st January, 1982, and had lived continuously in the United States since that date could apply initially for temporary residence. Their application was to be presented after 5th May, 1987 (180 days after signing of the law by Reagan), and before the closing date of 5th May, 1988. A prerequisite for achieving legalization under this program was the production of documents such as rent receipts, telephone or electricity bills which could prove "continuous" residence. Applicants also had to prove "physical presence" since the signing of the law, though there was a let-out clause for "small absences ... which do not break the continuity of physical presence."[8]

The first phase of the program (May 1987 to May 1988) gave provisional permission to work, pending a final decision on the application. The Immigration and Naturalization Service (INS) established 107 offices to receive applications, and a further 500 as entities designated to preselect candidates and assess their eligibility. The cost of submitting an application was U.S.$185 per person, with a maximum charge of $425 for a family of four or more persons. Legal representation costs, notaries, medical examinations and processing of documents were not included in the fee. Monica Verea estimated the likely total costs as $1,200 per person (García y Griego and Verea Campos, 1988: 32), a figure which proved to be accurate on the basis of data from the Ciénega de Chapala.

Once the work permit was issued, eligibility for most federal public assistance programs was revoked, with exception of the aged, blind people, pregnant women, or persons suffering an emergency medical condition or total incapacitation. State governments were promised up to $100 million per year for four years from the Federal budget to meet the costs of public assistance, health services and education arising from the legalizations. Application for permanent residence had to be made within the period of one year following the 19th month after granting of temporary resident status. Candidates had to demonstrate basic understanding of English and of the official history of the United States. Temporary residents who failed to solicit

---

[8] My description of the IRCA provisions is based primarily on García y Griego and Verea Campos (1988: 30–36), supplemented by information acquired from migrants who obtained legalization.

permanency within the prescribed period would be deported. Five years after initial documentation, amnestied entrants would become eligible for full welfare services and citizenship.

The INS expected to receive three million applications. By autumn 1987, only 600,000 authorizations of temporary residence had been issued, approximately half to Mexicans. Verea suggested that cost was a major disincentive, and that even those who were, in reality, eligible, might have to participate in the purchasing of fraudulent documents which the provisions of the law encouraged, given the difficulties of proving permanent "physical presence" (op.cit.: 34). In the case of Guaracha, some migrants who were amply qualified to apply for legalization under this program remained undocumented (and stayed in the United States, often with their families). Seasonal undocumented migrants were excluded, in principle, from legalization by this route.

The Special Agricultural Workers Program

There were two routes to achieving legalization under this category. Under the first, temporary residence would be granted to undocumented migrants who could prove they had worked in seasonal employment in agriculture for at least 90 days during the previous three years (1984–1986). In the course of the first year following the granting of a temporary visa, they could acquire an immigrant visa permitting permanent residence. Candidates could apply directly to the entity designated by the INS in the United States, or to U.S. consular agents in Mexico, during a period of 18 months between 1st June, 1987, and 1st December, 1988.[9] Candidates could not be expelled while their applications were being processed. Under the second scheme, undocumented migrants who had worked in agriculture for at least one year, from May 1985 to May 1986, would be permitted to acquire temporary resident status and could then apply for permanent residence a year after those in the first group.

Applicants legalized under the amnesty scheme were only allowed brief absences from the United States, but SAW migrants could travel outside the U.S. freely, commuting across the border daily if necessary. They could also accept non-agricultural employment, and in the case of Guaracha, did so on a substantial scale. The residence requirements of the SAW program were much easier to satisfy than the five years continuous residence needed for amnesty. The entitlement of SAW workers to social benefits was, however, also restricted. The limits the IRCA imposed on migrant workers' access to the public welfare system represented a

---

[9] A striking index of the unexpected volume of successful SAW applications is the fact that the Guadalajara consular office of the United States was forbidden to process visa applications from states other than Jalisco in 1991, in view of the "excessive" number of persons it had admitted in the previous two years.

distinctly negative facet of the legalization process. Although undocumented workers in the 1970s generally did not claim all of the benefits to which they were entitled, migratory status had repeatedly been deemed irrelevant to the rights which workers enjoyed under the law as workers by U.S. courts.

The other initial drawback of SAW legalization was that it did not give immediate residence rights to the worker's family. The architects of the law conceived of SAW migrants as a new kind of "bracero," for whom permanent residence would normally mean an extended work permit for a finite number of years, and not citizenship. The Mexican response to this limitation was, however, a substantial amount of undocumented entry by the wives and children of legalized SAW entrants, as is evident from the data presented in Figure 5.7 (see page 118). The Family Unity provision of the 1990 Immigration Act relaxed some of the earlier restrictions, and allowed SAW-legalized residents to bring direct family members into the United States legally.

The SAW program was created as a concession to the farm lobby, the major opponents of regulation. Yet it was not framed in a way which guaranteed the continuing supply of migrant farm labor, since once temporary residence was granted, the worker could not be forced to continue working in agriculture. Because of this, the continued use of undocumented farm labor was more or less guaranteed. There were, however, two other measures related to agriculture included in the IRCA provisions, the category of H-2-A seasonal agricultural workers and that of "complementary agricultural workers."

H-2-A Workers

H-2 legislation dates from the period when the Bracero Program ended. It was framed to allow legal imports of labor for jobs which no citizens were willing to do, whilst protecting the wages and conditions of citizen workers. H-2-A agricultural workers were, under the IRCA, guaranteed acceptable housing and protected by a labor contract. They should also be paid the same as citizen workers for the same kind of work, although their lack of unionization lends their use an obvious utility in depressing wage levels. Individual farmers present applications for employment of H-2-A workers, within 60 days of the date of their proposed employment. After a week they are told whether their application is approved, or whether more documentation must be provided to justify their case. According to the law, if an H-2 worker is displaced by a national, the employer is not obliged to pay him for the time for which he was contracted but did not work. Farmers using H-2-A workers are obliged to hire available U.S. workers until half the harvest is in, even if this means dismissing an H-2-A worker. Verea notes that there was a considerable increase in use of H-2-A workers after the program came into force in June 1987 (op.cit.: 38). Previously less than 10% of the 30,000 H-2 workers contracted were Mexicans, concentrated in Virginia and North Carolina, and the change indicated a broadening of the regions where this system of labor recruitment was important. Later evidence suggests, however, that undocumented labor was not replaced by H-2-A labor on any significant scale. Applications to the program were minimal by 1989, and the only significant contract labor schemes evident in Michoacán at the start of the 1990s involved work in the Alaskan oil-fields and Canadian agriculture, both of which offered vastly superior terms to that of the H-2-A program. No migrant from Cotijaran or Guaracha has entered on an H-2-A contract or would consider doing so.

Complementary Agricultural Workers

This program was intended to regulate future entry after the initial program of legalizing the existing "stock" of undocumented migrants was concluded. Implementation would begin in 1990–1993, when the actual number of workers legalized under the SAW program was known. The number of CAWs to be admitted was to be determined by the Secretaries of Labor and Agriculture, if and only if they determined there was a shortage of national agricultural workers, and strict ceilings were set on the number which could be admitted. CAW workers would receive temporary residence for three years, and had to work at least 90 days in agriculture. After three years, they could apply for permanent residence. Given the restrictions imposed on new admissions under this residual program, and what turned out to be massive oversubscription to the SAW program, it is evident that new migrants joining the ranks of those already going to the North after 1989 were mainly going to have to enter as undocumented workers again, without hopes of future legalization.

In their assessment of the likely consequences of the IRCA at the time of its enactment, García Griego and Verea Campos suggested that it would increase the socio-economic selectivity of undocumented migration, and that the entry of better-qualified legalized migrants would change the sectoral distribution of undocumented migrants, who would also restrict their mobility within the United States and prolong their stays beyond the 6-month "temporada," because of the added difficulty and increased cost of entry (op.cit.: 26). Their main emphasis was on the costs of acquiring false documents, given that the IRCA demanded that employers inspect documents demonstrating legal authorization to work. After paying the traditional costs of entry and securing work, the migrant would now have to make further payments to document traffickers. They doubted whether the IRCA would imply any significant expulsion of undocumented migrants and reduction of overall access to the U.S. labor market. These conclusions turned out to be broadly correct, but failed to recognize that a significant number of young men would secure legalization without having previously worked as undocumented migrants, and that some older men who had ceased undocumented migration some years earlier would now return to the North.

The Cotijaran Response to Simpson-Rodino

Almost all Cotijaran migrants applied for legalization under the SAW program, and most have now received what they describe as "la (mica) buena," a "Green Card" valid for ten years. A few see possession of a U.S. work permit as valuable in itself as a form of security. One migrant who returned early in 1990 to invest the lion's share of three months' U.S. earnings in sowing his own and his father's land, explained that he was returning shortly after the harvest to "put some more time in" to guarantee his continuing right of entry, although he did not expect to earn very much. Another made a brief trip to the North simply to ensure he had the documentation needed. For most, however, going to the United States is essential to their livelihood, and the data I will now proceed to present suggest that it is becoming the central dimension of the whole way of life of an increasing number of families.

Figures 5.5 and 5.6 show the numbers of married and single male migrants from Cerrito Cotijaran, classified by age group and migratory status. Eighty per cent of married migrants had been to the North prior to 1988. Seventy-seven per cent of the current legal migrants—including the *emigrados*, whom I distinguish here from the *rodinos* who legalized under the IRCA—had entered the United States without documents in the past. Three of the younger *emigrados* are children of the eldest, Ignacio, who works as a foreman on a ranch in Arizona. Ignacio has not returned to Cotijaran in nine years, although he has had two families there and one of his sons paid a brief visit in 1990.[10] He has, however, played a significant role in the migratory history of the community, although it is less important than that played by one of the two other *emigrados* in their fifties, Abruelio.

Abruelio made his career in Merced, California as a *contratista* of the "raidero" variety described in the previous chapter. He has not returned to the community for four years. In the years following his last return, his wife (a Guaracheña) has been travelling to the North to join him, and his two sons are now legalized migrants. Abruelio has been the most significant point of contact for migrants from Cotijaran over the years, since California has always been the most popular destination, and has progressively increased in popularity over Arizona. In 1990, 83% of the married male migrants, and 95% of the single migrants, went to Merced. Furthermore, many of the women who accompanied husbands, and all but one of those who went alone or with fathers, also worked in the tomato fields in Merced.[11] It is significant that Abruelio's sons, unlike Ignacio's, secured legalization under the IRCA provisions. This was because their father is an "emigrado chueco," a person who secured

---

[10] He has another family in the North, and his case is discussed in depth in the next chapter.

[11] The exception was a married woman who went to join a married sister working in a garment factory in Los Angeles for nine months. Her case is discussed in the next chapter.

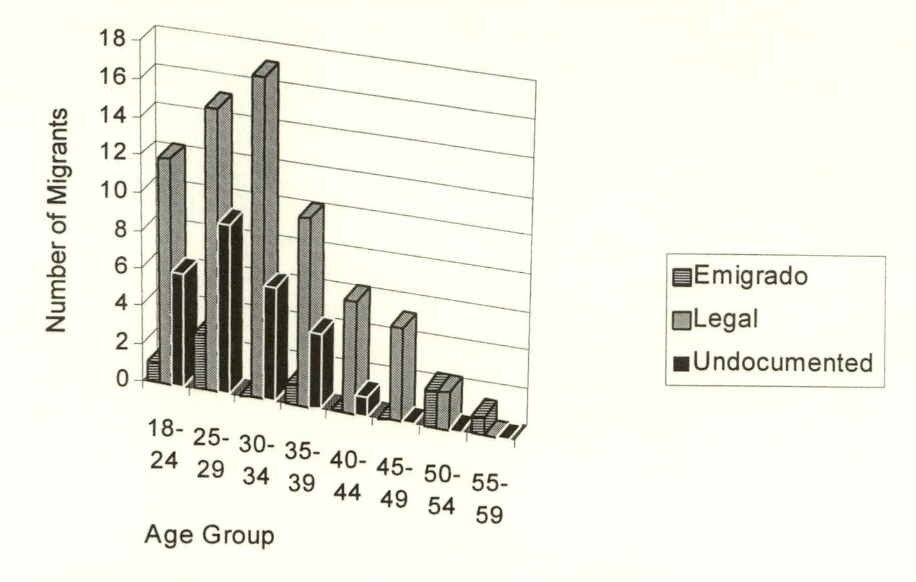

FIGURE 5.5 Married Male U.S. Migrants by Age Groups and Migratory Status, Cerrito Cotijaran, 1990

permanent residence rights using a false identity: two of the longest-established "emigrado" farm workers in Guaracha present similar cases.

Abruelio worked as an undocumented migrant for a period after the end of the *bracero* contracts, whereas Ignacio emigrated, with the help of his employer, before the contract system ended. He has brothers still resident in the village who also worked in Arizona, one of whom also worked as a foreman and explained that his *patrón* protected him from the *migra* in the years when he had crossed the border illegally. Arizona offered at least some of those who went to work there opportunities for permanent settlement which were not taken up. The California migrant farm worker network of the community has, in contrast, offered less security and stability. Of the four other Cotijaran *emigrados* in California who maintain regular contact with the community, three emigrated by marrying there, one abandoning his family in Cotijaran in the process. Only two are farm workers, the other working in the service sector in Los Angeles rather than in Merced. The one single man to have secured permanent residence rights as a farm worker is an anomalous case, since he was brought up in Mexico City and was able to mobilize contacts in the North not available to men in the village. Although his father had been in the United States for an extended period before land reform, the family's subsequent migratory behavior was determined by its much later movement to the capital, where the father found a job painting the railway station through a political patron.

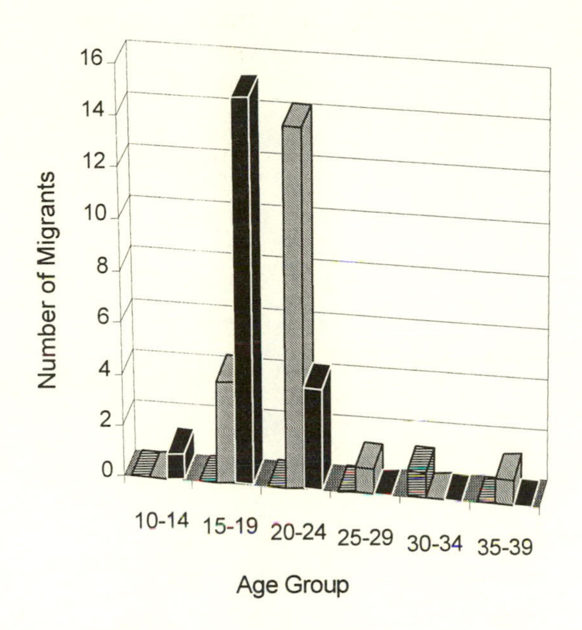

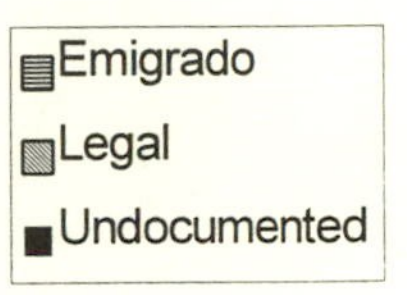

FIGURE 5.6 Single Male U.S. Migrants by Age Groups and Migratory Status, Cerrito Cotijaran, 1990

The Cotijaran migrant network into California has traditionally been orientated to supplying seasonal field workers, and these workers were mostly undocumented in the past. Today's undocumented laborers are not exclusively young men. More than half the married undocumented migrants in 1990–91 were between 25 and 35 years of age, although the vast majority of single undocumented migrants were less than 20 years of age.[12] Nevertheless, even discounting the not insignificant proportion of married migrants (25%) who remain undocumented, the Cotijaran data demonstrate the failure of the IRCA to "regulate" migration. Not only did some of the older men resume migrant careers after a lapse of years because it became possible to go legally, but fifteen per cent of those in the 25–29 age group and thirty per cent of those in the 30–34 age group only *began* their migration in the period of the SAW program. This pattern is consistent with the general picture on the results of the new immigration law. Originally, some 250,000 to 300,000 applications for legalization under the SAW program were anticipated, but the number actually received by the time of the program's closing date of 30th November, 1988,

---

[12] The one very young single male migrant, aged 13 years, is an unusual case. His mother died early in 1990, and he decided to join his father in the North, leaving his older brother in charge of the rest of the family at home.

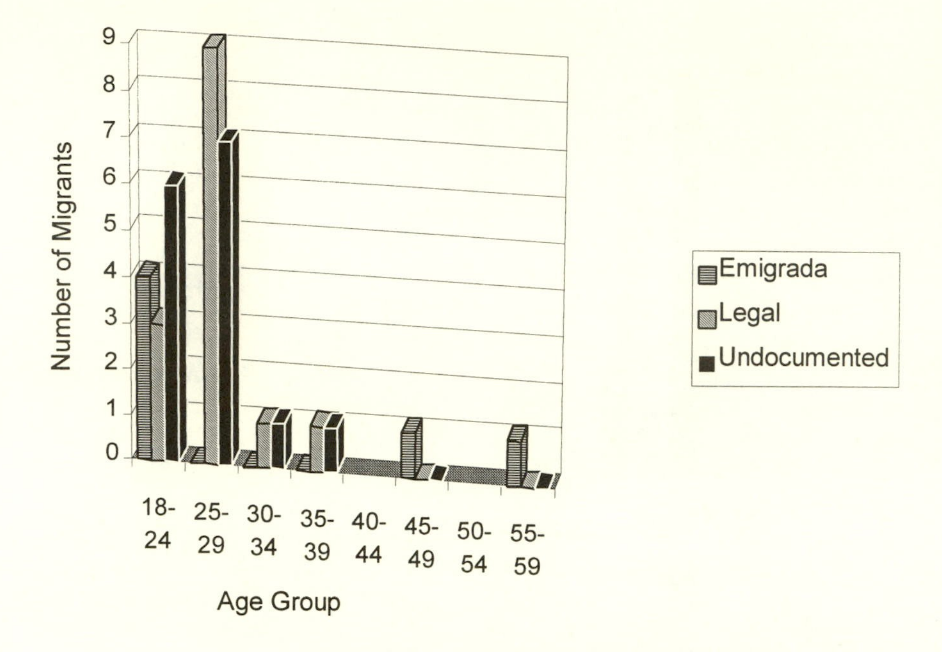

FIGURE 5.7 Married and Separated Female U.S. Migrants by Age Groups and Migratory Status, Cerrito Cotijaran, 1990

was 1,301,000. This discrepancy suggests *a priori* that a majority of the applications must have been fraudulent, although in practice only ten per cent were rejected (Cornelius, 1990: 107).

Both married and single men from Cotijaran found ways, described in more detail below, of obtaining false documentation to enter the SAW program, thanks to the facilities provided by their established migrant social network. In these processes there were some losers among the older generation of migrants, men who found the documents required to support their application had been sold to another person by the intermediary on whom they had relied to make the necessary arrangements. Yet the view of the community as a whole was that the IRCA facilitated migration. There are more Cotijaran (and Guaracha) migrants today than in 1987, and the legalization of the majority encouraged younger brothers to leave after 1988 as undocumented migrants, partly in the hope that with time they too could "arreglar," and partly because it rapidly became apparent that the employer sanctions aspect of the legislation was not deterring *patrones* from hiring new entrants.

The same logic might have influenced many married women who entered undocumented to join husbands who secured temporary work permits, and some of these couples saw the birth of a child in the United States as a step towards establishing permanent residence rights. Thirty per cent of Cotijaran's male migrants in 1990 had their wives in the United States, twenty-two per cent had children with them there, and sixteen per cent had children there who were born in the North.[13] Sixty-five per cent of the married women in the United States in 1990 had not been there prior to 1988. The proportion of those resident there earlier is almost entirely accounted for by women married by men from Cotijaran in the North. In the case of this community, therefore, the tendency for lone male migration to be replaced by the migration of couples and families which many analyses have identified as a general trend in recent migration from western Mexico is very recent.

The proportion of undocumented married female migrants from Cotijaran, broken down by age groups in Figure 5.7, exceeds 40% of a total which includes women who are U.S. residents of Mexican origin married by Cotijaran men. Just over a third of the married male migrants did not return to Cerrito Cotijaran in 1990 and had been absent for over a year at the time of my survey. More than two thirds of these men were with their families, and the vast majority of them (83%) were legal. Only a small proportion (less than 30%) had married in the North. A larger proportion of the movement of women[14] and children to the North was undocumented than documented, and little movement of this kind existed in this community prior to the Simpson-Rodino legislation. Some women were able to enter the United States on tourist visas, since they could claim to be visiting relatives there, but many were simply accompanied by their husband (or another relative) to the frontier, to be "passed" by a *coyote*.

In some cases, of course, the husband was undocumented as well, but such a situation does not necessarily imply total insecurity. One of the advantages of undocumented workers in the past was that employers could readily dispense with their services, and the IRCA may ironically have made employers less eager to pick up the telephone to the INS in order to expedite matters. A few employers still actively assist valued workers and their families to evade detection, as was the case with one of Cotijaran's few factory workers in Los Angeles. In the case of farm work, it seems that employer sanctions have little long-term effect on the hiring of undocumented migrants. A legal migrant farm worker from Guaracha, who prefers to work with a regular employer in Sebastopol in the San Francisco region of California rather than through the *contratistas* in Merced, told me that his *patrón* did refuse to hire undocumented migrants in 1989, but abandoned this stance in the

---

[13] Two of the older couples in the North are unable to have children according to their resident kin.

[14] The migration of single women from Cotijaran is less significant than in the case of Guaracha. This reflects the occupational and residential differences between the two migrant populations within the United States. Leaving aside children in school or of pre-school age, and women who are separated and migrated independently, only five single women went in 1990, three in the 15–19 age group, one in the 20–24 age group, and one in the 30–34 age group. All worked in agriculture, and accompanied fathers or brothers. Tomato picking in Merced employs substantial quantities of female and child labor.

next season. He was unwilling to prejudice his relations with his regular legalized workers by denying work to their undocumented kin. For different reasons, Merced's farmers appear to have been untroubled by the new law. The complaints of undocumented workers from Cotijaran in 1990 centered on low pay and shortage of work resulting from the constant increase in the number of migrants arriving.

In the case of married women who arrived undocumented, it might be presumed that the couple hoped to establish a more permanent residence in the North. It is not, however, necessarily the case that the wife's joining her husband forms part of a concerted plan. In some cases, women are apprehensive that their husbands will squander their earnings on vices, or even abandon their families if they continue to spend long periods in the North alone, both worries which have foundations in experience. The possibility of the husband's achieving permanent residence rights in the North through a new marriage exacerbated the stresses to which marriages were subjected by separation of the partners. Normally, however, a woman would not attempt to join her husband without his agreement, nor command the resources needed to enter illegally independently, though help may sometimes be obtained from a parent or sibling. In one case where a woman did leave independently in 1990 (with a single sister), she had concluded that her husband, whom she had only married "al civil" before his departure,[15] had abandoned her and their baby daughter, since he had not written for a year. On occasion, dramatic gestures may lead to reconciliations, and some wives certainly pressure husbands to agree to their joining them, but the issue of the determinants and consequences of growing family migration is a complex one. Although I will return to this issue in more depth in the next chapter, a few general observations should be made at this point.

It has been argued that much of the "undocumented" family migration which occurred in the immediate aftermath of the IRCA (1987 and 1988) was a response to a generalized fear in the sending communities that "the door was closing" to future emigration (Cornelius, op.cit.: 119). The data from Cotijaran suggest, however, that the process continued and, indeed, accelerated in 1989 and 1990. It is also clear, however, that the movement towards more permanent family settlement in the North in many other communities predated the changes in immigration legislation. One explanation of the general process would be the maturation of transnational social networks, and changing socio-economic and cultural patterns associated with that process. It is also important to stress, as Cornelius observes, that the evolution of the California labor market has increased opportunities for undocumented women to find work not only in agriculture, low-paid service jobs,

---

[15] Although civil marriage is the only form recognized juridically by the state, church marriage alone is considered fully binding by local people. The man will still be subject to criticism in his community of origin, particularly if, as in this case, he has already fathered a child, but less than if he had contracted a church marriage. Even so, return to the community is likely to be problematic without a reconciliation, which might entail abandoning another family in the North.

domestic outworking for the textile industry, and a range of other "secondary labor market" enterprises, but also in menial jobs in sectors of the "primary labor market" which display a preference for Mexican labor.

I will discuss these issues in more depth in Chapter Seven. The Cotijaran data make it clear, however, that increasing permanence of settlement is not necessarily related to the urbanization of the migrant population. California agribusiness is particularly suited to absorbing female and child labor on a seasonal basis, but it does not seem possible to explain these developments either in terms of the "response" of Mexican labor reserves to U.S.-generated demand, or the converse of a supply of labor generating its own demand north of the border. It is a question of a continuous process of "bilateral adjustment," which includes social and cultural processes with their own logic. The IRCA reinforced tendencies towards permanence of settlement because undocumented wives and children were likely to remain in the North pending legalization of their situation, and there seems little doubt that attempts at regulation have created more dilemmas for immigration policy than they have resolved. Yet the only conclusion that it seems possible to draw from the experience is that immigration policy needs to address the "deep structures" of the migratory process rather than attempt to control its surface manifestations through immigration law.

Thwarting the Legislators

This conclusion is reinforced when we consider the determinants of the anomalous results of the SAW program in more depth. Even before the IRCA, migrants used false documentation, and valid documentation was used by persons other than those to whom it was originally issued. It was commonplace, for example, for undocumented migrants to "borrow" credentials from documented kin and friends or even from dead people, in particular social security cards. I have also recorded cases of sharing of the documentation required to access the United States. A legal migrant uses his own documents to cross the frontier at a land border crossing, choosing a moment when there is a large number of entrants requiring the attention of the immigration officials, and the document is unlikely to subject to close visual scrutiny or computer-checking. He then proceeds to the home of a relative who has rights of permanent residence in the United States, who takes a trip to "visit friends" or "do some shopping" in Mexico. This person delivers the loaned document to a waiting brother of the first migrant, before returning using his own papers. The second, non-legalized entrant, follows the same strategy of crossing when scrutinization is likely to be perfunctory. Another, even more daring strategy, is to try to enter the North as a tourist with an older sibling's passport and visa, despite age differences and lack of a close physical match. Such persons often succeed in working illegally for a period and then returning without difficulty—in ironic contrast to a friend who lost his *Mexican* papers and only narrowly escaped deportation to El Salvador!

In the light of these traditions, it is not surprising that the IRCA's insistence on absurdly rigorous standards of documentation presented Michoacanos with a challenge to which they were more than equal. In the early days of the SAW program, forged documents were produced on a large scale for people from Cotijaran and neighboring communities. Although migrants were finding that "micas chuecas" were no longer effective against improved identification procedures in attempting entry to the United States by 1990, it remained difficult to control the "borrowing" of the identity of other persons. Most significant, however, were the mechanisms involved in obtaining the documents needed for official legalization. These produced differentiation between and within communities in terms of access to U.S. labor markets. Young men from communities with established migrant traditions had a far greater chance of securing an SAW permit than those with a shorter and more peripheral involvement with the North, even if they were technically ineligible.

The first point to highlight is the role of intermediaries of Michoacano origin in the United States as sources of the documentation necessary to support a legalization application. This was reminiscent of the situation in the *bracero* period (Gledhill, 1991: 252–3). Money was made illicitly out of the regulation process, and many people who obtained legal status had to pay more for it than the law stipulated. When the program was first announced, a number of local migrants residing legally in the United States asked their regular employers to help them secure legal entry for kinsmen with no previous (or recent) experience of work in the North, by providing documents which could be used to establish eligibility for legalization. The intermediaries were able to sell the documents in their local communities for U.S.$300 or more to would-be applicants, and at least some employers or their agents themselves turned the supply of documentation into a profitable sideline. One migrant farm worker from Guaracha who had secured permanent resident status through marriage in the United States bought a tractor with the proceeds of commerce in documents of this type.

A young man wishing to go to the North for the first time would normally collect the documents in the North, though a few had them sent to their homes in Mexico. This involved one undocumented crossing of the border, normally in the company of migrants with prior experience. The person then went to a private office in one of the main local migrant destinations in California, such as Stockton. Here a further payment of $30 would secure help with the completion of the official paperwork and an affidavit certifying the veracity of the documents covering past work experience. Thus equipped, the migrant would report to the office of the INS to declare himself (or, occasionally, herself) an applicant for legalization, and receive temporary work authorization pending investigation of the case. At this stage it was necessary to pay the legally stipulated fee of $185 to the Immigration Service, as well as $90 for a medical check-up. Three months later the applicant would be interviewed by an INS investigator, already well-briefed on the lies which it would be plausible to offer as support for a claim to have been an undocumented migrant previously—the nature of the work in different branches of California agriculture, and names of ranches, employers and *contratistas* with whom one could claim to have worked on a "cash only" basis. Given the nature of undocumented migration, the task of the investigator was almost impossible if the candidate was well coached, and could supply the requisite documentary evidence of his past "career."

Most of the "excessive success" of the SAW program can be explained in this manner. The cost to the migrant of obtaining access to the program was relatively high in the year of entry: undocumented migrants merely had to pay the *coyote*, whereas the legalized undocumented migrant would spend at least another $600. Few managed to remit much, if any, money back home in the year of entry after meeting these costs. Nevertheless, the costs would be recouped quite rapidly in subsequent years in terms of money saved in crossing the border, leaving aside the benefits of legal entry in other respects, although this benefit has to be set against the fact that the increased number of migrants made work more difficult to obtain, reducing the income secured.

Many would-be entrants were not, however, able to secure access to such a large quantity of cash. Village money lenders regarded a loan of this type as very risky, since the migrant might not return. Even at the level of individual communities, those who lacked the means to pay the "going rate" were discriminated against, and some genuinely qualified applicants were actually excluded from the program because an intermediary sold their documentation to another party.

This is not in any way to argue against the desirability of legalization. It was a preferable situation from the standpoint of the majority of migrants. It implied little sacrifice for the United States, beyond reducing the macro-economic significance of forms of domination of capital over labor based specifically on the migratory status of the worker. A considerable proportion of those whose legalization was based on false documents would have entered as undocumented migrants in any case. It is, however, necessary to emphasize the negative implications of the policy thinking underlying the IRCA. As academic commentators emphasized at the time of the original Simpson-Mazzoli proposals of 1982 (Cornelius & Anzaldúa Montoya, eds. 1983), the "documentation" of migrants serves little practical regulatory function, but imposes additional costs on relatively poor people. This benefits private intermediaries engaged in extra-legal practices which are, nevertheless, by-products of the legislation enacted. To the extent that it "regulated," what U.S. immigration law regulated was which Mexicans could enter the country legally and which could not. It therefore exacerbated social and regional disparities within Mexico.

From the perspective of communities like Cerrito Cotijaran, one might conclude that things "worked out in practice" in a way which was preferable to the *status quo ante*, but whether this is any cause for satisfaction depends on one's evaluation of the future the present situation offers in comparison with other alternatives.

Simpson-Rodino both stimulated migration and made it more problematic for future generations. Many young migrants who went to the North for the first time from Cotijaran in 1989 and 1990 and had not returned, were said by their parents to be unable to do so for lack of resources. They belonged to the substantial group of teenage migrants who remained undocumented (see Figure 5.6, page 117). The same problem is evident, and on a larger scale, in the data from Guaracha.

Guaracha: A New Wave of Emigration?

Family migration, and, in particular, the non-return of wives and children who entered without documentation, lends a greater air of permanence to the movement of migrants. It is very difficult to decide when a family has left for good, and even people who have stable jobs and rights of permanent residence in the North may still maintain close contacts with their kin, and return to visit them every few years, if not annually. Some, however, come to find life in the home village unattractive for a variety of reasons I explore in the next chapter. Nevertheless, it remains useful to attempt a preliminary classification, on the basis of separating those who remain seasonal migrants returning annually to reunite themselves with families in the village from those who are staying longer in the North.

In the case of Guaracha, I obtained data on a total of 392 male migrants who had been working in the United States during 1990. Of these 133 were seasonal migrants who had left and returned in the course of the year and regularly did so,[16] 159 were longer-stay migrants who did not return during the year, 82 were migrants who had not returned in years, and 18 were persons who were also permanent residents in the United States in the sense that they had stable work and residence there, but who did return annually to visit kin. The proportion of seasonal male migrants was therefore only a third of the total, although 14% of those who did not return during the year—22 individuals—were young men who had gone to the U.S. for the first time in 1990 without documents, and a few of these did come back before the end of fieldwork in July 1991.

Half the 196 male migrants were single, in the sense that they were not legally married either in Mexico or the United States, though a few of these were contributing economically to the maintenance of children they had fathered north of the border. One of the other subjects was a widower, and twenty, 5% of the total, were separated or divorced from wives in Guaracha. The remainder were mostly legally married, though a small number (3%) lived in "free unions." For the sake of simplicity, I will refer to all couples as "married" in this initial quantitative

[16] Some 20% of the seasonal migrants of 1990 had stayed for one or more years in the North earlier in their migratory careers, mostly while they were still single, though a few married men had been going for shorter periods since they had acquired legalization.

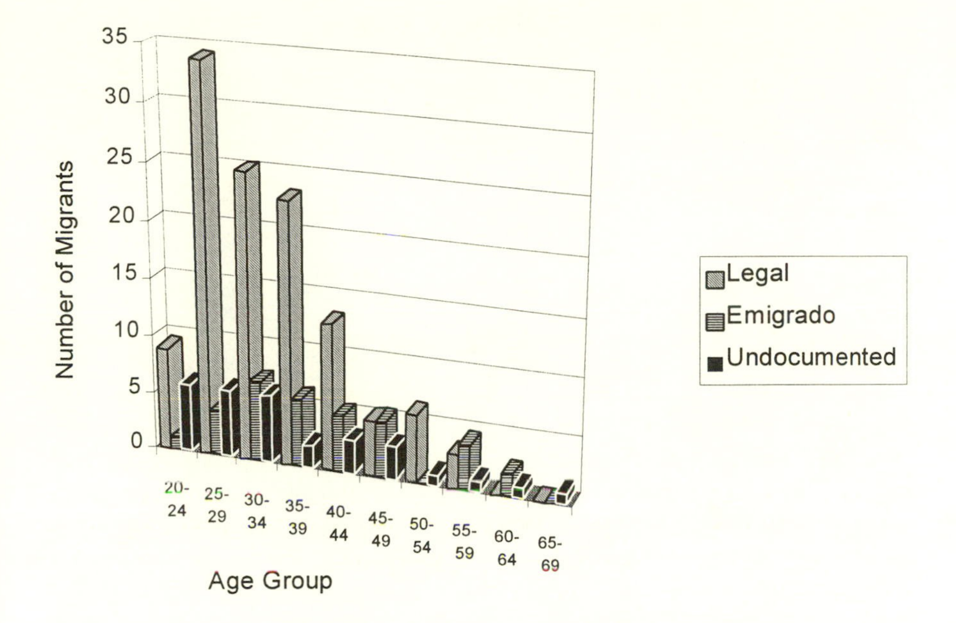

FIGURE 5.8 Married or Separated Male U.S. Migrants by Age Groups and Migratory Status, Guaracha, 1990

exposition, although the distinction has a qualitative significance which I examine in the next chapter. 41% of all married male migrants of Guaracha origin were in the North with their wives, but more than half of them were not married to women from Guaracha, and 39% had married women they met in the United States, excluding those men who had abandoned their wives in Guaracha for a new relationship there. Two out of three of the cases of migration of couples involved undocumented wives accompanying legalized husbands, although some did not yet have their children with them in the North. The growth of family migration was, however, evident relative to the situation at the start of the decade, as was a substantial increase in both the absolute numbers of international migrants from the village, and the number of individual households which were receiving economic remissions from the North.

I will begin by outlining the basic profile of contemporary migration patterns. Figure 5.8 provides a breakdown of the age-structure and migratory status of married male migrants born in Guaracha, including those who are separated or divorced from wives in the village and one widower. It will be noted that more than half of these 182 subjects are under the age of 35, but that more than 10% are over 50. 64% of the *emigrado* migrants had married outside Guaracha, and a majority of these, 71%, had married women they met in the United States. Of the sixty-four legalized migrants born in Guaracha and married to women of Guaracha, twenty-six

TABLE 5.1 Distribution of Male Migrants by Sector, Guaracha, 1990

Sector in which migrant worked in 1990	*Number of migrants*	*Percentage of migrants*
Agroindustry	15	4
Casual work	8	2
Construction	12	3
Industrial	113	29
Service	27	7
Other	4	1
Farm work	213	54
Total	392	100

(41%) had their wives with them in the North, as did four of the undocumented migrants. At least 54% of the wives of male legal migrants in the United States remained undocumented in 1990. Thirty-five per cent were known to be legally resident, and the status of the remainder was uncertain.

Seventy-one per cent of the family migrants were under 40 years of age, though the highest proportions of migrants with the families in the North were found in the age groups between 35 and 49. The proportion of family migrants never reaches 50% of migrants in any age group, and hovers around 30% for the 25–34 range, before ascending to 44% for migrants between 35 and 39. Guaracheño migrants are, however, more widely distributed between different sectors of the economy than Cotijaran migrants, as Table 5.1 indicates. Although work in agriculture continues to be the predominant occupation, the more so when work in canneries and other agroindustrial activities is included,[17] a growing proportion of Guaracheños sought work in industry in the 1980s. Service sector employment, generally in menial positions, was also quite significant in all age groups, though the largest number of service workers was found in the 20–29 age range. Yet between 30 and 36% of Guaracheño migrants were industrial workers in all age groups between 20 and 49 years of age. No older migrants were industrial workers, and although the highest proportions of migrants who worked in industry were found in the 25 to 39 age range, more than 50% of the total number of industrial workers in the sample were between 20 and 30 years old.

Table 5.2 shows the distribution of married, single and separated or divorced men between the different sectors. The highest proportion of married migrants still works in agriculture or agroindustry, but taking age differences into account, marital status as such does not seem a key variable in explaining occupational

[17] Some migrants work in the fields when there is no work to be had in the canneries, and so the division is far from clear cut. I have included only those who work full-time in agroindustry in the category.

Table 5.2 Sectoral Distribution of Migrants by Marital Status Category as Percentage of Total in Category, Guaracha, 1990

	Marital Status		
Sector	*Married*	*Single*	*Separated*
Agroindustry	7	2	0
Casual work	1	3	5
Construction	4	3	0
Industrial	26	31	25
Service	6	7	5
Farm	57	51	65

differences. More significant is that more than 50% of family migrants worked in urban occupations, 43% in the industrial sector.

Figure 5.9 shows the distribution of single male migrants from Guaracha by age group and migratory status. 70% of the single migrants in 1990 were less than 25 years old, and more than half of them, 72 individuals, were undocumented. Even in the older age groups, there were some undocumented men, in most cases people who had been going to the North for a long period, but chose not to seek legalization because of the cost.

28% of the migrants aged less than 25 had gone to the United States for the first time in 1990. Of these, 60% wintered in the United States, generally because they had not earned enough to return, though another significant factor was that the enactment of the IRCA made the position of undocumented migrants more problematic than ever, enhancing fears of the possible consequences of capture by the authorities.[18] Of the remaining 162 unmarried male migrants who had been to the United States before 1990, just under half (80 persons) had been to the North before 1988, and only 57 before May 1986. Of the 102 unmarried migrants who have secured legalization, only 46 had entered by May 1986, and 44 entered for the first time after the 31st of December, 1987.[19]

Of the pre-1990 unmarried male entrants, 40 (25%) were seasonal migrants returning annually. 72.5% of these migrants were farm workers, although shortage of work had forced some of them to find other jobs for part of the season, most notably tidying gardens for private homeowners. 79% of the seasonal farm migrants

---

[18] Violence towards undocumented migrants by the U.S. border patrol, as well as extortion by the Mexican police, became a major news topic in both countries during 1990 and 1991.

[19] In the case of married men, the situation was more favorable from the standpoint of supporters of the IRCA. Of the 118 legal migrants of Guaracha origin who were or had been married, only 8 had not entered the United States before 1988, although some had resumed migration after a break because of the prospect of legalization, did not formally fulfil the requirements of the IRCA, and presented false documents.

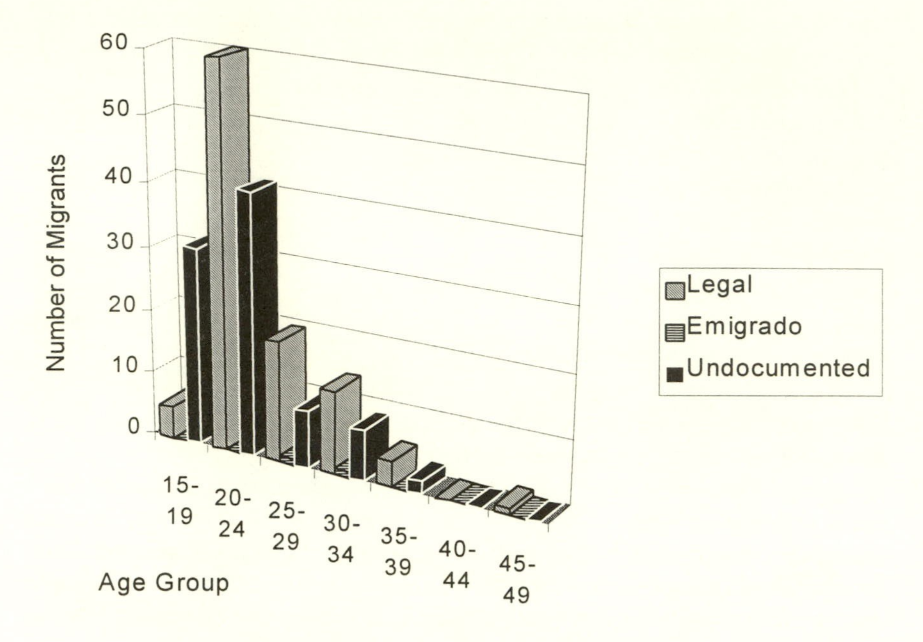

FIGURE 5.9 Unmarried Male U.S. Migrants by Age Groups and Migratory Status, Guaracha, 1990

had secured legalization, and so were entitled to unemployment benefits: the income from casual work like gardening was acceptable as a supplement to state benefits, and, indeed, was a necessary supplement given the level of the latter (between $80 and $120 a week in 1991). Two of the undocumented single migrants who had been returning annually since their first entries, in 1987 and 1989 respectively, worked in the industrial sector in Los Angeles, but all of the remaining six worked in the farm sector.

This leaves nine other single migrants who returned in 1990. All have now legalized, although four of them went to the North for the first time in 1988. One, who had been going since 1984, when he was 16, was a son of an original *ejidatario*. His older siblings were already committed to U.S. migration by the start of the 1980s.[20] He maintains no stable pattern of work or residence, drifting around between the city of Los Angeles and the rural locations where some of his brothers work, taking jobs as a janitor here, washing cars there, or spending a few days in the fields, as the mood takes him. Two others worked in similar service occupations, but one combined work as a mechanic with farm work when necessary, and the

---

[20] One of the older brothers, much to his father's chagrin, abandoned higher education in Mexico City for what was originally work in a gas station in Los Angeles.

remainder were factory workers. One of these, who began his migratory career in 1980, had been absent from the village for five years in the past, and several others had previously stayed in the North for extended periods.

Legalization makes return easier, and it is perhaps significant that a higher proportion of the returnee group were legalized than was the case in the age groups to which they belonged as a whole. The future of these single men will, however, also be influenced by the evolution of their personal relationships. The oldest migrant in the group was thirty-one, but three quarters were aged twenty-five or below. At least some were likely to form relationships with women they met in the United States, if they had not done so already. Three quarters of the returnee group were acquiring permanent residence rights.

The main disincentive to more permanent emigration from Michoacán is the state of the California labor market in general, and the farm labor market in particular, but the general picture from the data on migration of single men was of extended stays in the North. Of the legal migrants alone, sixty-eight did not return to the village even for a visit in 1990. Still excluding the case of the 1990 entrants, forty-nine of the undocumented migrants had been in the United States without returning to the village for more than a year, and fourteen had been away for more than two years, although only two had been absent for more than three years. In contrast, twelve of the legal migrants who did not return in 1990 had not returned since last leaving for the United States in 1989, fifteen had not been back since the year they achieved temporary resident status, 1988, and 60% had been away longer. Four had not returned since the start of the decade, and a total of eighteen had not returned since 1985 or earlier in the decade. Most significant of all is the fact that twelve—almost half—of the legal migrants who had not returned since 1988 or 1989, had not been to the U.S. *at all* before 1988.

A majority of single male migrants are, therefore, long-stay migrants, and those who have the facility to come and go from the United States freely are staying longer than those who remain undocumented. This is not to say that legal migrants are necessarily going to spend lengthy periods in the United States: both legalized married migrants, and the children of long-established *emigrados* whose families remain in Guaracha, may be relatively short-stay migrants, spending only a few months in the North each year. Some of the *emigrados* do not even go to the United States every year, if they have land or other interests in the region. In the case of legalized single men, however, the drift towards permanency in the North seems much stronger. Furthermore, excluding men whose partners considered themselves to be abandoned, eighteen married migrants whose wives remained in Guaracha could be considered relatively "long-stay" in 1990, in the sense that they had not returned annually in recent years. Ten had been absent since 1989, and one since 1988. Four left in the spring of 1990 but did not return during the same year, and the others had returned briefly in 1990 after an absence of eighteen months or more. Six of these men were undocumented, and one *emigrado*, but the remaining eleven were *rodinos*. Two-thirds of those who had not returned since 1989 were also *rodinos*.

The Guaracha data on the development of family migration and the behavior of single men certainly suggest that tendencies towards greater permanence in the North are strengthening. Of the single migrants with what appeared, in 1990, to be the greatest tendency to permanency in the United States, the predominant occupational sector was industry (55% of the cases), with farm work in a poor second place (26%), and services third (13%). A solitary worker in this group labored in construction, and another belonged to the "other" category of Table 5.1. He was a *coyote* earning U.S.$300 to $350 per head for passing undocumented migrants from Tijuana to Santa Ana, and had not returned to Guaracha for a decade.[21] All but three persons in this group were *rodinos*. One of the others was *emigrado,* and the other two were undocumented farm workers who had been absent for six and nine years respectively, Luis, who is rootless and has a reputation for drinking and fighting, and Eusebio, aged 32, who did not seek legalization, though his life in Bakersfield is quite stable.

The farm sector increases in importance, to 42% of the cases, if we include the larger category of "long stay" migrants. This includes some of the most recent entrants (though not those who went for the first time in 1990). In this larger group, legalized and undocumented migrants are encountered in equal proportions working in agriculture. Industrial employment still accounts for 36% of the cases overall, in comparison with an aggregate figure of 31% for all single male migrants, with a proportion of undocumented to legalized workers of 2:5. The "long stay" category includes four casual workers who seek their living from the street corner, all undocumented, and three workers in agroindustry, only one of whom is legalized. It also includes four more construction workers, three legalized, and seven more service workers, four legal and three undocumented. The proportion of service workers in the long-stay group was 9%, still slightly higher than the aggregate percentage of employment in the sector for single male migrants. There is one "other," a 30 year old undocumented migrant farm worker, who spent the last three years of his five year absence in San Quentin prison after a killing in a cantina, and did return briefly to visit his kin in 1990 following his release, before returning to his old haunts in Santa Rosa.

Putting these data together, it is clear from a comparison between the breakdown for long-stay migrants and the data on single male migrants in general presented in Table 5.2, that tendencies towards greater permanence in the United States are associated with a shift from rural to urban employment, and in particular, with the

[21] The occupational classification used in this preliminary analysis should be taken with a small pinch of salt, since there are a few others who combine "legitimate" employment with other activities. The absolute numbers involved are, however, small, and I have included the most notable cases, including those in prison, in the residual category.

industrial employment of legalized migrants. Nevertheless, a significant number of long-stay migrants from Guaracha still work in agriculture or agroindustry, a sector which both retains undocumented migrants of long standing, and continues to attract new undocumented entrants in substantial numbers.

It should be noted, however, that while agriculture retained the highest share of undocumented Guaracheño migrants of any sector (58%), the sector with the highest proportion (50%) of undocumented migrants relative to legalized migrants and *emigrados* after casual employment was construction. Only 34% of Guaracheño farm workers were undocumented: 55% were legalized and 11% *emigrado*. Industry accounted for only 24% of the employment of undocumented male migrants, compared with 32% of the employment of legalized migrants, but 27% of Guaracheño migrants who worked in industry were undocumented. 26% of service workers were also undocumented. The continuing use of undocumented labor is therefore not a peculiarity of U.S. agribusiness, but a general characteristic of those sectors of the American, and in particular, Californian, economy which use migrant labor.

Durand and Massey (1992) argue that, historically, agriculture has offered Mexican migrants the best prospects for securing legalization, because of the specific interests pursued by the grower lobby in influencing U.S. immigration policy. Agricultural work was, however, the majority choice for the new undocumented migrants who began their careers after 1990, recorded on my last visit to Guaracha in December 1992. As we will see in Chapter Seven, this has important implications for the position of migrant farm workers who opted for more permanent residence with their families in the North. Overvaluation of the peso should, in theory, have made seasonal migration less attractive by 1992, but in the case of Guaracha, there was a net increase of 6% in the number of international migrants relative to 1990. This is striking testimony to the bleakness of the regional economic panorama, and to the incapacity of U.S. immigration controls to stem the flow of undocumented migration from communities like Guaracha.

The final aspect of Guaracheño international migration in 1990 which requires comment is the movement of women across the border. The main kind of female movement was that of wives, and it is vital to recognize that many of these women (and their children) also work in the United States. One reason that young single women accompany older married brothers is to look after children while both parents work.

In the case of one family with a long tradition of undocumented family migration to Stockton by husband, wife and children, the wife, aged 44 and legalized, continued to go to the North (along with one of her sons), while the husband stayed at home in 1990 and 1991, dedicating himself to a battle with a professional brother over inheritance of his late father's *ejido* land. Another woman who migrated independently, aged 54, was the widow of a long-term farm migrant to Stockton who died of a heart attack in 1989. Two of her sons had already followed their father to the North, but the mother went with the rest of the family in order to claim social security benefits. She herself then started working in agriculture.[22] Her second son, aged 30 and still single, was the first to join his father, leaving in 1980. He had not returned since then, but remitted money sporadically to his mother, whose relative poverty was evidenced by the fact that she sold sweets in the village to make ends meet.

As we saw in the case of Cerrito Cotijaran, married or abandoned women may migrate independently of husbands in the United States, on occasion in pursuit of the disappearing spouse, and two other cases in Guaracha would fit into this category. Married women aside, however, most (79%) of the thirty-three remaining female migrants from Guaracha in 1990 were single, and more than half were under 25 years of age. Figure 5.10 shows the distribution of the unmarried female migrant population by age and migratory status. Only 15% of the female migrants who were single, widowed or separated went to the United States and returned to the village in the course of 1990.

One of the women who left and returned during 1990 was legalized. Aged 23, she had been working in a cannery in Stockton since her brother, an established migrant, bought her documentation in 1988. Also working in a cannery, though in the San Francisco region, since 1988, was a 31 year old woman who went for two months of the year during the vacations of the kindergarten where she works as a teacher. A single parent, her father is an *emigrado chueco*, and her mother also went to join the rest of the family in 1990. Her brothers became legal migrants, but she remained undocumented. The other three cases of short-term migration by single women are also related to the international migration of kin: one, aged 17, spent eight months looking after a sibling's children in Stockton, another went to join a brother working in a printing press, and the third joined an older sister working in domestic service in San Diego, though she disliked the work and returned after six months.

Six women who went to the North for the first time in 1990 and did not return in the course of the year were undocumented. One went to look after the baby daughter of her brother and his Salvadorean wife, who are both working in the industrial sector in Los Angeles. Another, aged 25 and trained as a secretary in Mexico, is one of two daughters who are the only children of a widow. She found work in a factory in Bernais through the son of a neighbor. The other four worked

---

22 This case provides further insights into the role of *contratistas* as intermediaries. The widow's husband had been a migrant for nine years, leaving for the first time after he had been responsible for killing two people in a drunk-driving accident. He stayed away for long periods, but had returned shortly before his death. He had been working with a "borrowed" social security card in his days as an undocumented migrant, and retained his rights when he legalized. His widow went to the U.S.A. initially because she was told that Eduardo, a leading Guaracheño *contratista*, was trying to sell the benefits to someone else. She had to borrow the money to go, passing with a *coyote*, and had to take her minor children, birth certificates and other documentation with her to prove her claim. She must now remain in the North to secure the benefits due to the younger children.

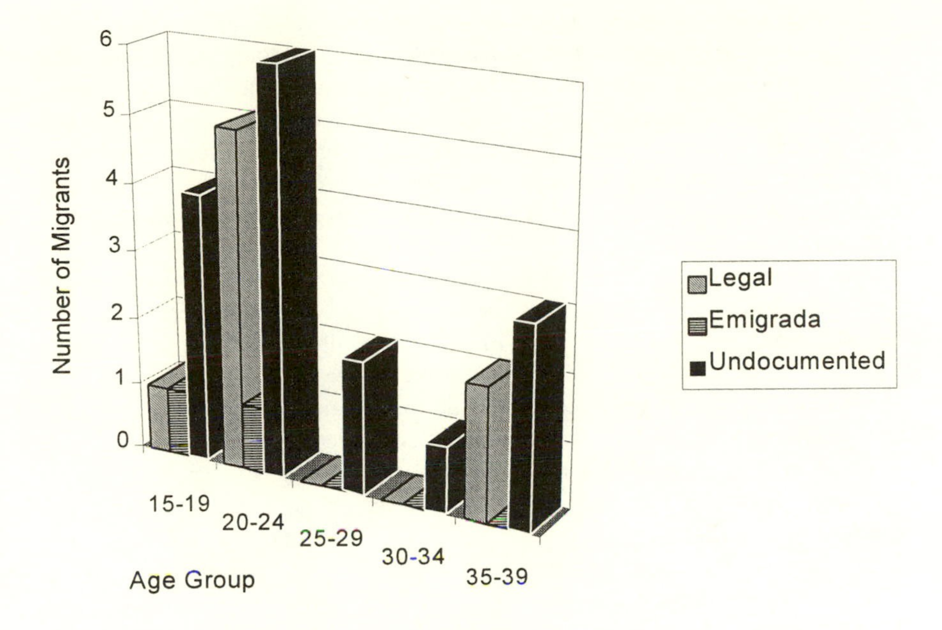

FIGURE 5.10 Unmarried Female U.S. Migrants, by Age Groups and Migratory Status, Guaracha, 1990

in agriculture. Two sisters joined their brothers in Sebastopol, in the San Francisco region, and worked in a plant nursery, accompanied by the unmarried sister of the wife of one of their brothers, who was already with her husband in the North. The last woman, aged 20, had worked in the fields for the tomato growers in Guaracha. She joined her two brothers in Bakersfield. Both brothers are long-stay migrants: one did not return from his first journey to the United States, and the other abandoned his family in Guaracha. How many of these women will stay permanently in the North cannot be judged with certainty. Nevertheless, of the women enumerated in 1990, all but the kindergarten teacher and the 17 year old who went to Stockton were still active migrants in 1992.

Of the remaining fifteen single female migrants, one, the 18 year old daughter of a man who achieved permanent residence rights in the 1970s, is in higher education. Five women, all legalized migrants with many years residence in the North, are aged thirty-six or over. Three of these women are sisters, and one of the others has a younger sister with her. All work in services: one is a domestic servant in San Diego, and the others work in private service and hotels in the Santa Ana region. A 19 year old undocumented migrant, who returned to the village only briefly in 1990 after more than a year's absence, and then returned to the North, also works in Santa Ana, but in a shop. Another of the legal migrants, aged 22, is a domestic servant in San Diego.

Services are the primary occupational sector for this group of long-stay, and in the main legalized or *emigrada*, single female migrants, but four more are industrial workers in Los Angeles, three legal and one undocumented, and the remaining two, one legal, one undocumented, work in the agricultural sector. Looking at the overall employment pattern of single female migrants, more than half of whom are undocumented, service sector employment still predominates (44%), but employment in agriculture and agroindustry is slightly ahead of urban manufacturing, at 32% and 24% respectively.

Including the occupational data on the few widows, all legal migrants, and separated or divorced women migrating to the United States independently, adds industrial and farm workers in equal proportions to the overall picture of female employment in the North. Women from Guaracha therefore participate in all three basic sectors of the migrant economy open to them in significant numbers. Although the agricultural sector was the chief employer of undocumented female migrants in 1990, particularly when undocumented working wives and children are included, followed by services, undocumented women are found in reduced proportions in manufacturing employment as well. In comparison with Cerrito Cotijaran, Guaracha has a higher proportion of female migrants in urban employments. This reflects the village's more heterogeneous patterns of male migration. Because the movements of single women are heavily influenced by the movements of married sisters and brothers, the stronger the tendency for men to move towards urban employment, the higher is the proportion of women working in cities. Tendencies towards urbanization of employment seem likely to continue, reinforced by the spread of suburban development into farming areas where migrants have settled (Eisenstadt and Thorup, 1994: 5). The evidence presented here suggests, however, that the employment of migrant women in agriculture and agroindustry will also continue to increase, although perhaps at a lower rate.

This, then, is the broad outline of current patterns of international migration from two rural communities in the Ciénega de Chapala region of Michoacán, organized by very general social and economic categories. This type of analysis tells us something about the scale of the phenomenon, its importance from the point of view of the economy of the United States, and its importance in the life of the sending region. It does not, however, provide us with a very complete picture of the deeper economic, political, social and cultural consequences of the migratory process. That is the task of the next two chapters.

6

The Family United and Divided: Migration, Domestic Life and Gender Relations

Different community-based studies have provided rather different pictures of the nature of Mexican migration to the United States. In an attempt to bring order to these apparently inconsistent results, Durand and Massey have analyzed the observed variation between communities in terms of four principle variables, each of which figured in the discussion I offered in Chapter Four: the historical age of the migration stream; the niche in the U.S. labor market where migrants first become established; the position of the community in Mexico's political economy; and, in the case of rural communities, the distribution and quality of agricultural land (Durand and Massey, 1992: 33–35). They argue that permutations of these variables explain differences in the class composition of migrant populations, the level of participation of women and children, the proportion of documented migrants and rates of legalization. They also suggest that they explain differences in the way migrant earnings are spent in the home community—whether they are invested in land, commercial farming or small business activities, or expended in consumption.

Durand and Massey argue that a consistent structural explanation of community-level variation provides a sounder basis for generalization. Generalizations are, however, also shaped by underlying theoretical conceptualizations of the social processes involved in migration. One that Durand and Massey themselves offer is that "agricultural labor is more conducive to a pattern of seasonal migration by families than urban employment," because it "has historically provided a more secure path to legal status" for both the migrant worker and his family, an advantage reinforced by the fact that growers offer work for wives and children in the fields and frequently supply low-cost housing (op.cit.: 24). I will discuss this argument in more detail later in this chapter. It clearly does not address the question of the increasing permanence of residence in the United States noted in contexts like Guaracha, which is as significant a question in the case of the farm worker population as it is in the case of urban workers,[1] but the point I wish to stress here is that it only considers the alternatives of lone male and nuclear family migration worth explaining. Yet some migrants marry in the North, some form a series of unstable unions, and some maintain multiple families. Some families established within Mexico break down entirely in the context of the migratory process.

It is true that some of these possibilities represent the behavior of a small minority, but the first does not, and even less frequent behaviors may be acute symptoms of social problems afflicting migrant communities which exercise a more subtle influence over social behavior in general. The structuring factors Durand and Massey consider do bring order to disparate data, but they also make migration seem a less contradictory process than it is, and reproduce the sharp distinction between "sending" and "receiving" regions which, as I suggested in Chapter Four, obscures the way contemporary migrant communities are constituted socially by transnational processes (Kearney, 1991: 59).

Marriage Breakdown and Multiple Liaisons

Twenty-one Guaracheño male migrants, and four from Cerrito Cotijaran, were officially separated or divorced in 1990, but in the previous chapter I noted that we need to define "marriage" and "separation" in a culturally specific way. The case concerned a young man from Cotijaran who contracted marriage only under the civil ceremony before leaving for the United States. Although a child was already born, when the father failed to write or remit money, his wife concluded that she was abandoned, and herself set off for the North in the company of her younger sister, leaving the baby with her mother. There were also two cases in Guaracha where the wife inferred abandonment after a husband who had been absent for an extended period failed to write or remit money, and began her own independent career of migration, albeit one linked to the presence of consanguine kin in the migrant destination.

Both Guaracheña women eventually took their children with them, and one has now formed a new consensual union in the North. She had already decided she never wished to set eyes on her husband again, and went North simply to secure a livelihood for herself and her children, in the same way that women abandoned by international migrant males may leave for the cities of Mexico and seek domestic service or other work. Nor do marriages necessarily fail only where men are absent in the North on their own. One Guaracha marriage broke down after the wife refused to stay with her husband in the North. There was, however, a pervasive fear of

---

[1] The data presented in the previous chapter suggested that the issue of increasing permanence concerns both single migrants and migrant families, and both documented and undocumented migrants, although the most recent drift towards permanency was strongest amongst the *rodinos* in Guaracha.

abandonment among women left behind in the two communities. In Guaracha, thirteen of the ninety-four married women who remained in the village while their husbands (mostly farm workers) were in the United States had not seen their partners for two or three years, and the proportion of women in this situation in Cotijaran was only slightly lower.

Fear of abandonment has a real foundation in community experience. In one of the Cotijaran cases, and at least two of the Guaracha cases, the husband formed a new liaison in the United States with the specific motivation of smoothing his path to legalization. One of the Guaracheños formed a liaison with a much older woman, whom he abandoned once it had served its purpose. The formation of new relationships (and often another or several other families) in the United States is, however, a much broader phenomenon, and does not necessarily lead to any formal separation or divorce, particularly where the migrant continues to support his original family. Survey methods often fail to record such behavior because questions are restricted to formal legal categories. Not all the cases of formal marriage breakdown I recorded were, however, prompted by the male partner's unfaithfulness. In one case, the stay-at-home wife's alleged unfaithfulness was the pretext for a rupture initiated by her husband. Such accusations may be premised on nothing more than sexual jealousy heightened by separation, or even be a pretext to legitimate abandonment, although there are cases in Guaracha where female adultery can be established as having occurred. Nor do women who take the initiative in breaking up with their husbands necessarily do so on grounds of unfaithfulness. Drinking and failure as a provider alone may cause a split. One woman, Maria, left her husband to work in domestic service in Guadalajara after publicly accusing him of being gay. The charge may have been largely metaphorical, although their sexual relationship was clearly not a happy one. Husband Ricardo worked in a restaurant in Los Angeles and returned annually. He failed to secure legalization after a *compadre* on whom he relied for delivery of his documents chose to give them to a nephew instead. Maria considered this symptomatic of Ricardo's lack of "manliness" and inadequacy as a provider, particularly since he failed to contest the matter, despite possessing pay slips and other documentary evidence of his eligibility.

Unfaithfulness, drinking, gambling and failing to provide for the family often go together, but it is important to recognize that marriages end because the husband refuses to continue living with his wife, whereas others end because the wife refuses to continue living with her husband, sometimes despite attempts by the latter to effect a reconciliation. Although 62% of the separated or divorced migrants from Guaracha no longer returned to the community, the remainder did come back regularly. Even when they remain absent, fathers may reestablish relations with their sons. At least three of the Guaracha men who abandoned wives in the village had regular contact with sons migrating to the same destinations, though none aided the sons to begin their migration, and they sent remittances to their mothers. One of the sons repeated his father's history and abandoned his Guaracheña wife. Father

Ezekiel, in his sixties by 1990, had not returned from the North since the late 1970s. He supposedly suspected his wife of infidelity and did not return for shame. The community believed him dead until his sons found him. All three of Ezekiel's sons have remained in the U.S.A. since the mid-1980s, the youngest two establishing free unions with women they met in the North.

That the circumstances of migration can lead to the breakup of marriages is not particularly surprising. What is more interesting is that marriages persist despite the fact that the wife knows her husband has other relationships. Some women also tolerate the fact that non-migrant husbands maintain other families in the local region. Although wives may not regard such a situation with equanimity, it is often the children, and particularly daughters, who express the greatest resentment, because conjugal relationships may, as we will see, be maintained without love. This raises further questions about the motivations of both men and women.

Firstly, whilst the migrant situation may create favorable conditions for infidelity, the formation of a second family cannot be explained in terms of sexual gratification, which could be achieved more cheaply by other means. Men often contribute financially to the support of two (or more) family units. By no means can all of the new liaisons formed by men in the United States in the past be explained by the desire to secure residence rights. Within Michoacán, the formation of multiple families is often associated with male power claims in the male community. It is behavior male *campesinos* generally expect of *caciques*, but although only relatively wealthy men can make themselves financially responsible for the maintenance of separate domestic units, male circulation between different women and families is not always restricted to particularly wealthy or influential members of the community.

This is the case in the Maya town of San Pedro Sacatepéquez in Guatemala (Ehlers, 1990). In San Pedro, in contrast to the Michoacán *mestizo* communities, free union involving no formal (civil or ecclesiastical) marriage ceremony has been the predominant form of marriage since records first began in 1925 (Ehlers, op.cit.: 144, 146).[2] What are known locally as *unido* relationships are typically established after the couple has had sexual intercourse. Women are ignorant of sex, and tend to assume a passive role when subjected to physical and emotional domination by men. Young men are pressured into making a commitment to their *novia* by families, but baptismal records in the community reveal that 7% of mothers give birth without benefit of spouse, *unido* or otherwise, and once a woman has borne

---

2 Eleven migrants from Guaracha were recorded as members of stable *uniones libres* in 1990. This was close to the proportion of free unions to legal marriages in the state as a whole according to the 1990 census: 7% of couples were in free unions. 79% married by both the civil and religious ceremonies, and 3% and 11% by the religious and civil ceremonies alone, respectively. The *municipio* of Villamar did, however, have a lower proportion of free unions and a higher proportion of marriages based on both the civil and religious ceremonies than the state as a whole, and free unions were more common among U.S. migrants than other people.

a child, her chances of a union with a man other than the biological father are slim (op.cit.: 147).

Under Guatemalan law, men can charge women who leave consensual unions with desertion of the home, even if they take the children with them, whereas no obligations whatsoever are imposed on the male partner. Women thus have peculiar difficulties escaping relationships in which men fail to contribute economically and subject them to physical abuse. Yet even without the legal sanctions, women can be locked into unsatisfactory unions by economic dependence. Both rich and poor men alike philander extensively, although only the wealthy can afford to maintain separate homes for mistresses. Marital breakdown is, however, rare in San Pedro. Men either leave their wives for short periods and then return, or establish *casitas* with their other partners and continue to make at least some continuing financial contribution to their wives (Ehlers, op.cit.: 150). Ehlers argues that women in this community do not find the sexual act—which they describe as men "doing their deed"—pleasurable. This is not only because men do nothing to foster female pleasure in sexual relations, but because women accept male ideologies of their inherent passivity. They thus become accomplices in their own subjugation, for Ehlers argues persuasively that overt enjoyment of sex by a woman would be construed by a man as a threat to his domination, "a switch in the balance of sexual power that suggests she might not be contained at home and might stray" (op.cit.: 150). Though women joke about the number of *novios* they have had—without reference to sex—and about the generic viciousness and puerility of men, the "game of love" belongs to the era before they take on the *santa carga* of the married woman and mother. Ehlers concludes that the reason that women welcome straying husbands into extramarital relationships is exactly the same as the reason they marry them: to achieve "productive and reproductive security."

What she terms a system of "parallel marriages" is therefore based on the coincidence of distinct male and female motivations in an economically stratified community. Women are searching for economic security, not merely through any direct economic contributions the man might make, but through the children that will issue from the union. In San Pedro, children are a continuing source of material support throughout their mothers' lives, even if their father eventually moves on (Ehlers, op.cit.: 152). Men achieve status from the maintenance of a parallel family because other men regard this as a measure of their power and virility, but they also ensure themselves permanent access to women who will tolerate their vices and perform the required services of washing and cooking without complaint. When one female partner loses her patience, the man can turn to another with similar "wifely" characteristics. The other woman or women may be termed a *querida*, but it is not passion that men are seeking, but something more mundane and ultimately more important in terms of their values.

The logic of "parallel marriage" in San Pedro rests on a particular combination of gender and sexual ideologies and socio-economic conditions. None of them are immutable. The economic value of women and children to men, for example, depends on particular labor market conditions and structures of production. Family structures are not products of unchanging cultural "norms," but adapt dynamically to changing economic conditions. As Escobar (1988) has shown in the case of Guadalajara, a shift of working class households towards more extended structures allowed adjustment to crisis conditions, by increasing the number of potential income providers under conditions of mounting employment instability and declining real wages. As Chant (1985) demonstrated for the case of Querétaro, the fact that male workers earn more than women tells us nothing in itself about the relative viability of nuclear, extended and female-headed households, since overall family welfare is a function of the consumer/worker ratio and the internal distributive relations of the household. If a significant proportion of the income of male heads does not benefit their dependents, families where several people work may be better off, even if those workers earn less *per capita.* Furthermore, male behavior may inhibit family income maximization by denying women opportunities to work when they wish to do so.

Gender ideologies therefore remain relevant to understanding how family and household structures adjust to changing economic circumstances, and *vice versa.* We should expect to find variations in the local situations produced by a dialectic of economic transformation, on the one hand, and negotiations over the meaning of gender and the roles of men and women, on the other. In the region of Guatemala where Ehlers's study is set, differences between the behavior of indigenous and *mestizo* communities do reflect differences in modes of production and articulation to the market. *Ladinos* were more inclined to withdraw financial support from their first partner when they established new relationships, and manifested a higher rate of definitive desertion. Ehlers notes Bossen's argument that the "traditional" rural Maya household was based on gender complementarity in the economic sphere (Bossen, 1984). The contributions indigenous women (and children) made in the sphere of production were significant for *male* economic security. "Economic modernization" undermined female production activities, and reduced women's cash incomes substantially relative to those of men, transforming them into economic burdens rather than assets (Ehlers, op.cit.: 157). Indigenous social patterns were increasingly converging with *ladino* patterns. As market-purchased substitutes became available for the domestic goods and services which women traditionally provided, their value to men became that of "symbols of affluence whose consumption activities and productive seclusion visibly express the conspicuous and independent success of their husbands" (op.cit.: 163).

Uneducated women generally lack opportunities to earn incomes comparable to men in the local economy around Guaracha. There has been a substantial amount of work for women and children in commercial agriculture, but pay is low relative to male wages, and in national terms. Another outlet for female labor has been the strawberry packing plants in Zamora. This type of work entails the movement of women outside the immediate confines of the village, and beyond the range of direct supervision by parents or husbands, contradicting patriarchal conceptions of the female role. Women with more education also work in professions such as nursing in the towns of Jiquilpan and Sahuayo, although they are likely to continue living at home.

Ciénega women have, however, also long had the opportunity to participate in long-distance internal migration, since the predominant form of emigration from the region since the 1940s has been movement to the metropolitan cities and young people have been able to lodge with kin in the cities whilst studying and/or seeking entry into the labor market (Gledhill, 1991). One type of urban work, domestic service, could be seen as preserving the character of a "domestic container," but still tended to undermine parental control. Migrant women achieved freedom in selecting their own partners from outside the community, often preferring consensual unions to legal marriage. There have been various cases of illegitimate births and divorce and separation. Although such problems sometimes bring women back to the community, it is more common for them to form a new relationship, once any children of the first have been deposited with their grandparents.

The contrast between the position of women who remain resident in the villages and those who migrate out of them is substantial. The participation of unmarried women in local commercial agriculture increased through the years of crisis, but its importance to household survival continued to be understated, through its classification as temporary work. Female participation rates in local farm work are higher in Cotijaran than Guaracha, in line with Cotijaran's greater poverty, but because the women work for men from the village acting as subcontractors for larger commercial interests, their paid labor is readily classified as work done under the supervision of a male kinsmen. In Guaracha, the few men whose mature wives continue to work in the fields or packing plants are downgraded in social estimation. Mature women who work in local agriculture or agroindustry are mainly women who have been abandoned or had children out of wedlock. Even widows and abandoned women who remain in the community still tend to search for ways of making income which do not force them to work outside the house—sewing or taking in washing, for example—or rely on the support of working children.

Greater participation in the outside labor market is not necessarily an unmixed blessing for women. For poor women with young families, this often, though not invariably, leads to daughters having reduced opportunities for education, because they take on their mother's domestic burdens (Chant, 1994: 210–11, 223–4). In the case of the rural Ciénega, however, male fears about the consequences of women escaping the tutelage of fathers or other male surrogates continue to influence their choices, since fathers frequently pressure their single daughters not to leave the family home.

Women are thus faced with real dilemmas in the face of misfortunes or in seeking a better future: staying in the village has different implications to various migratory options which are made available through kin networks connecting villages to distant communities. Even young women with little education can change their lives radically (for better or worse) by going off to live with an aunt or a married brother.

The early internal migrant strategy remains the choice of a minority. Within the communities, married women may make a decisive economic contribution to the household economy, by raising animals and engaging in forms of domestic production which provide a direct cash income, such as making and selling foodstuffs for sale in the village. There is even some participation of women in domestic outworking for manufacturing concerns. Yet objective circumstances and male ideology combine to promote a strong devaluation and domestication of the female economic role. Within the communities, women are drawn towards seeking male support. Men have little incentive to remain in a relationship which they find uncongenial, unless a notorious inadequacy as providers makes them unattractive to other women, and women who decide to leave an unbearable union face a difficult choice. They have limited opportunities to maintain themselves locally, and are unlikely to be able to marry again while their first partner is alive, unless they migrate and leave any children of the first union with kin in the village. Men, on the other hand, do enter into "parallel unions."

The women who enter into such relationships and bear illegitimate children suffer some social stigma, but if the male is a capable provider, even young single women, as well as those who are abandoned, may be willing to pay the price in terms of reputation. Irma was the eighteen year old daughter of the Cotijaran woman abandoned by a husband from Guanajuato whom she met working in the fields in Zamora, mentioned in the previous chapter. She had two children by a prosperous Guaracheño, Eduardo, one of four brothers known as the "broncos." Eduardo's interest in the relationship was to project his social persona as a "man of power," and Irma's acceptance of it was more than simply a response to being trapped in poverty. Her mother, Juana, aged thirty-four, came from a poor landless family, and her older brother went yearly, still undocumented, to Merced. Juana and her younger brother took what work was available with the local tomato growers. This family's particularly low social status in the community reflected the way Juana's history seemed to confirm negative stereotyping of women who go to live in Zamora to work in the fields or *congeladoras*. She had given herself to a treacherous stranger. Irma's behavior confirmed that Juana's lack of morals had rubbed off on her daughter, but Juana and women like her choose to stay in the community in conscious defiance of prevailing attitudes, and Irma had little more to lose in accepting the proposition which Eduardo made to her one day after she had been picking his tomatoes, because she was already stigmatized by her mother's reputation.

Not all wives will tolerate their husbands maintaining another family, particularly when it is close at hand, but their reactions are tempered by pragmatism and the underlying weakness of their position. The second family generally resides in a different community, and men may divide their time between households on a regular schedule tacitly or even explicitly accepted by all parties. That abandoned or poor women who bear children out of wedlock are downgraded but not ostracized, reflects the way female views about the viciousness of men create space for negotiating tolerance. It is evident, however, that women's options are limited if they remain in the community, whereas men with economic resources can benefit from female dependence. A less dramatic exemplification of this principle is the way widowers who are merely comfortably off by local standards consistently succeed in remarrying women decades younger than themselves.

When a wife leaves her husband over another woman, this is often because he is failing to provide for her and her family adequately. Such women can often depend on migrant remissions or other forms of economic support from children. They may even migrate themselves. Men from the Ciénega are likely to cease to support their original families altogether if the wife proves difficult. They see wives more as a burden than an economic resource within the villages, and may only think twice if the wife's kin are in a position to make trouble for them in the community.

International Migration and the Parallel Family

Distance does not do much to reduce public knowledge of second families in the North. The behavior of individuals is filtered back through village gossip networks by other migrants. Even men who make significant efforts to be presumed dead tend to be tracked down by the network eventually. Those who form new relationships during extended periods in the United States do so for a variety of often confused motivations. Some simply want to enjoy the kinds of domestic services they enjoy as married men at home, whereas others are making a statement to their peer group which is not dissimilar in spirit to the statement having a "second family" makes in their native region. Women in the North may, however, have a value women at home generally do not have, not only as a means to secure residence rights, but also as workers in the open labor market who are capable of bringing in significant amounts of money income, buffering male living standards against variable earnings and periods of unemployment.

Some cases, however, seem to reflect other motives, which are best illustrated by concrete examples.

> Julio started his migrant career in farm work in Stockton, leaving for the first time shortly after his marriage. He then moved to Dallas, where he found work in construction, and finally to Chicago, where he obtained particularly well paid work in a factory making car fenders with the help of an *emigrado* friend. With more money in his pocket, he found life in Chicago a revelation, and met a city-born woman who seemed to represent an entirely different, and infinitely more exciting, style of life, socially and sexually. [I should note here that men tend to project their sexual fantasies onto women associated with the North, especially *gringas* and *güeras*, although this sexual dimension is entangled with images of life-style difference and redrawn moral boundaries.] Julio and the *americana* moved into an apartment together. One of Julio's

older brothers (now in jail) was already established as a *coyote*, and got involved in the drugs business. Another educated brother worked for the Mexican tourist board in California. This generation within the family had a different vision of what the "good life" could constitute in the United States, a vision centered on bars, clubs and the life of the street. Julio's relationship with his new partner defined itself in terms of love and freedom. It lasted three years before they broke up, and he returned to the village with a drink problem and little feeling of fulfillment. Had the relationship he formed in the North been less important to him, less central to his new identity as a potentially permanent resident of the United States, he might never have returned. He found readjustment to life in rural Michoacán extremely painful. His wife, who had gone to live with her mother in Guadalajara during his absence, accepted him back, but their relationship has never recovered, and she left him two years after he returned.

Alberto enjoyed a much less comfortable life as a worker in the United States than Julio, roaming around in search of casual farm work, and often sleeping rough. He liked the sense of freedom he achieved, and adjusted well to the life of an undocumented migrant, but unlike Julio did not develop a sense that there was a new life to be built in the North. He lived for the day, drinking, gambling and going with women, remitting little money to his family at home. After he had been in the North for more than a year, this egotistical gratification began to pall. He felt lonely, and searched for greater stability in both work and life. He was drawn into a new relationship with a working woman who had separated from her own husband and provided him not merely with domestic services but with additional income. His security increased, but the new family's economic circumstances remained precarious, and there were frequent rows. He began to remember the woman and child he had left back in the village. In the end, he decided to return to Mexico and seek reconciliation, carrying, in his own account, a burden of guilt about the woman he abandoned in the North.

Some migrants can, of course, maintain separate relationships in the United States and Mexico for an extended period by virtue of regular returns to the village, but cases like Alberto's are not uncommon. The woman he met in the United States expected him to stay with her permanently, but in some cases, women may not expect (or even desire) a permanent relationship, or look on men as either a socially or economically necessary complement to their own role as providers and raisers of children. Whether this is true or not depends on the particular social and economic context in which they are living.

Matrifocal family structures based on female support networks and serial monogamy with a succession of transitory male partners are related both to specific labor market conditions (absence of stable male wage-earning capacity) and to specific social conditions (the decay of social mechanisms which support male intervention in household organization and control of female sexuality). The Ciénega villagers themselves often express the view that in the North: "La gente nada más se junta" (people only shack up with each other). This is, however, by no means a general pattern. The statement simply reflects the greater incidence of free unions in the North, relative to their rarity at home. A useful insight into family structures among Mexican migrants at the start of the 1980s is provided by David

Heer's research on Los Angeles County, which distinguished American-born citizens, legal immigrants and undocumented migrants.[3] Heer found that consensual unions amounted to 12.4% of 3,298 partnerships in which the mother was an undocumented migrant living with her spouse, and 13.2% of 2,752 cases in which the male partner was undocumented (Heer, 1990: 114, Table 7.9). These proportions dropped to 2.3% and 4.2%, respectively, in the case of legal immigrants. They were slightly higher, at 4% and 5.9%, respectively, in the case of the U.S.-born citizens of Mexican origin, though still much lower than in the case of undocumented migrants. Households headed by single mothers were, however, most prevalent among U.S.-born citizen women, at 29.3% of the total, and again lowest in the case of legal immigrants, at 9.9% (ibid.). Households with no male partner present constituted 15.3% of the undocumented households. The ethnographic evidence I have presented indicates that single mothers from Mexico may still be drawn into new relationships with migrant men, despite the insecurity of their position.

Although female-centered support networks within migrant communities in the United States may be important, these data suggest that this is largely in the context of households which include men. That female-headed households were most prevalent amongst American-born citizen women of Mexican origin in Heer's sample is consistent with the argument of Hayes-Bautista (1993) that it is the most "assimilated" members of the Mexican origin population who take on the social characteristics ascribed to the urban "underclass" in the United States. I will discuss the issue of the "underclass" in more depth in the next chapter, but even the figures presented so far indicate the vital importance of keeping a sense of proportion. Overall, Latino households in California had the highest proportion of households consisting of a couple and their children of any ethnic group up to 1980, at 47.1%, compared with 24.6% and 21.8% for Anglos and Blacks, respectively (Hayes-Bautista, 1993: 134). Heer's data show that 72.1% of the Mexican households in which the mother was undocumented, and 86.6% of the households in which the father was undocumented, consisted of legally married couples, with the spouse present. The proportions were even higher for legal immigrants. One other significant fact which emerges from Heer's study is that extended family structures which permit resource pooling amongst their members are more frequent among undocumented migrants in the United States than they are in the rural home communities. 35.9% of all undocumented mothers lived in extended households, and 71.1% of undocumented mothers who did not live with the father of their children did so (Heer, op.cit.: 117, Table 7.11). Non-nuclear households were less frequent (53.7%) among legal immigrant women without a resident partner than in

---

[3] Los Angeles County was the place of residence of 44% of the undocumented Mexican migrants enumerated in the 1980 U.S. census, for which special provisions were made to encourage undocumented persons to respond (Heer, 1990: 30).

the case of both citizen and undocumented mothers, and the proportion of extended households amongst migrant families in which an undocumented woman lived with her partner was higher (29.8%) than for both legal immigrant (18.2%) and U.S.-born women (17.7%) living with their partners (ibid.).

Julio and Alberto's histories do, however, reveal the price some women pay for male egotism. In both cases, one suspects that had things turned out better for them in the United States, they would have abandoned their families at home. Yet these examples also suggest that male behavior has deeper determinants than pure egotism. It may be bound up with fantasies about life-styles related to the dislocation inherent in the migrant experience, the notion that the North exists beyond the boundaries of a moral community of reference, and is a place where desire might be fulfilled. It may not even be a question of liberation of repressed desire, though men of the region do feel that some sexual acts are unacceptable to women of their native communities. Displacement itself may invoke desires that might not otherwise be felt so strongly. Some individuals clearly opt for migration not out of immediate economic necessity, but with a conscious or unconscious aspiration to reconstitute themselves as persons. Since displacement itself may awaken a felt need for reconstitution, even amongst those who harbor no initial ambition to change their lives, such considerations are more broadly relevant.

Here, however, we should consider the question of historical change. Abandonment of families in Mexico for new liaisons in the North dates back to the earliest phase of emigration from Michoacán before the mass deportations of 1929. Yet in general, recognition of kinship connections and common local origin (*paisanaje*) was central to the social strategies of past generations of migrants.[4] Through the formation of *compadrazgo* relations, marriage alliances and associated life-cycle rituals reaffirming social bonds between families, such as baptisms and fifteenth birthday celebrations, those who settled in the North re-established social linkages which defined expectations of mutual moral obligation. The lone male migrant situation fostered innovations in kinship practices, and strengthened the significance of certain bonds, in particular, those between fathers and sons, brothers, and uncles and nephews (Massey et al, 1987: 140–1). Yet most migrants continued to live obstinately "Mexican" lives in many cultural domains.

The importance of kinship networks in providing individual migrants with support and reconstituting communities did not, in itself, guarantee the stability of conjugal bonds formed in Mexico. Even where conjugal units remain intact, domestic authority structures and gender roles can be transformed. Nevertheless,

---

[4] It is important to stress the way family and group membership is conditional on *mutual recognition* of a relationship (Alvarez, 1987: 98). As I stress in the next chapter, a focus on the way migrant social networks underpin systems of mutual aid and group solidarity can obscure the fact that mechanisms underpinning solidarity also define *boundaries* of strong moral obligation and the possibility of *refusing* aid.

the argument that the spatial and social displacement involved in migration leads to a "breakdown" of the family is as invalid in the case of international migration as it is in the case of rural-urban migration within Mexico (Alvarez, 1987: 165). Adaptation to displacement through reconstitution of social and familial bonds has been a major historical feature of Mexican migration.

Contemporary social and economic conditions on both sides of the border are, however, now radically different from those experienced by earlier generations. There is now greater scope for migrants with families at home to form non-casual liaisons in the North than in earlier periods, because lone male migrant stays in the North have become more extended and the stock of women has increased within the migrant and refugee communities formed by Mexicans and Central Americans. Nevertheless, the fact remains that the majority of marriages contracted in Mexico do survive the migratory process, and growing tendencies towards family migration in communities like Guaracha are reducing the number of women left at home. Although many wives cite fear of abandonment as their motive for wanting to go to the North, others have positive aspirations for improving their own lives, and in both cases the women often prove more reluctant to return to Mexico than their husbands.

I will return to the issue of the situation of women later on, but there is more to be said first about men and the implications of migration for male identities.

Marriage in the North and Migrant Identity

Leaving aside men separated from Guaracheña wives living with other women in the North, twenty-three men from Guaracha had contracted legal marriages, and a further nine entered free unions, with women they met in the United States. Only two women from Guaracha had married men they met as migrants in the North. In the case of Cotijaran, only four male migrants have married women met in the United States. Relatives in residence knew the origin of only one of them, a woman from a Jiquilpan family, since none of the others had ever visited the village. Of Guaracha's U.S.-born spouses, six or seven had actually visited with their husbands, and the names and backgrounds of around half of the total were known to the migrant's resident kin. They included a Salvadoreña, Guatemalteca and Puertorriqueña, as well as spouses from other regions of Mexico, including Veracruz, Sonora, Zacatecas and Oaxaca.

Although some of the partners Guaracheños met in the United States came from communities in the same region or state, the number of spouses from culturally distinct backgrounds indicates a greater openness of the Guaracheño community in the North. This might at first sight seem likely to correlate with the community's greater involvement in the urban economy. The marriages with non-Mexicans were indeed contracted by urban industrial workers, but the number of farm workers marrying women they met in the North was more or less identical to the number of urban workers. The marriages with women from other states of Mexico also mainly involved farm workers, although the number of cases where the background of the partner was not known in the village prohibits any definitive conclusion.

Forty-two per cent of all Guaracheño couples in the United States consist of partners both born in the village. The remaining cases represent marriages between members of the village and surrounding communities, or, in a few cases, unions contracted during internal migration to Mexico City or Guadalajara before movement to the North. Nevertheless, that forty-three per cent of male migrants with partners in the North have contracted unions with women they met there, a majority of whom have never visited the village, is an index of the extent to which migration has transformed itself into a more permanent process of emigration, and is producing an emigrant population which is no longer definable simply as "Mexican American," much less as a series of "daughter communities" with distinct local origins within particular regions of Mexico. Such colonies do still exist, and are reproduced by the emigration of entire families formed in the villages, but the geographical dispersion of Guaracha migrants, and their intermarriage with other members of other groups, is producing a generation which will not have unambiguous ties to a particular Mexican homeland or even, where a parent is not Mexican, to Mexico itself.

The place of the modern Mexican migrant population in U.S. society is a complex issue which I discuss more fully in the next chapter, but the increasing permanence of residence north of the border of migrants and their families makes it an important issue for rural Mexico itself. Emigrants may continue to influence life in the villages even after years of absence, particularly, though not exclusively, where they play a role as intermediaries providing access to jobs in the United States, but a certain social distance may develop between long-term absentees and their kin and *paisanos*.

As a first illustration of this, I will take the case of Refugio, aged 39, and son of a Cotijaran *ejidatario*. His father, Rafael, spent twenty years going annually to Texas or California, first as a *bracero* and later as an undocumented migrant, until the end of the 1960s, when he decided to dedicate himself to the land he acquired in La Beneficencia and La Palma. Rafael's wife, Gloria, offered a rather different interpretation of his decision to end his migratory career, to wit that he had become so fat that he could no longer run fast enough to escape the *migra*, but there is a third, since she suffered a serious accident at this time. This probably helped convince Rafael that his place was at home. Although Rafael was a seasonal migrant, he established regular working patterns, particularly with an employer in Fresno, who paid the costs of the *coyote* on his behalf. His regular contacts enabled him to act as a recruiter of other workers.

Refugio started migrating at the end of the 1960s, and married in Cotijaran in the 1970s. His wife, Maria, twelve years his junior, was sixteen when their child was born. The couple were betrothed, as was common in Cotijaran at the time, when Maria was in her early teens. The marriage did not prosper. According to Refugio's mother-in-law, he was away for years on end in the United States, drank heavily and beat his wife when he did return. Refugio's own mother and brothers confirmed the drinking problem, which became so serious that he finally sought the aid of Alcoholics Anonymous in 1988. By this time, he was separated from Maria, who went with her mother to work in domestic service in Guadalajara.[5] There she remains today, now in a new relationship with one of Refugio's cousins.

Refugio himself returned briefly to the village for a few days in the winter of 1990, his first return in several years, but stayed only a few weeks before setting off for the North again with his younger brother Cecilio, a legalized migrant who only stays the *temporada* in the North before returning to his family in the village. Although Refugio's past migratory experience included a spell grape-picking in Sonora, he had a regular job on a ranch in Buckeye, Arizona. This is the region to which Cotijaran migrants have gone because of the presence of Ignacio, the foreman on a cotton farm mentioned in the previous chapter, whose case is discussed in more detail below. Refugio himself is now a deputy foreman. The Buckeye ranch provides its workers with free transport to the fields, air-conditioned cabs, and subsidized accommodation. Hourly rates are lower than in California, but the work offers few uncertainties to those who can acquire it, providing that they can tolerate the hot climate. Yet, in contrast to his rather easy-going brother, Refugio is still not a happy man.

As his mother put it: "He is more from *there* now than from *here*." Rafael and Gloria's home is by no means the most humble in the village, but it is a simple adobe dwelling, teeming with chickens and other animals, bereft of the solid furniture and tile floors some houses now possess. Refugio admitted that he was ashamed of the way his family lived, and wouldn't feel comfortable inviting friends he had made in the North to come down on holiday to see the *rancho*. Refugio's dilemma was not, however, simply one of social embarrassment. The collapse of his marriage, and continuing inter-family recriminations this was causing, left him particularly rootless in a closely-intermarried community riven with envy (*envidia*), of which his own father was also a victim.

---

[5] Mother Consuelo was the woman abandoned for another woman in Jiquilpan by her *ejidatario* partner, Federico, mentioned in the previous chapter. She had never been legally married to Federico, but continued to live in her mother-in-law's house, looking after the old lady, after he moved out. Federico only went to the United States once, with his son-in-law Refugio. He had worked in a private capacity for the deputy director of BANRURAL's Jiquilpan branch and set down roots there. His legal wife had been childless, and went to Mexico City after Federico broke up with her, where she is now living with a singer. Consuelo bore Federico six children: two sons are now in the North, the elder having set off at age fourteen, while her two younger daughters work locally in the fields. Consuelo went to Guadalajara to work in service for five years after Federico left her, but returned to the village with Refugio and Maria's daughter. Refugio's parents tried to take the child away, however, and she was sent back to her mother in Guadalajara.

Some classified Rafael as a labor contractor benefiting from exploiting others. The limited returns on migration for the majority sharpened antagonism towards even those who were modestly more successful than the norm. In reality, Rafael was not even relatively rich, and harbored his own resentments towards those who had achieved economic advancement through clientage relations with members of the agrarian bureaucracy—which included the father of his daughter-in-law Maria. Refugio's own discomfort was exacerbated by the tension between his parents and former mother-in-law, as well as by gossip about his drinking and domestic violence. He had also lost peer group respect because his ex-wife's new partner was a kinsman and his parents had failed to recover his child. Nevertheless, as a key migrant capable of helping people find work, he still had friends with whom he could associate on visits. What he did not have was a place in the life of the village. His only meaningful *local* identity was that of the successful migrant farm worker in Buckeye, Arizona.

Neither of the two leading migrant intermediaries in Cotijaran introduced in the last chapter has been back to the village for some time. Ignacio, the Arizona foreman, emigrated in 1955, with the aid of his employers, but still had land and a household in Cotijaran, headed by his second partner and mother of his two youngest children, Leticia, to whom he was not legally married. Ignacio supported Leticia financially, although he also had another family in the North, and she had not seen him for nearly a decade.

Three of Ignacio's sons by his first marriage were working in Arizona. A son by Leticia, aged 18, worked as a *jornalero* in the village, and had not been to the United States. Two of the three migrants married women they met in the North: they had permanent residence rights through their father, and their wives' names and origins were not known to his second family. The other married a woman from Cotijaran, and returned for a brief visit to his in-laws in November 1990. He works with his father and has a secure, permanent job. Marriage within the community fosters maintenance of contacts, but bridges can be rebuilt after a great lapse of time: the son of a Guaracha *emigrado* who was born in the United States met the woman whom he married on his first ever visit to the village, in his twenties. Ignacio, however, had apparently cut his ties with the abandonment of his second local partner in favor of his family in the North.

Many felt resentment towards him not simply because of his unusual success as a migrant, but because of his failure to "accommodate" kinsmen and *paisanos* with work. One of Ignacio's brother Davíd's sons, who worked (still undocumented) in Merced and had recently taken his wife with him, did start out in Arizona, but moved to California because, as his father darkly put it, uncle Ignacio "refused to help him." Evidently, Ignacio would have difficulty accommodating the stream of migrants sent annually from Cotijaran, given the kind of facilities he possesses as a farm foreman in a heavily mechanized branch of U.S. agribusiness. Even in the absence of alienation from life in the *rancho*, or of positive feelings towards aspects of life in the North, *emigrados* in this kind of structural position find maintaining regular contacts with their community of origin less congenial with the passage of time. Marriage and family formation in the North can only reinforce this process. The son of Ignacio who did return had the advantage of having married a woman from a family with a social network embracing many who might feel some hostility towards his father. Only a little wagging of malicious tongues was evident during his visit.

As I noted in the previous chapter, the other Cotijaran intermediary, the Merced *contratista* Abruelio, did not achieve emigrate as a *bracero,* but entered as an undocumented migrant until he acquired permanent residence rights with a borrowed identity. He had not returned to Cotijaran since 1986, when he was robbed, an event he ascribed to *envidia*. His wife, from Guaracha, had remained resident in a modest house in the village, and was title-holder of *ejido* land in her own right. She had twice visited her husband in the United States prior to her third visit, in April 1990, from which she had still not returned three years later. Both their sons had now taken their village-born wives with them to the North, and one had not returned for three years. Abruelio's one remaining resident child, a daughter, is married to a seasonal migrant who now works in Arizona. Abruelio's family is, in comparison with Ignacio's, more firmly rooted in the village than in the United States, all the children having married in Cotijaran. Both husband and wife have additional kinship ties with families in Guaracha. If they are now shifting their residence permanently to the United States, Abruelio's interpretation of the motivation of the 1986 robbery seems the key to explaining their behavior, since he does not maintain a separate family there.

The migration brokers and their children constitute a special category of persons who are not simply drawn towards greater permanence in the North by the labor market niche they occupy, but also find continuing involvement in their home communities problematic. As one old Cotijaran *ejidatario* and U.S. migrant in the 1920s, notable for his lack of antagonism in principle to the capitalist wage labor relationship and belief in the worker's obligations to his employer, once put it to me:

> There are some people from here who serve as *mayordomos* in the North. They kill the people there, the poor who only go for trips up there. Yes, they work them all right, they earn money bringing people to work, and then the *Migra* comes and throws them out and they put others to work in their place. That's how they become naturalized (sic).

The implication of this diatribe is that the *mayordomos*' success was illegitimate. They profited not merely from an excessive exploitation of the worker, but also from the misfortunes of undocumented *paisanos* who were expelled—a common experience for Cotijaran migrants. This made them accomplices in an unjust system. Nevertheless, the relationship with the brokers remains ambiguous, since they also "help" migrants to find work. Yet this positive side leads to accusations of moral failure if no work can be delivered.

Some of those who earn their livelihood entirely in the United States do return regularly to Mexico. Excluding cases where husbands returned only briefly during the year to see resident wives, seventeen migrants in Guaracha who were permanently resident in the United States paid regular holiday visits to the village, to keep in touch with kin, in particular aged parents. Two were widows, and two single women, but four were women with partners from outside the community, the remainder being single men. Nevertheless, the returnees are heavily outnumbered by those who stay away. A total of seventy-seven Guaracheño couples in the North belonged to the "permanent," "long-stay" or "brief visit" categories.[6] Since only a minority of these couples consist of unions between migrants from Guaracha and partners they met in the United States, the emigrant tendency within the population is running deep. I now turn to explore its implications in terms of the quality of domestic relations in general, and gender relations in particular.

The Family That Stays Together

The movement of entire families from Michoacán to the United States is not a new historical phenomenon, but the Great Depression and mass deportations marked the end of the demographically heterogeneous emigration of the 1920s. The Bracero Program sought to secure male labor power divorced from the family unit. Yet the fact that demographic patterns of migration from some communities had begun to change again before Simpson-Rodino is evident from the undocumented migrant population counted in 1980 U.S. census, which was 45% female and 21% under the age of fifteen. Some community studies undertaken in the Seventies and early Eighties were beginning to reveal substantial proportions of women and children in the migrant population, although others continued to report that migration was virtually restricted to undocumented males (Durand and Massey, op.cit.: 20–21).

---

6 My December 1992 fieldwork confirmed the tendency towards permanence in the data for 1990–91. Only seven (0.04%) of the migrants recorded as "long-stay" in the original study had returned by the end of 1992. Only one of them was a family migrant and he was undocumented, as were four of the other returnees. Two-thirds of the new migrants of 1990 were still migrating in 1992, and more than half of them were working (undocumented) in urban occupations and staying for extended periods. Fifty-six migrants recorded in 1992 had not been migrating in 1990–91. Two-thirds of them were young, undocumented, single men following in the footsteps of older siblings and seeking work in the fields, as did three young women. Of the seven new urban migrants, two were married women who left to join husbands already established in the North, and a third was a woman who migrated to join kin while still single, and had a failed relationship with a Salvadorean she met in Los Angeles.

Durand and Massey argue that these differences are explicable in terms of two key variables: the historical depth of the community's migration stream "which determines the maturity of the networks and the particular U.S. immigration policies to which it is exposed" and the "niche in the U.S. occupational structure in which the community's migrants first become established." As far as the first variable is concerned, they suggest that as migrants acquire more experience in the U.S. and expand their support and employment networks, the costs and risks of migration drop, whilst "the life of a solitary migrant worker eventually becomes difficult to sustain" (op.cit.: 20).

It is unwise to assume that whether women and children go to the North depends solely on decisions by family patriarchs. There are certainly cases where women overcome initial resistance on the part of husbands to their going, and male members of the woman's family may also play a role in the process. The latter are often directly responsible for organizing the passage of undocumented wives and Mexico-born children to join husbands already in the North. Furthermore, some female migrants are unmarried women accompanying fathers or male or female siblings. Assuming, however, for the moment, that male decisions are the primary factor in determining the movement of women and children across the border, some of the additional insights which Durand and Massey offer into the structural factors which might promote such movements are worth exploring.

The historical impact of different phases of U.S. immigration policy is an important determinant of the demographic composition of contemporary migrant populations. Communities which have been migrating longest have higher proportions of legal migrants, simply because more people entered when policies were more liberal. Much of the movement of women and children in the late Sixties and Seventies consisted of the families of former *braceros* who emigrated, often with the help of employers, once it became clear that the contract labor system was to end (Durand and Massey, op.cit.: 22).

The village of Jaripo, discussed in Chapter Four, is a spectacular example of this phenomenon, because of the special advantages its people received from political patronage within Mexico. A tendency towards diminished frequency of return to this community by families resident in the U.S. was associated, first, with the abandonment of grower-provided housing in favor of rented accommodation in the suburbs, followed by a shift, on the part of younger people, out of farm work into industry. It was then reinforced by the fact that the fourth generation of Jaripo migrants had been educated and socialized primarily in the United States. Fonseca remarks that though many families were returning less frequently than before by the mid-1980s, visiting remained normal, but that value system clashes between *norteños* and the remaining villagers were increasingly evident. My own visits to Jaripo have certainly provided evidence that flaunting *norteño* success provokes *envidia*: sports cars, for example, tend to produce mutterings on the lines of: "Only those who get involved in drugs can buy these things!" Fonseca is, however, inclined to see the main thrust of *emigrado* identity as being in the direction of "resistance and recreation of Mexican national culture" (Fonseca, 1988: 371), and it is interesting that Jaripo provided staunch support for the PRD in the December 1989 municipal elections, despite a vigorous campaign against the party by the local priest, under the banner of "anti-communism." Nevertheless, Jaripo is clearly an extreme case because of the comprehensive legalization of its migrant population.

As I noted earlier, Durand and Massey argue that agricultural labor promoted seasonal family migration because of the facilities it offered for legalization, and because farm work offered employment to all family members, making "family migration for U.S. farm labor ... a rational strategy for maximizing family income" (Durand and Massey, 1992: 24). Urban employers do not normally act collectively as a political lobby to ensure the continuity of their labor supply, nor make efforts to secure legalization for their workers. Durand and Massey assume that undocumented status discourages family migration, along with the absence of employer-subsidized housing, and they contend that these disincentives are reinforced by low entry-level wages in urban occupations, and by the existence of fewer opportunities for children to work and contribute to family income. They conclude that the migration of wives and children to cities lowers rather than maximizes total net earnings, making it harder to accumulate savings quickly. Nevertheless, the lesser initial economic rationality of family migration to cities would, they argue, be offset over time by the factors mentioned earlier, promoting a greater diversity in the demographic composition of migrant streams to urban areas as lengths of stay and number of trips increased (op.cit.: 24–5).

Durand and Massey assume that whether people migrate to urban or rural destinations is primarily a function of where pioneer migrants establish the first nodes of an evolving migrant social network, which structures the particular points of entry of other community members into the U.S. labor market. It is undeniable that the factors of the configuration and historical maturity of migrant networks do play a major role in shaping community patterns, although network-mediated migration may be "multilocal," with individuals going to different destinations where they have kin or friends at different points in their careers (Wilson, 1993: 112). The data from Guaracha and Jaripo suggest that there is also a generational effect, with younger people tending to prefer urban work, but Durand and Massey's analysis fails to take into account the occupational mobility of individuals between urban and rural work. Such mobility was characteristic of the Mexican population in California even in the early decades of the century, prompting Ricardo Romo to suggest that it was a concomitant of the equally long-established pattern of low rates of upward mobility for Mexicans through the occupational structure of the United States (Romo, 1983: 128).

Juan-Vicente Palerm has argued, however, that migrant networks tended to bifurcate between urban and rural destinations during the 1970s and 1980s. An increase in the numbers of Mexican and Central American migrants moving direct to the cities made it more difficult for rural workers to move on to urban jobs. Prior to this, there was a considerable amount of two-stage migration, with farm workers shifting in time to urban employment, requiring a constant replenishment of the farm labor force through new migration (Palerm, 1991: 34–35). This argument is primarily concerned with migrants who settled more permanently in California. Settlement in rural locations was reinforced by growing inner-city blight, rising costs and deteriorating wages, which reduced the comparative advantage of urban areas, but it was made more viable by the increasing interest of U.S. agribusiness in possessing a more sedentary workforce equipped with the specific skills needed for highly technified production of fruits and vegetables (Palerm, op.cit.: 78–80). Palerm's analysis offers a different way of looking at Durand and Massey's association between agricultural migration and family migration, but it does not resolve some apparent problems with their explanation of why urban migrants also began to take their families with them.

Even assuming that the relative "profitability" of family migration in urban and rural contexts is sufficient to explain observed patterns of behavior, some criticisms can be made of Durand and Massey's argument. The farm migrants of Jaripo chose to move to the suburbs despite the costs, and although it is true that high urban rents are a frequent source of complaint, multiple occupancy of housing units does allow economies to be made. Acute deficiencies in low-income housing provision in some parts of California no longer seem a deterrent to migration of families, and growers have been looking for public incentives to provide facilities to match the need (Eisenstadt and Thorup, 1994: 20–21). The political economy of late capitalism favors a growth in the part-time employment of women within industry, and the "postmodern" economy of Anglo California offers migrant women from the South not merely "traditional" female work in domestic service in abundance, but a plethora of jobs in retailing, catering, office cleaning and the hotel sector. The proportion of Guaracheña women migrants working in agriculture and agroindustry combined is not substantially higher than the proportion working in industry, and industrial and urban service occupations account for the majority of female employments. This casts some doubt on Durand and Massey's assumption that the growth of family migration in the urban context is explicable simply in terms of the difficulties men experience sustaining "solitary lives," along with reduced risks and costs, but even if we accept their contention that maximization of family net earnings is not a primary determinant of family migration in the urban context, it seems necessary to bring other factors into the equation.

The Social Causes and Impact of Female Migration

Even if developments in the U.S. urban labor market have made women more of an economic asset to men, neither this nor the cumulative impact of maturation of migrant networks seems capable of explaining the overall increase in family migration in recent years. It also seems unlikely that the increase can be attributed exclusively to the effects of the IRCA. Another factor worth considering is generational change, and ideological and cultural transformations which have affected women as well as men.

González de la Rocha (1989) has argued that extended male absences necessitated a certain delegation of power on the part of migrant males to women left behind to raise their families in rural communities. This gave rise to a process of female "empowerment." By being forced to solve problems of economic survival, often in the absence of regular male remissions, women unable to rely on support from resident parents and kin took on new roles. Some women became domestic outworkers and wage workers. This reduced their economic dependence on the absent husband, and brought established patterns of male authority into question, even if the wife relinquished "masculine" tasks and adopted a ritualized deference to male authority on the occasions of her husband's return. Wives' struggles to raise families in the extended absence of men were seconded by their daughters. Daughters were not only even more likely to engage in wage work and be used to having their own income from work, but also experienced their socialization in a largely fatherless setting.

González de la Rocha suggests that this situation produces two reactions in the young: women do not want to repeat their mothers' solitary lives and heavy economic burdens, and young men do not want to repeat their fathers' experience of being strangers to their children and losing authority over them. She goes on to suggest that the wave of family migration which this generation has produced is likely to lead to ironic consequences. Patriarchal authority was weakened by long male absences and the need for women left behind to be self-reliant. This produced a generation of women who escaped traditional controls over courtship and choice of a marriage partner, and tasted economy autonomy. Yet their enthusiasm for family reunification north of the border, in part premised on their expectations about obtaining paid work there and building a better material life for their families, may lead to a re-establishment of patriarchal domination.

There are symptoms of shifts in gender relations throughout rural Michoacán, such as delayed marriage and increasing use of contraceptives. These can be linked to women's increasing involvement in local salaried work and to their being left to raise families during increasingly protracted male absences. An interesting case to compare with the evidence from Guaracha and Cerrito Cotijaran is Quiringüicharo, a *mestizo* community located between the two Michoacán agroindustrial centers of Zamora and La Piedad (Mummert, 1992). Quiringüicharo has in recent decades become a comparatively prosperous community, on the basis of international migration and the development of a modernized commercial agriculture based on extension of irrigation and mechanization, in which some of the older migrants have invested. At the same time, the development of the strawberry packing plants in Zamora in the mid-1960s enabled unmarried women to enter the regional labor force and contribute significantly to family income—despite strong male opposition (Mummert, op.cit.: 2). In these respects, Quiringüicharo clearly resembles the Ciénega, but it is a community where private landholding is much more significant, and its rates of participation in Zamora's agroindustrial labor force have been higher.

Quiringüicharo's international migration remained predominantly one of lone male movement even at the start of the 1990s, although it had changed its shape considerably in other respects. From the mid-1970s onwards, the number of migrants in the village population increased, and the average age at first departure fell, producing the same pattern found in the Ciénega communities as young men follow brothers, cousins, uncles and fathers to the U.S.A. straight from school. Quiringüicharo also replicates the Ciénega communities' tendency towards occupational shift: more and more younger migrants pass through the Stockton-Merced corridor to seek urban service sector work. The main destination of the Quiringüicharo urban migrants is, however, Chicago rather than the California cities. Groups of unmarried or lone migrant males pool their resources and share rented apartments on the outskirts of the city.[7]

Mummert argues that most married migrants prefer to leave their wives behind in Mexico, both to maximize net earnings and to "shield them from the corrupting effects of U.S. society" (op.cit.: 3). She also notes that men complain about the U.S. government's intervention in the private domestic sphere and the judicial sanctions imposed upon them for "disciplining" wives and children by striking them. This suggests that factors other than simple economic rationality shape the attitudes of men. Mummert found even fewer of the twenty-five young migrants to Chicago she interviewed receptive to the idea of a Mexican wife's working in the North than they were to the idea of her accompanying her husband in the first place. Yet, as she points out later in her analysis, if net earnings maximization were central to male migrant decision-making, few Quiringüicharo migrants would work in the service sector in Chicago rather than Californian agribusiness. Work in restaurants and janitoring might offer greater continuity of employment and day-to-day stability of earnings than seasonal agricultural work, only some of which is paid by hours, but the migrants themselves generally conceded that potential earnings were higher in agriculture. They emphasized the nature of the work and associated life-style as the key factors in their personal preference.

In Quiringüicharo, "containing women" seems a major male preoccupation. Husbands often insisted that stay-at-home wives lived with their own parents in the interests of guaranteeing fidelity. Living with in-laws is a problem for both men and women, but the contradictions of a woman living in her mother-in-law's house

---

7 This pattern is also typical of Ciénega migrants in California and family migrants from both Quiringüicharo and the Ciénega. A focal point of Anglo hysteria towards immigrants is the conversion of buildings constructed as a single-family homes into multi-family dwellings, as migrants seek to reduce accommodation costs by turning every available space within housing units, including garages, into living space, but both this practice and the growth of migrant squatter camps in the suburbs are consequences of homeowner resistance to construction of low-cost housing (Davis, 1990: 208–9; Eisenstadt and Thorup, 1994: 18).

are particularly acute. She lacks authority in the domestic sphere, is not subject to a well-defined authority relationship with her father-in-law, and is unlikely to contribute financially to the household from her husband's remissions.

There is, however, a growing movement of single women from Quiringüicharo to the United States, generally to live with older siblings. Mummert relates this trend to the earlier development of female work in the strawberry agroindustry, which had also encountered initial opposition, because it meant that women escaped from the domestic space in which they were supposed to be corralled under parental vigilance. Acceptance of female work in the plants was eventually assured by its economic utility to the household, but the first generation of female workers, predominantly from poor landless families, had to fight for the right to enter the regional labor market. Women had their own agendas in such struggles and their success had significant consequences. In Quiringüicharo, the Ciénega and González de la Rocha's Jaliscan communities alike, women have increasingly been able to retain control over their earnings and use them for personal consumption rather than hand them over to their parents.

In Quiringüicharo, women's earnings are not be used to equip a home after marriage. Any furniture bought remains in the parental house and the husband's migrant earnings alone are used to equip a new residence. Mummert suggests, however, that spending on make-up and clothes "constitute an investment in [a woman's] future by allowing her to more effectively enter an increasingly competitive marriage market." This scarcely bespeaks a revolution in gender relations, but changes have occurred. Courting is now open and parental supervision of *novios* has diminished in scope. The normal age of marriage has risen from 14 or 15 to 19 or 20, for reasons which are at least partly concerned with the changing goals of young people themselves. Neolocality is made more feasible by male migrant earnings, although if the husband continues to migrate, wives are, as already noted, often returned to the supervision of their in-laws. Most importantly, Mummert suggests that important changes have taken place in definitions of gender roles within the domestic unit and in kin obligations.

In Quiringüicharo, work in the strawberries has not been restricted to single women, widows or abandoned wives. Although they remain a minority, married women do sometimes seek paid work while their husbands are absent in the North, sometimes without his knowledge. The participation of married women is increasing. This echoes González de la Rocha's data from Jalisco, although there, as in the case of Santiago Tangamandapio to the east of Guaracha (Wilson, 1990), the development of clothing production in rural areas with large female labor reserves provides the wives of migrants with salaried work in their own community. At the same time, married women have learned how to manage money remissions in the banking system and organize work on improving the house. Mummert argues that the changing economic role of women has led to an increase in their participation in family decision-making, reduced submissiveness in the face of physical abuse or adultery, and weakened the claims parents can make for filial support. The weakening of the web of obligations between parents and children is the product of a number of different dimensions of the commoditization of social life, as I have argued in the case of Guaracha (Gledhill, 1991), but international migration and female participation in salaried work is particularly important for giving young people control of autonomous monetary resources.

Since migration by single women to the North seems to replicate the earlier pattern of movement into the packing plants, female international migration from Quiringüicharo might be expected to increase further in the future. It is clear from Mummert's discussion that family migration was not entirely negligible even at the start of the Nineties. What remains most striking about this case is, however, the strongly patriarchal quality and defensive tone of the rationale men offer for not wishing their wives to join them in the North. Yet their position would seem misguided if González de la Rocha is correct to hypothesize that family reunification re-establishes patriarchal control whereas leaving women at home weakens it.

The grounds offered by some husbands in Cotijaran and Guaracha for wanting their wives to stay at home have resonances with those of Mummert's interviewees. Even legalized husbands often stress the hardships of life in the North. In the case of seasonal farm migrants, the husband's argument often centers on the inadequacy of some of the facilities which Durand and Massey suggest are facilitators of family migration—the poor standard of the accommodation offered by their *patrones* and the impossibility of maintaining a proper family life in the migrant *ranchos*. The bottom line of their argument is, however, the unruly nature of migrant society: crime, drugs and drinking, and, above all, threats to a woman's virtue posed by the continuing presence of large numbers of unaccompanied male *cabrones*.

These latter arguments can be made with a vengeance in the urban context, but the crucial point is that they are made in a patriarchal spirit. From the woman's point of view, however, the alternative of staying in the community can be equally oppressive, and González de la Rocha herself concedes that young women do not wish to repeat the experience of their mothers.[8] Where female sexuality is rigorously policed by the community and its gossip networks, stay-at-home women whose husbands are absent for extended periods of time can find themselves in a peculiarly unenviable situation, fearful to participate in any kind of social activity of a public nature, like a dance or *fiesta*, lest a malicious voice accuse them of flirting, or worse, when they encounter potential sexual partners. Even venturing out in the company of other women in a similar situation is not entirely free of risk. These considerations have to be set against the claim that women necessarily achieve a greater capacity to assert themselves because the increasingly extended

---

[8] Another issue raised by the data on permanence of single men in the United States which I have presented is whether single women will actually be able to find a desirable marriage partner among a diminishing number of regular returnees.

absences of their husbands create certain spaces for female empowerment, and undermine younger women's willingness to conform to traditional gender roles.

Crucial variables are the degree to which women can achieve real economic independence, and the extent to which patriarchal control is undermined in the home community as a consequence of the overall process of social change characteristic of the locality. In the case analyzed by González de la Rocha, there were very high rates of migration, and very extended absences by a high proportion of male migrants, with particularly good opportunities for women to earn money. Yet even here it seems that patriarchal values were deeply sedimented enough to be reactivated as social and economic circumstances changed, and men and women renegotiated the meaning of the "Mexican family" in the United States.

A Broader Crisis of Patriarchy?

That women seek to assert themselves and negotiate new arrangements with men only creates the possibility of a fundamental shift in gender relations. It could be argued that women have always negotiated, even where they have opted for a strategy of apparent submission to male domination. Browner and Lewis (1982) suggested that women gained better economic and social rewards in some contexts by opting for a stance of Marian self-sacrifice rather than self-centered assertiveness. In communities where men and women are differentiated by social status and economic situation as well as age, different strategies may be appropriate for different women. Patterns of social control may be challenged by individuals with varying degrees of success, and the best available strategy for some women may be to accept assignment to a socially recognized deviant category. This is, as I showed earlier, how some poor women achieve economic security.

As practical circumstances change, the negotiated redefinition of gender roles and kinship obligations is likely to raise broader issues which pertain to many different dimensions of personal and social existence (moral categories, sex and relations with children, honor and worth, *mexicanidad* and the *gringos*, materialist life-styles versus objectified and valorized cultural lifeways—the list is almost indefinitely extensible). Negotiation may draw on contingent elements of the continuing flux of cultural representations, including mass media messages which may be given quite diverse local readings. For the poor, the final resolution must be practical, but there is no reason to think that it must be purely utilitarian.

Negotiation will, however, remain subject to some specific structuring principles. One of the most deeply sedimented structures influencing gender relations in the Ciénega de Chapala is religion. This is still a conservatively Catholic zone, despite some historical association between extended absence in the North and abandonment of Catholicism. In a study of the indigenous community of Tlayacapan, Morelos, Ingham (1986) has shown that folk Catholic beliefs provided a symbolic framework for thinking about reproduction as fertility and sexuality, and thereby for thinking about community sociality and the relations between the sexes within the family. Folk Catholic practices were strongly reflective of patriarchy and the "double-standard" of male and female sexual conduct. Almost everything men did in the street—which was a male world after dark in Tlayacapan as it is in *mestizo* communities in Michoacán today—was symbolically focused on sex and male attitudes to sex, in a social world in which female sexuality was repeatedly denied and negated, whilst men's sexual activities outside the home were not restricted to the symbolic level.

Ingham suggests that male drinking on the street is sometimes a substitute for sex, almost invariably accompanied by homosexual joking with other men, but there can be few women anywhere in rural Latin America who have not experienced the other consequence of male sociality based on alcohol, enforced sex with a repellently drunken husband returning late at night. This is not simply an unpleasant experience in itself: it violates the symbolic association between the mother and the Virgin. Thus, whilst men were traditionally allowed both symbolic and real expression of their sexuality, women had few opportunities to express either their sexuality or their discontents, even at a symbolic level.[9]

Ingham argues that women were not entirely passive in the face of their unenviable situation. The way they traditionally expressed their frustrations about the denial of their own sexuality, the unsatisfactory experience of sex within marriage, and their ambivalence about motherhood and the burdens of child care, was by being possessed by the spirits known as *los aires*. The curing process associated with *los aires* possession was heavily imbued with eroticism. In *mestizo* Michoacán, women are more likely to complain of a disenchanted condition such as *nervios*, but much of what lurks beneath this veneer of "modernity" remains redolent of the world of *aire* illness, *susto* (fright), *mal de ojo* (evil eye) and libidinous *duendes* which Ingham describes.

The traditional situation in Tlayacapan was influenced in a significant way by the now defunct practice of extended post-partum sexual abstinence, but extended absences by migrant spouses may actually recreate some of the tensions generated by this type of practice under contemporary conditions. Male absences certainly replicate the tensions arising from women's knowledge that men enjoy both symbolic and real outlets for their sexuality, whilst their own are curtailed by surveillance and threat, as they simultaneously struggle with added burdens of domestic responsibility and worries about when, or even whether, their husbands will send them money.

---

[9] A *ranchero* family in Los Reyes held a Christmas Eve saturnalia in which men dressed as domesticated women, equipped with aprons, to be berated personally and sexually by both their wives and daughters, but I have yet to encounter anything of this kind in other types of communities in the region.

If rural women today are less willing than they were in the past to suffer traditional forms of patriarchy in complete silence, we should not exaggerate the extent of the change. The counterpart to *machismo*, defined as the cult of male virility and dominance of the public sphere, is supposedly *marianismo*, a cult of female spiritual superiority. Some writers have interpreted *marianismo* as allocating women a dominant role in the domestic sphere, and as a source of power, since women might be able to influence public life through their domestic influence on men, and I have already noted the argument that women can manipulate the Marian role. Yet the notion that women could exercise disguised power over husbands seems alien to Mexican ideas simply in the light of the way mothers indulge their male children. Many young women still express their agreement with the view that men should dominate the household in arguments amongst themselves, on the grounds that they would not want to be married to a "weak" man. Male ideologies in the Ciénega still stress the desirability of containing female sexuality within the confines of the home. Women from these communities who participate in external labor markets remain susceptible to charges of sexual looseness, despite the fact that such participation is now long-standing.

This male obsession with control of female sexuality can ultimately be traced back to the links between Spanish notions of status honor and "purity of blood" in the racial ideology of the colonial period (Lomnitz-Adler, 1992: 278). Arrom (1985) contends, however, that *marianismo* was a 19th century innovation, designed, as I noted in Chapter Three, to deal with the problem that a liberal constitution should have abolished traditional patriarchal authority and given women equal rights and opportunities under the law. The principle of women's equality was undermined by the principle that women were "different" to men. *Marianismo* thus limited the gains of middle and upper class women from modernization. Working class urban women in 19th century Mexico City were not strongly affected by the ideology, since they were forced to work outside the home and often had no home in the middle class sense, living in tenements where relations with other women were often more central than relations with men. In the *mestizo* villages of rural Michoacán, however, it became practical for men to view domesticity and motherhood as the ideal destiny of their partners, not because male incomes were secure or adequate, but because the economic contributions women made as workers and household managers could be classified as belonging to a "domestic" sphere. It has not, however, been easy for men to maintain a completely successful defence of these containers under modern conditions, and their problems have been exacerbated by the growing problems they themselves have experienced in fulfilling the role of provider.

Guaracha and Cerrito Cotijaran are certainly not the most sexually repressive communities in rural Michoacán. In Cotijaran, young couples sometimes live together, within a parental house-lot, before marriage. Both communities tolerate pre-marital sex of a more covert kind. Although this is generally on the understanding that men marry women who become pregnant, there are unmarried mothers and illegitimate children in the communities. "Going with different men on the street" is certainly stigmatized, and when a child is born, the offending woman is usually packed off into domestic service and the child brought up by its grandparents. Yet some women do enter illicit sexual relations, as the "double standard" and existence of parallel families dictate they must. Once a woman is actually married, however, tolerance is only extended to women judged to have been abandoned. They are thus doubly victimized, since bearing children to other men is the price of economic support, and the most powerful critics of women who take this way out are likely to be other women.

Women who suffer at the hands of vicious husbands do enjoy support and sympathy from other women, and friends may encourage a woman to leave a man whose behavior has become intolerable. Female mutual support is not, however, unconditional. Other women are subject to pressures from their own husbands, and fear that those husbands may stray into the beds of the unattached. It is one thing for women to sit together joking about male worthlessness and another for them to act collectively to challenge it. Individual decisions to leave a bad marriage are no easy option, as some of the data presented earlier indicate: in this context female migration may seem the best way out.

We have seen that growing female participation in the regional labor market may be followed by a growing desire on the part of women to go to the United States. It is also becoming common, as I noted earlier, for younger sisters to be taken North to look after children when migrants' wives are working. This latter practice may undermine domestic authority relations, since, in the majority of cases I recorded, the young woman sought paid work after arrival, even if this provoked a family row. Closer analysis of the varying situations of female migrants in general suggests, however, that González de la Rocha is correct to warn against assuming that international migration by women inevitably strengthens the undermining of patriarchal values.

As I showed earlier, some female migrants went independently to the North after being abandoned by their husbands, although they do not necessarily seek their partners out, and in some cases form new relationships. A few married women go whilst husbands stay at home. A particularly dramatic case is that of a teacher's wife in Cerrito Cotijaran, who left to work with her sister in a Los Angeles sweat-shop while her husband was on strike. In this and other such cases, the risks of going were moderated by the migrant social network, but what is most interesting about the case is the woman's reaction when she returned. Other women criticized her for humiliating her husband, even though he consented to her going. She refused to leave the house for several weeks.

This example highlights the fact that there is still a long way to go before patriarchal attitudes are stamped out from *both* sexes. Those women who forge independent working lives in the North tend to be victims of envy and gossip, making reincorporation into community life difficult. Accumulation of female migrants in the United States facilitates further female movement: women can often secure support from other women, even if they are notionally "taken" to the North by fathers or brothers assuming the role of "protectors." Women frequently seek to escape such tutelage by shifting residence once they arrive, though mature women find it easier to make their own journeys to visit and work with female kin resident in the North than younger ones. Yet an emphasis on women's support networks as systems facilitating autonomy and adoption of new roles would be one-sided. Within the villages of origin, women's networks are loci of social control as well as sources of mutual support. This remains true in some types of migrant community in the North, where the density of settlement of households from a single community in Mexico fosters a certain replication of home conditions. Furthermore, when a women does undergo a radical transformation of social persona in the North, she may face difficulties of reincorporation into the village community. This encourages permanent emigration and marriage in the United States, which is the dominant tendency among women from the Ciénega communities who went North to work when they were single.

Even women who live in Mexican colonies in the United States surrounded by neighbors from their home communities may still be better off in some respects. They may, for example, seek more effective protection against domestic violence, backed, as Mummert's informants lamented, by the law, although the sanctions established by U.S. law are evidently not sufficient to eliminate this pervasive social problem.[10] Though most of the examples I possess of female-initiated marriage breakdown in the North led to the woman's return home, a woman who split up from her husband should have greater prospects of sustaining herself and her children in the North, which is, after all, the destination of some women abandoned in Mexico. Nevertheless, close-knit migrant enclaves inevitably reproduce some of the practices and ideologies found in Mexican rural communities.

The urban setting appears to offer greater freedom because of the greater heterogeneity of residential districts, but not all women achieve greater freedom in this context. Working women may be able to establish new networks through friends at work, but those who do not work may be consigned to relatively isolated lives in urban settings, divorced from networks of kin and friends. Even working

---

10 A particularly tragic example is that of Cristina, a young woman from Guaracha who belonged to a family with a long migrant tradition. She first went to the United States with her undocumented husband, a man from the village, before the enactment of the IRCA, and they had a child there. The marriage went sour, and Cristina came back for a time to the village with her baby, but subsequently returned to the North. After further reconciliations and quarrels, marked by increasing physical violence on the part of the husband, Cristina's kin and friends urged her to have nothing more to do with him, since his behavior was a reflection of a serious drink and drugs problem. Yet just when it seemed that the marriage was definitively over, there was a final meeting in a motel room. Cristina's kin thought that the husband might have lured her there under some pretext concerned with their child, but whatever the truth of the matter, the encounter proved fatal. Cristina's lifeless body was found next day. Cocaine had been forced into her nose and mouth, to give the impression that she had died of an overdose.

women may find themselves more imprisoned than before within oppressive domestic relationships after the day's work is done and they are confined to the apartment to perform domestic chores or watch TV. There are some advantages for women in urban living, particularly in terms of simplification of shopping and diversions, but there are other negative factors: social discrimination, bad working conditions, and what is often a particularly exhausting "double burden," not to mention the rising tide of inner city social problems. There is no simple scale on which the people themselves can compare the life-styles offered by the village and the diverse forms of social existence available in the United States.

Nevertheless, patriarchal ideologies are not just a problem for women. Under modern economic conditions, men frequently find themselves unable to fill the stereotype of provider and decision maker for the domesticated woman. At the present time, this is as true for many in the North as it is in Mexico, as the number of men pursuing migrant jobs continues to increase in a period not simply of temporary recession, but of major structural change in the labor market. If women are more likely to leave situations of domestic violence and alcoholism than they were in the past, men may also be more likely to behave that way if they cannot live up to their ideologically ascribed role. Much of the literature on *machismo* fails to make any clear distinction between relatively enduring ideologies and practices of male domination, on the one hand, and the heightened expressions of male violence towards women produced by changing socio-economic conditions, on the other. The latter leads us to view *machismo* exclusively in the terms suggested by Oscar Lewis (1959), as a response to economic insecurity, or as a reaction to a greater female participation in the non-domestic economy which challenges a male monopoly on the provider role. This argument captures a partial truth, but it is ultimately undesirable to reduce *machismo* to its more brutal manifestations. Men behaving badly by leaving their wives in villages with inadequate or irregular economic support, while they satisfy their manly needs in the North, may make life no more oppressive for women than those who apparently behave well and accept the desirability of family reunification "on the other side." The sedimented cultural premises of gender subordination run deep, and impact on both sexes in subtle ways, as human actors struggle to negotiate the compromises that make the continuation of individual unions possible, and are caught up in the strategizing of others as whole communities strive to reforge identity, coherence, *and* systems of social control.

7

American Dreams and Nightmares: The Fractured Social Worlds of an Empire in Decadence

From the vantage point of rural Michoacán, American power seems overwhelming. As I observed in Chapter Four, the Gulf War provoked considerable local comment about *gringo* projects of global economic domination. It is not difficult to appreciate why America should be seen as the world's economic colossus in an area with a high rate of international migration, but this long-standing tendency to view the United States as the economic metropolis *par excellence* does not account for the virulence of the characterization of American motives in the Gulf, as those of economic imperialism and controlling the resources of other nations. That seemed to be a response to the NAFTA negotiations and the apparent abandonment of economic nationalism by the Mexican government. Small businessmen, managers, and peasant farmers alike were anxiously posing the question: "How can we compete?" Pessimism about surviving the opening up of domestic markets to stronger competitors was reinforced by a suspicion that U.S. interest in the NAFTA was not confined to increasing exports and using cheap Mexican labor. Few people seemed to believe President Salinas's pledges that Mexican oil was sacrosanct.

In symbolic terms, oil is central to popular nationalism. The country's possession of a "wealth of natural resources" keeps the possibility of autonomy and development alive, and the fact that oil was wrested back from the control of the *gringos* by Cárdenas is generally seen as one of the major achievements of the Mexican revolution. That a broad range of provincial social actors remained skeptical of their government's pledges on this question is significant. It implied a lack of faith in the ability of the neoliberal elite to represent the nation, premised on a perception that they were allied with foreign economic interests. The government's secrecy on the details of the NAFTA negotiations naturally tended to encourage suspicion, which was aggravated by rumors and by independent press comment during the negotiations that foreign control of Mexico's oil industry was being increased by stealth, through the reclassification of petrochemical products.

The logic of suspicion itself was not, however, based primarily on material facts, but on a deeper interpretation of the meaning of the neoliberal project.

The actual global economic position of the United States does not correspond precisely to the Mexican view, although the NAFTA itself can be seen as an important part of a new project to rebuild U.S. economic power. The collapse of the Soviet empire has ultimately only served to highlight the contradiction between maintaining economic hegemony on the global stage and maintaining global political hegemony by military means, coupled with the logistical support of client "counter-insurgency" regimes (Gledhill, 1994: 153–5). The growing demands for U.S. intervention in an increasingly conflictive and crisis-ridden world are all the more burdensome because of the recessionary impact of the end of the Cold War on key sectors of the U.S. economy, particularly, though not exclusively, in California. America is thus itself involved in a "difficult transition." In this chapter, I focus on the way Mexicans in the United States are bound up in its national and imperial contradictions.

Crisis in California

In his survey of the impact of Eighties crisis in Mexico on patterns of international migration, Wayne Cornelius noted that most of the new jobs likely to become available to migrants in the future would be "relatively poorly paid, unskilled, of low prestige, in restaurants, hotels and other areas of the urban service sector" (Cornelius, 1990: 109). At the same time, however, he echoed the conclusions of an earlier Urban Institute study (Muller and Espenshade, 1985) in offering a relatively up-beat picture of California's economic future, stressing its high rates of employment growth in comparison with the national average and the continuing strength of demand for migrant labor on the part of the agricultural and manufacturing sectors. Cornelius fully acknowledged the evidence that "Hispanic"[1] immigrants in California usually earned less than "native" North Americans employed in similar work, that real wages for undocumented non-agricultural immigrant workers fell during the 1980s, and that factors such as union membership, gender and "ethnicity" were more important than migratory status *per se* for determining patterns of disadvantage at work (op.cit.: 124–25). Yet the emphasis throughout his discussion is on the opportunities California offers relative to Mexico, and its advantages in comparison with other possible migrant destinations in the United States. The latter are said to include "less racial discrimination in comparison with

---

[1] The term "Hispanic" is, as I stress later in this chapter, a particularly problematic political construction. Since short-hands are useful for simplifying exposition, I will use the term "Latino" here when talking about people who can trace their origins to a Latin American country, although this label might also be said to carry some ideological load.

other potential destinations, such as Texas," as well as "abundant jobs in agriculture and industry" which are "quick to obtain and relatively well paid in comparison with other states in the Southwest" (op.cit.: 110). Cornelius concluded that, short of an "economic catastrophe" befalling the United States, the old pattern of a predominantly seasonal lone male migration was bound to continue its transformation towards a stable, urban and more socially heterogeneous "immigrant community" (op.cit.: 128).

This might seem a strange diagnosis in the aftermath of the Los Angeles Riot of 1992. On closer inspection the riot turns out to have been more than an uprising of urban Blacks against the racism of the Los Angeles Police Department (LAPD). To judge from the published arrest figures, an even larger number of Latinos took to the streets, to vent their rage on shopkeepers as well as agents of "law and order," in a moment of madness which was fuelled, in the opinion of a school teacher interviewed by Mike Davis, "by economic desperation and class resentment" (Davis, 1993b: 37–39). Among the epicenters of the riot was the Mexican enclave of Lennox, a square mile of overcrowded bungalows east of the International Airport, which has the distinction of having the highest residential density of tourism and hotel workers in the state. Long deaf to residents' complaints about the depredations of crack dealers from Inglewood Boulevard, the sheriff's deputies finally exhausted the community's patience by shooting a fifteen year old boy in the back (Davis, op.cit.: 47). Caught in a web of exploitation which stretches from the *coyote* to the Korean grocer, and may even filter back into the life of the community of origin, many of today's Latino migrants have preoccupations beyond discrimination in job opportunities and wage rates.

The teacher quoted by Davis was insistent that the attacks on Korean businesses by Central American immigrants were not driven by "race" antagonism, since attacks were targeted on grocery and liquor stores rather than other businesses. The businesses hit were seen as adding to the burdens of the poor by overcharging for basic necessities. His interpretation suggests that these Latino immigrants were reasserting a principle of "moral economy" appropriate for the postmodern world. Even so, antagonisms of this kind can harden into antagonisms expressed in terms of race, given that this kind of explanation for structural social inequalities is a logical consequence of the egalitarian individualistic creed of the hegemonic Anglo order (DaMatta, 1991: 130). The teacher described the other target of the crowd's violence, the LAPD, as a "sadistic occupying army." This phrase captures the way in which public power enters into the construction of Californian class structure. Perceived cultural differences ("ethnicity") are translated into essentialized differences of "race," in which skin-color betokens an ascribed group character and innate behavioral propensities. It suggests that the way the agencies of public power behave responds to a perceived crisis of power within Californian society.

Such a crisis is predictable on the basis of the analysis of the impact of immigration into the metropolis from the periphery as a transnational process by Michael Kearney which I discussed in Chapter Four. In 1994, the Rodney King incident was repeated with a Latino victim, when a bystander videoed a policeman dispensing four blows to the head of Felipe Soltero, aged 17, with a metal truncheon. In this case, however, the officer was black. Although it is important to pay particular attention to the sub-culture of law enforcement agencies, as I will show later, such incidents are reflections of more generalized community antagonisms. White vigilante attacks on Latinos in California are attracting increasing public concern, and it seems likely that attacks perpetrated on undocumented immigrants are seriously underreported because of the victims' reluctance to submit themselves to the documentation processes involved in filing charges and fear of law enforcement agencies (Eisenstadt and Thorup, 1994: 51). Yet there is also a disturbing pattern of increasing low-intensity violence between Blacks and Latinos and between Latinos and Asian immigrants. Anti-immigrant feeling is, however, more manifest as a political force in socially heterogeneous suburban neighborhoods than in the poorer inner-city neighborhoods (Eisenstadt and Thorup, op.cit.: 42). The suburbs provided the bedrock of support for Proposition 187, approved in November 1994 in the context of Republican governor Pete Wilson's stridently anti-immigrant reelection campaign. This state legislation withdraws access to public education and non-emergency health care from undocumented migrant families—and thereby seeks to turn teachers, doctors, nurses and social workers into appendages of the INS—but its likely ramifications go beyond its formal provisions. Should Proposition 187 survive the legal test of constitutionality, it will reinforce patterns of surveillance and discrimination which are prejudicial to all persons of Mexican origin in the United States, irrespective of their legal status.

In fairness to middle class Californians, I should concede that they have some genuine grounds for both concern and complaint. The IRCA was a federal policy which has had a disproportionate impact on particular states. The fiscal burdens on state and local government of providing social services to the legalized migrants are not insignificant. Californians argue that the costs of immigration have, in fact, proved greater than the architects of the national policy anticipated, and certainly had cause for complaint in the fact that part of the $4 billion promised by Congress to "cushion the blow" of the legalizations as part of the IRCA package had still not been disbursed seven years after the passage of the Act (Eisenstadt and Thorup, op.cit.: 72). It is also necessary to be realistic about suburbanite opposition to the construction of low-cost housing projects for immigrants in their neighborhoods: individual homeowners cannot escape the consequences of the way the real estate market works, and do face the possibility of finding themselves with negative equity. On the other hand, as we will see, the past political behavior of white Californians has made a major contribution to the shape of the evolving social crisis, and their present behavior may deepen it, as Eisenstadt and Thorup have pointed out. Depriving children of public education does not enhance their value as "human capital" or the likelihood of their remaining docile members of the "working poor." Reducing access to preventative medicine makes little sense in fiscal terms if it leads to increased costs for emergency treatment later on. Since the evidence suggests that usage of social services other than education by undocumented migrants is in fact minimal, the anti-immigrant position might more rationally direct itself towards repatriation of legalized migrants and their families, whose needs for services will continue to increase, although it could readily be retorted that this is not practical, sensible, civilized, or even economically rational, because migration in fact brings net benefits to Californian economy.

Understanding the point of view of Anglo Californians is necessary to understand their role in the politics of immigration, and I have no wish to denigrate the efforts of academics and concerned citizens who are trying to formulate immediate and practical proposals for abating tensions and ameliorating the lot of immigrants. Finding proposals which are viable may, in the short-term, entail circumventing broader political debates (Eisenstadt and Thorup, op.cit.: 21). It is, however, necessary to take the bigger picture into account in order to assess longer term prospects. It includes the structures of class inequality which some of the actors will wish to defend, and the inequalities of political voice which will continue to shape public policy. These are the enduring bases of discrimination and inequality.

Anti-immigrant hysteria is nothing new in Californian history, but present tensions should not be seen as simply another chapter in a cycle. The crisis currently afflicting Californian society may not dissipate with economic revival, nor be readily resolved by political efforts to convince people that they must accept the change in the demographic composition of their state, and respond to it in a rational way in terms of "cost-benefit" analysis. What Cornelius describes as the growing "cultural objections" of "native" Californians towards the presence of Mexican and other "Hispanic" workers are not explicable simply in terms of the immigrant workers' changing role in the Californian economy and greater "visibility" (Cornelius, op.cit.: 129). Nor are they explicable simply as a consequence of the way class structure has been spatialized and ethnicized in the post-industrial United States, although this is an important issue. They are rooted in the way the United States is structured as a nation which, as DaMatta argues, can only be brought together as a "comprehensive and complementary society" in the sphere of politics, as a territory in which diverse social segments are subject to the authority of a single state, united by the fetishized symbols of the President and the Flag (DaMatta, op.cit.: 121). Both the absolute and relative numbers of immigrants from Mexico are important, because they exacerbate the problems of the "indigestibility" of persons who are systematically "othered" to which Kearney refers. Exploring these issues in more depth will take us a long way beyond the economic issues on which Cornelius mainly focuses, but even his economics offer a rather partial vision of reality, and perhaps not simply with the benefit of hindsight.

It would be unfair to criticize anyone writing in the 1980s for failing to grasp the scale of the problem the end of the Cold War would pose for California. One fifth of the industrial workforce lost their jobs as a direct consequence of the "Peace Dividend," nearly 200,000 workers, 40% of them unionized (Davis, op.cit.: 46). Although Blacks and Latinos constituted less than 20% of the aerospace industry workforce, more than 50% of the lay-offs have been of persons in these groups (ibid.). More than a quarter of national job losses in 1990–93 fell on California. It was not, however, simply high-tech jobs which went, but jobs in non-durable, non-military manufacturing in sectors in which Latino workers predominated. Movement of production to *maquiladoras* south of the border did not wait for the ratification of the NAFTA to put the final seal on the transformations initiated by Mexico's entry into the GATT. Male unemployment in the predominantly Latino manufacturing districts where Guaracheño migrants were concentrated, such as El Monte, was running between 15% and 25% by the end of 1992 (ibid.). The NAFTA is not, however, the root of the mounting problems facing Blacks and Latinos in California.

Cornelius's up-beat scenario failed to consider the broader impact of neoconservative policies on an ethnically segmented Californian labor force. This was already visible before the end of the 1980s, as de-unionization and public sector budget cuts proceeded, as was the structural character of a trend towards the spatial reorganization of production, based on the transfer of higher-income occupations to the suburbs and "edge-cities" around the metropolitan urban cores (Davis, 1993a). This trend, not limited to California, underlies the tendency towards restriction of new jobs for Mexican immigrants to the service sector. Nor, as we will see, is the tendency towards "white flight" to the periphery and creation of poverty in the core restricted to the non-agricultural conurbations: it is also characteristic of farming communities.

The restructuring of production and labor markets cannot be understood as a "natural" development towards a post-industrial economy which simply reflects the historical maturity of the system. It reflects both long-term contradictions of the capital accumulation process on a global scale and the specific political forces which shaped public policy in the United States in the Reagan-Bush years. In order to highlight the place of Latinos in this unfolding process of structural change, I review some of the issues which a more structural account of the changes California has experienced should address. I begin with a closer examination of the data on labor markets which Cornelius himself cites, in order to emphasize the point that much of the transformation responsible for the darker horizons of the last few years was already underway by the mid-1980s.

Labor Market Development and Ethnic Segmentation

The analysis of the California labor market at the start of the Eighties provided by Muller and Espenshade (1985) draws our attention to labor market segmentation by ethnicity during the period when employment was growing rapidly. These writers also provide information on the underlying composition of employment growth at this time. They estimate that 440,000 of the immigrants who came to the United States during the 1970s were employed in Los Angeles County. Some

210,000 of them were Mexicans, and 74,000 non-Mexican Latinos. Although employment growth in manufacturing in Southern California was more than three times the national average rate, the number of machine operator jobs in Los Angeles County actually declined slightly, and blue-collar employment growth was slight. Two-thirds of the job growth was in white-collar jobs, and jobs demanding greater skill expanded at the expense of unskilled and semi-skilled jobs (Muller and Espenshade, 1985: 58). From the point-of-view of Latino migrants seeking urban employment, the only bright spot in manufacturing was the above average rate of growth of jobs in low-wage, non-durable manufacturing in Los Angeles County, the kinds of jobs which are now being lost to the *maquiladoras*.

The service sector accounted for more than 31% of overall employment growth in Los Angeles County in the Seventies. Since the number of Mexican immigrants moving into unskilled blue-collar jobs exceeded the number of new jobs of this kind being created by a substantial margin, Muller and Espenshade concluded that "the presence of migrants willing to accept wages unacceptable to natives" was sustaining and fostering low-wage service and manufacturing sectors (ibid.). They argued that there was little direct competition for jobs between "native" and immigrant labor, except in the case of low-skill Blacks, because most Blacks had superior education to immigrants and, like Anglos, were achieving upward mobility (op.cit.: 101–2). The Urban Institute study did not, however, attempt to distinguish the specific impacts of legal and undocumented migration. Heer argues that the pattern of out-migration from California to other states in the period 1975–1980 indicates that undocumented immigration from Mexico did lead to job displacement for non-Hispanic Whites, as Mexican foremen hired more undocumented *paisanos* and any remaining non-Mexican workers felt themselves "culturally out of place" (Heer, 1990: 67–69). Drawing on the 1980 census, he also associates undocumented migration with job displacement because of the lower mean family income of undocumented workers relative to other workers of Mexican origin, a reflection of the larger numbers of undocumented workers in lower paid jobs (Heer, op.cit.:155, Table 8.9). What he fails to ask, however, is whether the jobs the immigrants took would otherwise have existed at wages acceptable to "natives."

Undocumented Mexican working mothers were concentrated most heavily in the apparel industry, as sewing machine operators, and in other machine operator and assembly jobs outside the electrical goods industry (Heer, 1990: 147, Table 8.3; 150, Table 8.5). The proportion of legal immigrant women working as sewing machine operators was not far behind that of undocumented women, but 7.1% of the latter were in service in private households, an occupation few legal immigrant women pursued (Heer, op.cit.: 147). Over half the U.S.-born women, in contrast, worked in administrative and clerical occupations: only one per cent were sewing machine operators. The most significant type of employment for undocumented fathers was as machine operators and assemblers (38.3%), followed by the "handlers, equipment cleaners, helpers and laborers" category (16.9%) and "service occupations" (13.4%). Legal and U.S.-born migrants were less prevalent in the

TABLE 7.1 Percentage Distribution by Industry for All Employed Men in Los Angeles County, Compared with All Fathers of Mexican Origin by Legal Status, 1980

		Legal Status		
Sector	*All men*	*Undocumented Fathers*	*Legal Fathers*	*U.S.-born Fathers*
Agriculture, forestry and fisheries	1.5	4.6	1.1	0.5
Mining, construction	7.4	12.5	7.9	10.0
Food industries	1.5	4.4	4.8	1.4
Apparel and finished textiles	1.2	5.0	5.0	0.8
Other non-durable manufacturing	5.4	11.1	7.5	11.6
Furniture and fixtures	1.3	4.6	4.2	1.7
Primary and fabricated metals	3.6	5.7	9.0	8.5
Machinery except electrical	3.4	2.8	5.5	4.3
Electrical machinery and supplies	2.7	2.9	3.4	4.2
Aircraft, space vehicles and parts	5.6	3.6	3.6	1.4
Other transport equipment	1.5	3.6	2.3	0.8
Other durable manufacturing	3.6	12.3	12.2	6.8
Transport, communications, public utilities	8.6	2.1	4.5	9.8
Wholesale trade	5.7	3.0	2.6	0.0
Eating and drinking places	3.9	8.9	3.6	2.4
Other retail trade	10.8	5.1	10.3	8.3
Finance, insurance, real estate, professional services	17.4	0.7	5.0	10.7
Business and repair services	6.7	5.6	4.9	7.3
Personal services: entertainment and recreation	4.7	1.7	1.2	1.6
Public administration	3.6	0.0	1.5	7.9
Total	100	100	100	100

Source: Heer, 1990: 151, Table 8.6. Data derived from U.S. Bureau of the Census, *1980 Census of Population*, PC80-1-D6, Pp. 1423–5.
Reprinted by permission of Cambridge University Press.

latter two categories, although the first accounted for the largest share of employment in all groups (Heer, op.cit.: 148, Table 8.4). Undocumented fathers did, however, participate in a wide range of manufacturing industries, as Table 7.1, reproduced from Heer's study, shows, although they had minimal presence in the financial, real estate and professional services sectors relative to legal and U.S.-born male family heads, and, unsurprisingly, zero participation in public administration. Nevertheless, the overall picture from the table indicates that the differences in occupational attainment between undocumented, legal and U.S.-born men should not be exaggerated, and that it remains fruitful to look at aggregate patterns of Latino disadvantage and at the impact of ethnicity, along with the other factors Cornelius emphasizes, unionization and gender, on household income differentials.

The value of capital investment per production worker in Los Angeles County industries declined in 1970–80 compared with the nation. This indicates that firms were substituting labor for capital in the production process, although the associated fall in value-added per hour of labor relative to the national average (6%) was offset by the fact that average wage increases were 16% less than the national average (Muller and Espenshade, op.cit.: 113). At the same time, the gap between rich and poor widened substantially, turning Los Angeles County from a region with a lower percentage of its popular in poverty than the national average into a region with above average poverty. During a period in which the proportion of people living in poverty was declining nationally, the proportion in Los Angeles County actually increased, from 10.9 to 13.4% (Heer, op.cit.: 71).

No doubt undocumented migrants figured prominently in this growth of poverty, but the changing structure of the Los Angeles County economy as described by the Urban Institute study did not enhance the earning capacity of many legal immigrant households either. Table 7.2 summarizes data Muller and Espenshade derived from the 1980 census on occupations and earnings for different "ethnic groups" in Los Angeles County. The occupational and income disadvantages suffered by Mexican migrants are apparent enough from the figures, not merely in comparison with Asians and Whites, but also, apparently, in comparison with Blacks, because of the larger proportion of Blacks working in the better remunerated occupational categories. The picture presented for Blacks is, however, deceptive as a guide to the long-term, because public sector jobs were important in improving their aggregate position. Such jobs were soon to be lost in large numbers. Although the earnings of Mexican migrants showed some improvement with greater length of stay, even long-time residents showed no signs of catching up with white Californians.

These findings are consistent with those of a longitudinal study of Mexicans who entered the United States legally during the 1970s. Drawing on the theory of labor market segmentation, Portes and Bach (1985) demonstrated that 75% of all immigrants entered a "secondary" labor market, distinguished from the "primary" labor market on the basis of differences in pay, place of residence, English-language competence required, and perception of opportunities for advancement. Those migrants who entered the primary labor market immediately did not do so for the

TABLE 7.2 Occupations and Incomes of Different Ethnic Groups in Los Angeles County, 1980

	Mexican Migrants[a]	*Mexican Americans*	*All Hispanic*	*Blacks*	*Asians*	*Whites*
Occupations (%)						
Professional, Technical, Managerial	3.1	13.2	10.9	21.4	34.3	35.2
White Collar	9.0	31.0	20.7	33.0	30.6	33.0
Skilled Worker	14.9	13.4	15.3	9.3	9.2	11.8
Other	73.0	42.4	53.1	36.3	25.9	19.8
Total	100	100	100	100	100	100
Income[b] ($)						
Mean Household Income	$15,250	$17,840	$17,238	$15,965	$24,018	$25,456
Persons per Household	4.31	3.78	3.73	2.77	3.10	2.28
Household per capita Income	$3,538	$4,720	$4,621	$5,764	$7,748	$11,165

Source: Muller and Espenshade, 1985: 46, Table 3
Reprinted by permission of The Urban Institute.
[a] Mexican Migrants are 1970–80 immigrants
[b] Income figures are for 1979

reasons predicted by human capital theory—the individual skills they had acquired—but largely because of the social networks they had established prior to legal entry. In consequence, entry into the U.S. labor market correlated with a substantial amount of downward occupational mobility for many immigrants who had been skilled workers or professionals in Mexico. The most important finding of the Portes and Bach study was, however, that once Mexican migrants were in the United States, labor market returns did not differ significantly for those Mexicans who worked in the primary labor market, since they tended to be confined to "secondary-like" occupations within primary sector firms. Thus Mexican immigrants enjoyed a "uniformly subordinate" position in the U.S. labor market, any significant social differences which emerged in the population having more to do with residential and social variables than conditions of employment (Portes and Bach, op.cit.: 259).

This pattern was found to contrast with another population of Latino immigrants which Portes and Bach analyzed as a comparative case: Cuban immigrants in the

1970s fared better overall than Mexicans, they concluded, because many were incorporated into an ethnic enclave economy dominated by immigrant business networks, which provided a basis for entrepreneurship and self-employment as well as for wage labor. The Cuban pattern of immigration created greater class differentiation. For Cubans in the primary sector, working for, and alongside, Anglos, knowledge of English and prior formal education significantly aided obtaining a higher income after six years, but secondary sector workers' positions were determined largely by the "inertial effect of economic resources transferred from Cuba and, over time, acquired in the United States." Cuban secondary sector workers competed with other ethnic minorities in firms which provided few rewards for individual skills and tended to penalize past educational attainment (op.cit.: 239). Those who worked in the enclave were, however, in a better position to translate formal training into more desirable jobs. In the case of Mexicans, there was no substantial enclave business sector, and their incorporation into the "open" economy was a more uniform process of absorption into a menial "underclass."

The term "underclass" captures the way occupational possibilities are restricted on an enduring basis for persons assigned a particular ethnicity. It is not simply that Mexican immigrants are willing to do low paid jobs of a kind that more affluent members of society might define as "menial," but that they tend to be denied better paid jobs and career advancement. The way Mexicans are incorporated into the labor market has influenced the historical development of the California economy, underpinning forms of capitalist production which might not otherwise have flourished. As Heer points out, undocumented migrants are defined as an "underclass" in legal terms (Heer, op.cit.: 106). Nevertheless, the term has acquired particular connotations in debates on urban poverty in the United States which make its application to Mexican migrants undesirable. It will be useful to explore what is wrong with the underclass concept in more general terms, because some of its ideological premises filter into both academic and non-academic discourses about the "problem" which Mexican migration supposedly poses for the larger society.

Constructing "the Underclass"

In both the United States and Britain, the dominant discourse on *the* "underclass" is framed in terms of unemployment, welfare dependence, lack of "normal" family organization, homelessness, and various indices of "pathological" social behavior such as drug abuse and alcoholism. As Joan Vincent points out, the "underclass" concept is a model of the "non-working class," constructed in opposition to a model of the working classes which is itself heavily ideologically loaded. The working class family is nuclear and possesses a home, and working class people respect the law, are thrifty and value independence (Vincent, 1993: 220). Vincent notes that this construction of a class "residuum" has historical parallels in earlier phases of capitalist restructuring: the "undeserving poor" of earlier eras, such as the Irish, were also ascribed innate "racial" characteristics and associated with "dysfunctional" single-parent families.

Some recent contributions to the debate on "the underclass," such as Auletta (1982), replicate the intellectual vices of Oscar Lewis's account of the "Culture of Poverty" and Daniel P. Moynihan's *The Negro Family* : false statistical comparisons, socio-centric interpretations of lower class behavior, refusal to cede legitimacy to any aspect of popular culture, and inference that any behavior which differs from the norms and values of society's dominant groups is necessarily "pathological" (Leacock, 1971; Leeds, 1971). At first sight, the major contribution to the debate of William Julius Wilson (1987) appeared to move the discussion on. Focusing on the contemporary problem of the poverty of the black population of America's inner cities, Wilson located its specific cause in deindustrialization. While middle class Blacks could move out of the ghettos and into the better-paid service jobs being created in the Seventies and early Eighties, working class Blacks found their low skilled production jobs disappearing, without being replaced by anything else.

Nevertheless, Wilson also revived some aspects of Lewis's culture of poverty argument (Maxwell, 1993). He argued that where a large number of people are concentrated together in the same social situation, joblessness and participation in the underground economy took on social meanings in themselves, and become an alternative way of life and the basis for a "ghetto subculture." A "vicious cycle of maladaptive behavior" was perpetuated through socialization, but not only in the family, as Lewis argued, but in the schools and the wider community (Wilson, op.cit.: 58). This effect was reinforced by the departure of middle class, upwardly mobile Blacks from the inner-city areas. The young people left in the inner-city were deprived of the "role models" provided by Black people who make it in the mainstream society in mainstream ways.

Wilson's argument is that public policy changes can eliminate the problem of the "underclass," but he sees the key issues as not simply ones of economic policy, but of social engineering to reintegrate inner city Blacks into the social mainstream. There is no questioning of the "normality" of the values of the independent, self-realizing individual and the privatized consumer family, and the approach ignores the existence of heterogeneity of behavior, social patterns and values within the population defined as the "underclass," in favor of a general emphasis on "pathologies." Nor does Wilson's framework allow us to reflect on the role of dominant societal values in producing some of the "pathological" forms of behavior. It might be argued that today, as in the era of the zoot-suiters, gang sub-culture offers a positive form of identity to youth, but it could also be argued that the apparent "anomie" which leads to "excesses" of violence is the mirror of the experienced moral order of late capitalism, a well-policed order which denies marginalized youth"normal" forms of social recognition yet encourages them to seek alternative ways of participating in its materialist values. The "underclass" inhabits a world in which everyone is bombarded by the same consumer culture and media messages, but not everyone has the chance of regular and well-paid employment. Drugs are big business, the profitability of which is premised on criminalization, and there are several respects in which it might be argued that the impact of drugs on the lives of the marginalized is quite "productive" in a Foucauldian sense, from the point of view of facilitating their exclusion and domination.

The bottom line of Wilson's analysis is that groups and persons should be objects of programs of social control, to ensure that they have access to the right messages and symbols: if the upwardly mobile role models had not moved out, community values would be different. There is little space here for recognizing that poor people adapt to poverty in different ways, and can pursue their own strategies for reconstituting themselves as persons and communities and for making their existence meaningful, some of which might be worthy of official support.

Vincent argues that the underclass in the United States is (wrongly) seen as "a pathological feature within a progressive capitalist economy rather than as a routine feature of capitalist crisis" (op.cit.: 228). As I have already stressed, the existence of persistent poverty among an identifiable group in an egalitarian-individualistic society creates an ideological dilemma, which can best be resolved by attributing responsibility for their situation to the poor themselves, either as a result of inherent incapacity, as in the racist formulations, or as a result of transmitted social incapacities induced by circumstances, as in Wilson's formulation. The latter line of argument does not, however, seem to offer an appropriate explanation of the persistent limits of the social mobility enjoyed by Mexican immigrants.

David Hayes-Bautista (1993) has argued that the "underclass" model should not be applied to Mexican migrants in Southern California, because first and second generation migrants do not display the behaviors and characteristics associated with the "residuum" category: they have strong families, a strong "work ethic," and lower rates of welfare dependence. Despite poor access to health care, their health profile is also impressive, in part because Latina women smoke, drink and take drugs less than Anglo and Black women (op.cit.: 138). Hayes-Bautista argues that these strengths reflect the legacy of Latino-Catholic culture and the fact that Latinos have resisted Anglo pressures towards full monocultural assimilation, preferring "biculturalism," a pride in both Latino and American identity (op.cit.: 143). His most significant contention in the light of Wilson's emphasis on the need to bring the poor into the "mainstream" is, however, that it will, in fact, be disastrous if the advocates of full "assimilation" on mono-cultural terms have their way, since the evidence on highly assimilated third-generation Latinos is that this group does display a greater incidence of "underclass" characteristics. Hayes-Bautista is also very clear about the threats posed to Latino futures by the past absence of social mobility commensurate with the Latino "work ethic," along with the new barriers to mobility created by loss of unionized jobs and an immigration policy that not only impedes the mobility of the undocumented, but may also be costing legal immigrants and U.S.-born Latinos job opportunities (op.cit.: 145).

Mexican immigrants have been brought into the underclass debate by virtue of the fact that "undocumented" work can be depicted as "pathological," and because their presence supposedly contributes to the "welfare burden." The perceived injustice of their economic situation and victimization through rhetoric has, however, prompted many Mexicans themselves to accept the more extreme neoconservative depictions of the *Black* "underclass" as a racially constituted, welfare-dependent and work-shy population, exploiting the privilege of citizenship to rip off the American taxpayer and the hard-working but underpaid Mexican, whilst profiting from drug-dealing and the other opportunities offered by the underground economy.

Popular discourses may therefore internalize the classifications generated by hegemonic political groups and the public institutional order through which their power of classification is implemented as a structuring force on society. They reflect a different "point of view" from that of the hegemonic order, and are, indeed, simultaneously accusing it of prejudice and failure to recognize true deservingness. The fact that all the actors are engaged in a common process of construction and misconstruction in which certain categorizations and values are hegemonic does, however, have an impact on real social practices, which academic deconstruction of the terms of the discourse scarcely begins to address. To appreciate the magnitude of contemporary problems, it will be useful to examine the changes which have taken place in California since the early 1980s in more detail.

The State, the Taxpayer and Immiseration

Muller and Espenshade concluded their study by arguing that the net contribution of immigration to Los Angeles County at the start of the decade was positive, despite the negative picture which was already being presented by nativist voices at that time, particularly on the costs of undocumented migration to the social welfare system. They estimated the benefits received from state and local government by Mexican immigrants enumerated in the 1980 census at an average of $4,842 as against $2,597 paid in tax, a fiscal deficit approaching 2:1 (Muller and Espenshade, op.cit.: 143). This fiscal deficit was produced by the combination of low migrant earnings, which meant low income and sales tax payments, and their large families, which meant more children in school. The Mexican immigrant population enumerated in the census was, however, biased towards families. Of the almost 500,000 undocumented persons in California whom Muller and Espenshade estimate were not counted in the census, a high proportion were single and working. Their per capita service demand would thus be lower, and their tax contribution higher, reducing the size of the fiscal deficit calculated without including them. The increase in family migration during the 1980s would have diminished this mitigating factor, but Davis maintains that legal and undocumented migrants combined now contribute more in taxes than they consume in local services, the Federal government creaming off the net surplus in payroll taxes (Davis, 1993a: 13). Furthermore, the tax burden created by the deficit identified by Muller and Espenshade did not fall primarily on Los Angeles County, but on the state treasury. There was also wide variation between the county's seventy cities in the level of services provided and local revenues collected: El Monte, 62% Hispanic, spent $193 per capita in 1980 and collected $130 per capita in local taxes, while Newport Beach spent $416 and collected $345 (Muller and Espenshade, op.cit.: 135). Official Los Angeles County studies had already estimated that the per capita outlays to undocumeed migrants for welfare services paid for with local (rather than state or federal) revenue were minimal, and that their total cost as consumers of services, at $48 per capita, was less than the County average overall. Muller and Espenshade argued that they had little access to the Aid to Families with Dependent Children (AFDC) program and food stamps, although Heer argues that undocumented parents did apply for AFDC benefits for their American-born children in increasing numbers between 1979 and 1983 (Heer, op.cit.: 161–62).

Public school costs emerged as the crucial local government cost of Mexican immigrant families, $404 as distinct from $197 for all households. Bilingual education represented an extra $200 per pupil cost per year, but this additional cost was offset by the Federal aid provided at the start of the Eighties, and by the fact that elementary school costs per pupil were lower than High School operating costs, since there was a higher than average proportion of Mexican children in elementary school and Mexicans had a higher than average high school drop-out rate. The number of students per household was therefore the basic determinant of higher per household locally funded costs for Mexican immigrant families in education, not costs per pupil. The main local government revenue source (42% of all revenue) was property tax, followed by sales taxes. Preponderance of occupancy of rented housing and low incomes produced a lower than average tax contribution from Mexican immigrant households (Muller and Espenshade, op.cit.: 138–40). From the Los Angeles County point of view, however, these effects were compensated by the transfer of $261 million in revenue from other parts of California. Although local residents also had to pay higher taxes, the greater part of the burden fell on other parts of the state, and the fiscal stimulus paid for the employment of the extra teachers and health professionals needed to supply services to immigrant families. Immigration therefore boosted white-collar employment for non-Hispanics.

Muller and Espenshade argued that the contribution of Mexican immigrants as workers reinforced the view that immigration was beneficial to the local society. They estimated that more than a quarter of the 210,000 jobs in low wage manufacturing and services occupied by Mexican immigrants in 1980 would have disappeared abroad, or never existed, in the absence of international migration. Immigration had reduced the prices of some goods and services in Los Angeles County, reducing the rate of increase in the cost of living below the national average. Despite the presence of low wage Mexican immigrants, per capita income and living standards rose faster in Los Angeles County than they did in California and the United States as a whole (Muller and Espenshade, op.cit.: 155). The fact that this progress was achieved, as I noted earlier, at the cost of an increase, against national trends, in the proportion of families living in poverty undoubtedly reflects the way Los Angeles County prosperity was built on the exploitation of Mexican migrants, particularly the undocumented.

Surveying projections for future demand for labor in Southern California, Muller and Espenshade anticipated a higher than national average increase in manufacturing employment, a third of which would be in labor-intensive low wage industries as against half in the high-tech and defence industries. Some 160,000 of the new assemblers, construction workers, machine tool operators, waiters, kitchen help, cooks and fast-food counter workers needed in the country as a whole during the 1980s would be needed in southern California. Few 1980 residents except Hispanics would be available to take unskilled jobs, and given likely trends south of the border, they estimated that unemployment rates would have to increase to levels similar to the 1930s for unemployment to be a serious deterrent to undocumented migrants (op.cit.: 173). Muller and Espenshade argued that only the most draconian employer sanctions could influence rates of undocumented migration significantly, a view which has been justified by the ineffectiveness of the provisions of the IRCA in this regard. They did not regard the fiscal impacts of Mexican migration as significant causes for concern, and concluded that the most serious problems lay in Anglo responses to the perceived challenge to their political and cultural hegemony posed by growth of the "Hispanic" population.

Although Muller and Espenshade took the view that it would be problematic if Mexican migrants refused to be assimilated into the "mainstream of society" as defined in Anglo terms, they did at least recognize that Anglo attitudes had played a major role in defining a spurious "problem" of Mexican immigration, and were themselves part of the real problem which their research identified. The main problem with their analysis was that its assumptions about the way the Californian economy would develop were based on an inadequate reading of how political trends would affect the profile of public finances and the role of national government.

Mike Davis has argued that the fiscal situation of the big U.S. cities today reflects the domestic political agenda of the Reagan-Bush years (Davis, 1993a). The Republicans sought to destroy core Democrat constituencies and programs sustaining support for the Democrat party, such as Urban Development Action Grants. At the same time, a policy of disinvestment permitted the rise of a new "postindustrial" economy, restructured on the lines of the "flexible accumulation" model, with a substantial growth of subcontracting and secondary labor markets in manufacturing, and dynamism in sectors such as financial and commercial services and real estate development (Harvey, 1989). The rhetoric of Republican policy-makers appealed to the logic of the global economy and comparative advantage, but many Democrat politicians were drawn to support the policy, because those it hurt most were of scant political significance in their particular constituencies. This fostered the convergence of Republican and Democrat positions, visible in the continuation of policies of abandoning the inner city cores by the Clinton administration, which paid a conspicuous lack of attention to courting the votes of the disadvantaged in an electoral campaign which aimed itself at "Middle America." In consequence, the federal share of the budget fell from 22% in 1980 to 6% in 1989 for a city with more than 300,000 inhabitants.

In Los Angeles, federal contributions to the budget fell from 18% in 1977 to 2% in 1985, the smallest contribution in any of the ten biggest metropolitan cities. By the end of the Eighties, as I noted earlier, the Bush administration was refusing even to help Los Angeles with additional costs imposed by national policies, failing to allocate the additional funds promised by the IRCA to Los Angeles as one of the two principal ports of entry for immigrants (Davis, 1993a: 13).

The fiscal shortfall produced by Federal budget cuts could only be made good by raising regressive sales taxes and user fees, given the refusal of the Anglo middle and upper classes to countenance increases in other forms of taxation. At the root of the emergent crisis of the inner cities in the 1980s was the suburbanization of economic growth and a massive shift in the ethnic composition of city cores. Between 1970 and 1990, the ten largest metropolitan cities in the United States lost 900,000 inhabitants overall, but gained 4.8 million Latinos, 1.5 million Asians and 800,000 Black inhabitants, reflecting the movement out of 8 million whites. Whites represented 70% of the population of these cities in 1970 and under 40% in 1990, by which stage Latinos had become nearly 22% of the population. In 1970 Latinos and Asians combined made up less than 3% of the total (Davis, 1993a: 15). By 1990, Latinos had become the largest ethnic category in Los Angeles (39.3% against 37.2% White).[2]

Virtually the entire white working class of the old southeastern industrial belt of Los Angeles moved to the suburban fringe in the 1970s and early 1980s, to be replaced by 328,000 Mexican immigrants, mainly employed in non-union manufacturing and services (Davis, 1993a: 16). The Black population of the city had by this stage tasted the degree of social mobility the new programs of the Johnson era provided, and were concentrated in public sector jobs. Since 1980 core cities have lost 30% of their job base, while suburbs have experienced 25% employment gain and suburban commuters take high proportion of high wage jobs in the cores. Local public sector jobs and jobs in the armed services provided the most important compensatory opportunities for Latinos and especially for Blacks unable to move laterally into new suburban jobs. These are precisely the kinds of jobs that budget cuts have been eliminating, along with the Comprehensive Employment Training Act programs which provided an alternative to the underground drug economy

---

2 Blacks were the largest category in Chicago, the cities of the San Francisco-Oakland-San Jose manufacturing hub in northern California, and Detroit. Whites remained the majority population in Dallas and Houston, New York and Philadelphia, though barely so.

TABLE 7.3 Ethnic Power Disparities, Los Angeles, 1992

Latinos	
Public School Enrollment	65%
Population	41%
Active Electorate	8%
Federal Jury Pool	7%
Capital Gains Tax	4%
Anglos	
Public School Enrollment	12%
Population	37%
Active Electorate	70%
Federal Jury Pool	80%
Capital Gains Tax	90%

Source: Davis, 1993b: 53. Data compiled from 1992 Los Angeles Unified School Board (population and school enrollment); County Registrar of Voters (vote, June 1992 election); ACLU (federal jury pool, second King beating trial); and Los Angeles *Business Journal* (capital gains income).
Reprinted by permission of *New Left Review*.

(Davis, 1993a: 12). Although second and third generation Mexican-Americans have lower mobility than Anglos, their mobility has proved higher than that of Blacks, who have been excluded from the edge-city boom. "Black suburbanization" mostly represents an expansion of the southcentral ghetto, with only a small movement into blue-collar suburbs in comparison with the exodus of Chicanos to the San Gabriel Valley. Yet this difference counts for little in terms of the scale of Latino immiseration, given the vast numbers of new Latinos entering the city over the past decade.

Suburbanization of economic growth over the 1980s divorced the postmodern "bourgeois utopias" of the edge-cities from the crisis of the core, and sharpened the racial definition of the Californian class system. The suburban electorate can finance their own service needs from locally generated revenues, severing their ties at this level with the so-called "underclass." Table 7.3 reproduces a series of measures of the power disparities between Latinos and Anglos in the Los Angeles of 1992, calculated by Davis from a combination of public and private sector sources. In the face of these figures, it is unsurprising that the suburbs are the effective arbiters of public policy in California, the only majority which counts in politics (Davis, 1993a: 18).

The consequences of this shift of political power and income from the urban cores to the suburbs are reflected in a set of figures which contrast sharply with the projections of the Urban Institute study. Since 1970, minimum wage and median state benefits have lost 40% of their real value. Median welfare benefit for a family of three now equals barely one third of the official poverty threshold, and 28% of those who live below the poverty line receive no public aid at all (Davis, 1993a:

24–5). The center cities now have six and a half times as many households living in poverty in comparison with the suburbs, compared with a difference of three and a half times in 1980. Per capita income in the core has deteriorated over the decade from 90% of that in the suburbs to 59%.

Union membership in California has declined from more than one third in 1973 to barely one seventh.[3] The percentage of male workers earning less than $20,000 a year has tripled, and the ratio of low wage service jobs to high wage industrial jobs changed from 2:1 in 1970 to 5:1 in 1990 (Davis, 1993b: 47). Tourism, with a turnover of $7 billion, is now the largest employer, supplanting aerospace. Anglo California's rise to economic glory began not with industrialization, but with its climate and real estate speculation (Davis, 1990). Even when its high-tech, military industries became the leading edge of its economy, another low-tech, labor-intensive production sector was developing by drawing in surplus labor from the South and manipulating its ethnic and migratory status. The trend towards suburbanization and the decay of core city manufacturing has led California to a new phase of development, in which the function of immigrant labor is increasingly one of serving the boundless consumption and service needs of an Anglo economy which is returning to its roots, with a renewed emphasis on real estate development and financial and commercial services.

These economic transformations have their roots in the late Seventies, as metropolitan cities throughout the United States were transformed from manufacturing centers into "global cities" by the new international division of labor (Sassen-Koob, 1983). The giant new office complexes, elite apartments and consumer facilities which loom so incongruously over an increasingly squalid core urban sprawl are nerve centers for coordinating world-market factory production and providing financial and insurance services for the international corporate market place. California's development of immigration-based labor-intensive manufacturing influenced the pace of transformation, but did not eliminate the forces promoting it in the longer term: wages in Tijuana are U.S.$5 a day rather than $5 an hour, and the Salinas government pursued a forceful campaign of repression against independent unions in the *maquiladoras*. Yet the logic of the market place does not explain the whole of the logic of change through the Eighties, despite ideological emphasis on privatization of remaining public assets and services, and largely empty promises of a private sector "fix" of the inner city problem. The American response to de-industrialization and the fate of the inner cities represents a political choice, determined by the fact that some residents of the country are more politically significant than others.

---

[3] Although the transfer of manufacturing production offshore has been the dominant tendency, some Californian manufacturing jobs have also been relocated in non-unionized industrial parks within the United States, around Phoenix, Las Vegas and Salt Lake City (Davis, 1993b: 46).

The inner-cities have become the epitome of poverty in America, particularly as far as media images are concerned, but rural poverty remains significant in the United States, and has an increasingly Mexican face. As I noted in the previous chapter, the generalized shift of California agribusiness towards fruit and vegetable production after 1975 created a demand for workers possessing specific skills who would remain year round in the region (Palerm, op.cit.: 78–80). The problems of the inner cities reinforced tendencies for migrants to settle in rural locations, but some Mexican-dominated rural enclaves have now themselves become sites of poverty and social problems not dissimilar to those of the urban cores. The first reason for this is that rural communities have also been affected by "white flight." Non-Latino medium to high income residents have moved out of the districts where Mexicans settled, along with local agricultural industries. As better paid jobs and the tax dollars to fund services have been lost, "relatively prosperous, self-contained and diverse" farm communities have turned into "depressed farm worker bedroom communities" (Palerm, op.cit.: 21). The expansion of the suburbs into space occupied by farmland is adding a further twist to this process.

The second major cause of rural decay is the IRCA. Palerm's data from Californian farming communities confirm the conclusion suggested by my data from Michoacán: far from discouraging migration, the IRCA stimulated it and flooded the farm labor market (Palerm, op.cit.: 89–90). Palerm argues that the position of settled migrants has been undermined by the arrival of the *rodinos* and their families and new undocumented entrants. This is not simply a question of the depressive effect of numbers on wages. The extra paper work created by the IRCA, along with employer sanctions, led growers to rely even more on the mediation of labor contractors, at least in Southern California and the Central Valley. The contractors could also supply the false but adequate documentation which enabled growers to claim compliance with the IRCA. Some were old established agents and firms, but others were new, some of them "fly-by-night" businesses (Palerm, op.cit: 113). Although many contractors recruit from particular regions in Mexico, all need to make profits, and Palerm argues that the emergent pattern was for contractors to recruit the cheapest workers available, either within Mexico or the border areas, even where this meant putting established settled workers out of a job (op.cit.: 113–14). The personal bonds between settled workers and growers shattered as the former lost security of employment, and considerable tensions emerged within the farm communities between "old" and "new" migrants, with particular hostility manifest towards the undocumented.

As Escobar has demonstrated, flooding of the labor market has also had a negative impact on the prospects of American-born Mexican Americans and long established Mexican immigrants in the Californian cities (Escobar, 1993: 79–80). Emphasis on the growth of Mexican migration to urban destinations has, however, distracted attention from the continuing importance of farm worker migration, and the way it is both deepening and "Mexicanizing" rural poverty in some parts of the United States. In the light of this evidence, a further shake-out of population from the Mexican countryside towards the farms of the United States seems highly undesirable, and it seems the height of complacency to continue to regard the social consequences of neoliberal policy towards the rural sector as inconsequential whilst the "safety-valve" of migration remains open.

Nativism, Ethnicization and the Links Between Hegemonic and Subaltern Ideologies

Up to this point, I have been considering broad structural trends. The use of highly aggregated "ethnic" constructs has a number of dangers. Firstly, it homogenizes and abstracts from internal social differentiation. Secondly, it can reinforce a view of those who are subject to discrimination as passive victims rather than actors who play a role in shaping the conditions under which they live. Thirdly, it considers only certain dimensions of the construction of identities and their relationship to social action and practices. I argued in previous chapters that migrant populations reconstitute modes of life and the person in the process of displacement, but that even those who come from the same region do not necessarily do this in the same way. In this chapter I have already noted how the "ethnicization" of Californian class structure promoted by the Anglo-dominated social and political order can provoke a mirroring of hegemonic values in emergent antagonisms between different subaltern groups at a relatively high segmentary level such as "Mexicanos" versus "Blacks," and that there is also ample scope for additional segmentation, not merely within the "Latino" population as a whole, but even within the "Mexicano" group.

The conflicts within the Mexican migrant population I have just been discussing reflect changing social conditions within the United States, and some analysts have made general arguments that "culture" is no more significant than "human capital" when it comes to explaining the social strategies of the heterogeneous set of persons who might be brought together under a catch-all category like "Latino migrants" (Salzinger, 1991: 140). People of the most diverse social backgrounds in their country of origin, and of diverse migratory statuses (refugees and asylum seekers, legal, spuriously legal and undocumented migrants), may be found pursuing apparently similar occupations. In this case it seems necessary to give analytical priority to the way the social and economic environment into which they have moved has an overriding impact on their strategies and expectations.

Salzinger examined two separate cooperatives for women who do domestic cleaning in the Bay Area. She found that their radically different attitudes to work and life reflected the way the market for domestic services is bifurcated. One cooperative was engaged in a "professionalization project" for cleaning, and catered exclusively for the market created by young and upwardly mobile professionals, whereas the other regarded the work as simply a way of surviving until something better could be achieved, displaying little "esprit de corps" or willingness to organize collectively to improve pay and conditions. This second group filled the lower paid jobs offered by elderly people living alone and by two-wage working class and single parent households whose own participation in the labor market now depends on cheap child-care.

Salzinger explains the development of a bifurcated market for immigrant domestic workers in terms of Sassen's analysis of how de-industrialization has transformed the nature of the middle class and with it the role of recent immigrants (Sassen, 1986). In the "global city" the middle class becomes service-based. The urban office infrastructure creates new jobs, but access to them is differentiated by credentialing which is seldom transferable across national boundaries. At the same time, the decline of U.S. manufacturing and other changes associated with the Reagan-Bush years which I have already discussed, generated an increasing demand for services from hard-pressed households lower down the income scale. The Eighties may have produced the "yuppie," but they have also ended the dream of continuing improvement of living standards for the lower middle class and skilled manufacturing workers. Immigrant labor has thus become integral to moderating the "domestic" class contradictions of a process of economic restructuring which has profoundly affected the class situations and life-styles of all Americans. The immigrants themselves have responded to this situation in different ways, which reflect differences in their social backgrounds. The group of women who were pursuing a collective strategy of professionalizing their role as service providers tended to come from more middle class backgrounds in their country of origin, and had been resident for a longer period in the United States (Salzinger, op.cit.: 154–5).

This example suggests that a purely socio-economic analysis may explain significant differences in the way migrants organize themselves collectively. Some may be able to change the terms of their incorporation into the capitalist economy, although, as Salzinger notes, the processes she describes might lead to a reclassification of (some) domestic work, but have no immediate implications for wider barriers to social and economic mobility (op.cit.: 158). It was acceptance of the immutability of those barriers which led some women to construct a positive identity around work, rather than the issues of gender, ethnicity and power which had originally attracted Salzinger to study collective organizations of this type.

This leaves us with some significant questions about how far self-ascribed identities based on possession of a distinct culture or ethnicity are important to migrants, and in what sense. It is often assumed that such identifications should be the basis for solidarity and even "resistance"—collective struggles for social mobility, justice and political power. Yet "resistance" is a slippery concept, since actions consciously aimed at modifying the terms of one's insertion into a social order may deepen conformity with the underlying structural principles of a hegemonic "mode of life" (Gledhill, 1994: 91–93). As I argued in Chapter Three, even where "solidarity" is manifest at one level, we need to be careful to examine its limits.

It is, however, not entirely satisfactory to draw a sharp distinction between the respective roles of migrant "culture" and socio-economic conditions in determining adaptations, because this line of thinking embodies a static conception of what "culture" is. People are assumed to possess a culture—the product of socialization in their homeland—which travels with them, but becomes a less significant determinant of their behavior as they adapt to new conditions of life. Yet the individuals concerned cannot cease to attach meaning to their experience and situations, or to interact with other persons in terms of meaningful constructions of their situation. Some particularly significant processes of cultural reconstruction at work among migrant populations do center on homeland-focused identities, but they are products of imagination rather than inertia. One of the most important issues in the study of the impact of modern mass migrations is the way the "deterritorialization" associated with sedentarization of immigrant communities in the metropolis is associated with what Arjun Appadurai terms "exaggerated and intensified senses of criticism or attachment to politics in the home-state" and "fundamentalist" recreations of cultural identity (Appadurai, 1990).

As Appadurai points out, these processes are not explicable simply in terms of the way migrants are placed in enduring positions of structural economic disadvantage in relatively wealthy societies, and might thus be expected to develop compensatory ideologies to reclaim dignity and respect. They are promoted both by the hegemonic politics of the state and by the capitalist commoditization of culture and cultural difference (Appadurai, op.cit.: 300–1). Appadurai's "sociology of displacement" suggests ways in which the creation of "transnational communities" not only fosters a proliferation of the micro-politics of identity, but provides the basis for novel kinds of counter-hegemonic or nationalist imaginaries in both "peripheral" and "metropolitan" societies, which may have significant consequences for national states. At this point, however, I want to focus on two particular issues: how do the hegemonic projects of metropolitan states influence the identities of immigrant groups, and how far any does development of collective identities premised on ethnicity or regional origin provoke further segmentation and fragmentation within the subaltern classes? I will argue that the identities people produce for themselves, and the ways they oppose themselves to other groups, are significantly influenced by hegemonic politics.

Since the late Seventies, the official categories of the American census have assigned people of Mexican origin to the racial and ethnic category "Hispanic." As Forbes (1992) argues, this category corresponds to no coherent set of distinctions of race, ethnicity, or nationality, but it is a useful political tool. The classification is not, strictly speaking, new, nor an invention of government. It developed in parts of the Southwest in a context of class alliance and political accommodation between Anglo and "Mexicano" elites (Foley, 1988: 282; see also page 196 below). The "Hispanic" identity distinguished the emergent elite group from *peones*, along lines of "culture" (more correct Spanish, education, and subscription to an Anglo-Saxon ethic of entrepreneurship) but also on lines of "race," for the "Hispanics" classified themselves as pale-skinned Europeans and the *peones* as darker and more "Indian"(ibid.). A similar political logic gave the category its broader appeal to the institutional political leadership of the Mexican-American population and the state alike during the period of Republican administration (Forbes, op.cit.: 67). Dangerous "Chicanos" became hard-working, self-realizing mainstream "Hispanics," duly enhancing the political capital of those speaking in their name.

The "Hispanic" category not only suppresses the Native American antecedents of the vast majority of *mestizo* Mexicans, but also the possibility of discussing the practices of discrimination, in particular the relationship between differential rates of social mobility among different segments of the "Hispanic" population and skin color (Forbes, op.cit.: 75). As we have already seen, there are other explanations of the differential rates of mobility between, for example, Cubans and Mexicans. Yet, as I showed in Chapter Three, valorization of whiteness does remain significant within the migrants' countries of origin. Its continuing significance is even visible within the *mestizo* household itself in western Mexico, where the birth of a child with fair complexion and blonde hair often evokes an effusive discourse on the beauty of the new addition to the family from the parents, who remain doggedly insensitive to the trauma they may be causing to a darker sibling. The hegemonic politics of the American state have therefore added another level to systems of social distinction already deeply rooted in the societies of the South, with the active complicity of some of their political representatives.

This is a paradigm case of the way modern societies politicize ethnicity. Official bureaucratic categories define "legitimate" group identities, which determine entitlements to resources. Power within institutional politics accrues to those who represent the recognized categories. The internal political manipulation of identities in the North does, however, come up against certain structural limits, imposed not merely by denial of social mobility, but by the continuing inability of the dominant society to digest its colonial "Other."

American society was founded on immigration from Europe, but it was also founded on slavery and militarism. The military dimension of U.S. power has not been confined to operations against the exterior, but has also been central to internal social pacification. Although Fordism produced the individualized consumer-worker and the privatized family consumption unit at the same time as it produced automobiles, the birth of a new capitalist social order under the auspices of economic corporativism was also supported by a class repression as violent as anything experienced in the South. Furthermore, the historical development of the U.S. economy has involved significant internal colonial processes.

Its first capitalist phase involved Blacks moving from the South to the Northeast and the former Mexicans left on the northern side of the frontier after the annexations. In both cases the process of displacement continued through well into the twentieth century, but as Sarah Deutsch (1987) has shown, amounted to more than a simple reorganization of the labor supply for an expanding capitalism. As more Mexicans entered from the South to take over the jobs vacated by the Negroes who had departed in the previous wave, they came not only to work on the farm and on the railways, but began to move North from Texas towards the industries of Chicago and the Northeast. Their presence helped Anglo employers implement a strategy of social and occupational stasis for Chicanos. This, in turn, helped to defeat attempts to build more assertive Chicano organizations in the original Southwestern homelands in the 1930s (Deutsch, 1987: 204–5). In the next, post-Depression, phase, there was further restructuring. Negroes began to enter California, while the Mexicans now entered in a different way, as *bracero* contract laborers. And so the process continues. U.S. labor markets are subject throughout to ethnic segmentation processes. Although the social and economic positions of different groups are redefined from time to time, one principle is reproduced continuously, that Mexicans entering the United States do so in terms of a strictly neocolonial relationship, as an "external" population which not only offers certain advantages to capital as a labor force, but is a key element in manipulations designed to secure the political containment of Chicanos and more recently naturalized citizen Latinos.

Episodes such as the "Brown Scare" of the period 1913–1918 in Los Angeles indicate that the intensity of nativist hysteria correlates with moments of perceived threat to the dominant social and political order, rather than simply economic difficulties (Romo, 1983: 90–2). The second decade of the twentieth century was, admittedly, one of substantial economic structural change for Los Angeles as well as depression. The large influx of Mexicans responded to the development of an industrial and manufacturing economy, but the "scare" was not merely centered on the purported contribution of Mexicans to labor unrest and the dangers of a growing army of the unemployed. It also focused on the threat posed to the border by the Mexican revolution and Mexico's supposed ties to America's German enemies in the European war. In this early case, then, the integrity of the Anglo nation-state was posed as the underlying problem, through the linkage made between the alien "enemy within" and a menacing exterior.

Not only has military power has always been central to U.S. global hegemony, despite the economic contradictions which have arisen from that fact, but the role of the United States on the global stage has been shaped by a cultural logic, which also manifests itself in internal pacification. The Los Angeles Police Department is a case in point. Davis's school teacher is not the only commentator to observe that the force has acquired a military character and ethos, very much in the style of an army of occupation. Members of the force reside together in neighborhoods outside the city, and according to interviews conducted by the American journalist Marc Cooper, see the social world they police as one divided between "normal" people and "assholes" (Cooper, 1991). The "assholes" are the Black and Latino "underclass," whose members are believed by the officers to have racially determined criminal propensities, and an innate lack of affinity with the values of the nuclear holy family of Anglo society which leads to reproductive incontinence.

The discourse which characterizes an agency of internal social pacification like the LAPD thus reveals a striking homology with the discourse which has defined

America's recent view of center-periphery relations, and legitimized U.S. backing for, and participation in, state terror (Petras and Morley, 1990: 49). The political imagery of the post-Cold War United States has shifted from a vision of a world threatened by rational subversion organized by communist states towards what Deborah Poole and Gerardo Rénique characterize as "a world made up of *sui generis* madmen and terrorists, warlords and drug barons, charismatic leaders and fundamentalist mass movements" (Poole and Rénique, 1991: 160). No systematic connections can be recognized between processes in the center and those in the periphery, for the separation of "irrational" periphery and "rational" center disguises:

> the unutterable connections (or "linkages") ... between drug economies and the international capitalist economy, between Third World debt, metropolitan banks and financial institutions, between Third World dictators like Saddam Hussein and the military industrial complex (Poole and Rénique, 1991: 191).

Yet even academic debates about "a domestic situation of class and racial polarization" also display "structural and discursive features [which] mimic those of imperial center and colonial periphery" (Poole and Rénique, op.cit.: 173).

To some extent, this homology is rooted in the historical processes which have constituted the "United States" as a political entity, reflecting a long-term dialectic of neocolonial and internal colonial relations. Demonization of "aliens" is a long-established feature of American history, as are variants on modern constructions of the "underclass." Romo notes, for example, how Samuel Bryan, of Stanford University, wrote in 1912 of the Mexican community in Los Angeles that:

> Their low standards of living and morals, their illiteracy, their utter lack of proper political interest, the retarding effect of their employment on the wage scale of the more progressive races, and finally their tendency to colonize in urban centers, with evil results, combine to stamp them as a rather undesirable class of residents (Romo, op.cit.: 92).

What is different about the contemporary convergence of discourses about the inner cities and the periphery is that it reflects the implosion of the periphery into the core, and the collapse of the boundaries separating the United States and its colonial "Others." Latin America and Los Angeles are now cognized through homologous metaphors of order versus disorder and civilization versus barbarism, which have become fatefully ingrained in the consciousness of ordinary Anglo-Americans. It is, however, ironic, though no cause for surprise, that the agents who terrorize the urban poor of Panama, and assault innocent Somalis in intimate displays of the implacable rationality of American power, are often soldiers recruited from the demonized Black and Latino urban "underclasses." The hegemony of Anglo and European "hyphenated Americans" over contemporary society is embedded in the national state order, and the nature of that order remains at the heart of the matter.

In the first place, the U.S. social formation is becoming more and more *self*-segmenting. The social mobility achieved by a portion of the Black population has not resolved problems of discrimination and poverty, nor strengthened national unity. This is not simply because American capitalism has been based on the ethnic segmentation of labor markets and extended reproduction of "underclasses." It is because the nation has been constructed in terms of "Anglo-Saxon" historical myths, in a way which has yet to permit a new synthesis based on genuinely multi-cultural myths. Attempts which have been made to rescue an alternative Black-African national and universal history tend to prove the point, since they usually invert Europe-focused dominant narratives of "manifest destiny." Most "white" Americans today are not of "Anglo-Saxon" stock, and many of the "hyphenated Americans" of European origin themselves experienced discrimination in the past. Nevertheless, the boundaries of the majoritarian project in the United States could include them—without building too much of their cultural traditions into the nation's foundational myths and values—because of the way internal and external colonial boundaries were constructed in the consolidation of the American state-nation.

The contradictory nature of this mode of being a nation is increasingly evident. Even if new immigration stopped dead tomorrow, natural increase alone guarantees a further shift in the ethnic composition of the U.S. population. Such shifts were not unknown in the old empires of yesteryear, which appeared, by and large, to be able to cope with them. These were not, however, "societies" constructed as Anglo-Saxon nations and committed to extreme egalitarian individualism. The Anglo population will, however, increasingly have to face up to the responses of its Mexican "Others" to their continuing exclusion. That response *could* promote a new pluralism: socio-economic aspirations tend to converge, and in many respects the "forms of life" of different segments are not highly differentiated. Yet the way the whole society is structured makes such an outcome more difficult to achieve.

In a world in which almost anything can be commoditized, inter-culturalism of one kind can be promoted by market forces. In the fields of consumption and recreation, "ethnic cultures," fragmented into commoditizable elements and styles, borrow from each other in the postmodern collage which many cultural studies writers place at the forefront of the process of "globalization." Subaltern groups can actually achieve a kind of hegemonic position in defining styles, as the case of contemporary popular music demonstrates, although these are precisely the cases where the ultimate hegemony of giant corporations in the process of commoditizing culture and style asserts itself most vigorously. Even the kind of social critique which comes out of the ghetto these days can be marketed to white middle class youth. It is possible to exaggerate the extent to which symbolic "communication" actually takes place across social and cultural divides. Young Michoacanos return to their villages with bumper stickers expressing propositions of a level of sexual indecency which they clearly failed to grasp at the time of purchase. The main "statement" their choice of tee-shirt may be making is that this is what was on offer at the second-hand stall. No doubt every act of consumer choice is expressing something. There are conscious attempts to emulate fashions seen as "American" in general, and the enthusiasm Mexicans showed for imports after the country's entry into the GATT suggests more than a search for the lowest price. Yet much that is Mexican (including the genre of movie represented by *El Mariachi*) appeals to other groups and, more significantly, can be fused with other traditions. At this level, Mexicans "fit," but at another level difference is reproducing itself in a violent and destructive form.

One obvious example is gang warfare. Core city Black and Latino youth face a common situation of deprivation, and there is some interchange between them at the level of "youth culture."[4] Yet despite the much publicized attempts of the Cripps and Bloods to foster a unity movement, youth violence has escalated in the high schools of Los Angeles and its environs since the riots, and new conflicts have emerged, in particular the sanguinary gang conflicts between Cambodians and Chicanos in Long Beach (Davis, 1993b: 41–2). Although Asians are usually depicted as enjoying greater economic success than Mexicans, it is important to note that some of the refugees produced by American intervention in south-east Asia have found themselves facing problems of large-scale male unemployment, and have ended up living embattled lives as an ethnic enclave, not merely in cities like Los Angeles, San Francisco and Oakland, where the minority who secure employment compete for the same kinds of jobs as Mexican and Central American migrants, but in Mexican-dominated agricultural communities like Stockton (Ui, 1991: 164–5). Davis notes that in addition to a persistent pattern of ethnic violence in Los Angeles jails, public housing projects have begun to manifest symptoms of an "ethnic cleansing" process of which all groups have been victims (Davis, 1993b: 42). The pattern of Mexican stigmatization of Blacks for "underclass" characteristics I noted earlier is now complemented by Black discourses about the way they are being displaced from the job market by Latino immigrants. Even some supposedly radical Black writers are now either echoing Anglo nativist discourses or arguing that Latinos are beneficiaries of white paternalism and a lower level of racial prejudice (Davis, op.cit.: 43).

That these are false diagnoses is less material than the fact that they reflect ways in which subaltern groups are made complicit in Anglo hegemony. There is little incentive for Black politicians to argue that the fortification of Anglo political and economic privilege in the edge-cities is the root of their own community's problems, whilst they are continuing to support the exclusion of Latinos from access to

---

4 The rise of Chicano Rap was followed by a Mexican derivative, and the music of Black rappers seemed to be quite popular among young migrants in the town of Los Reyes, along with the Norteño music favored by Ciénega migrants.

political power and are unable to defend city finances from further cuts. As Davis grimly concludes:

> Confronted with a virtual melt-down of local government, Latinos wonder, not surprisingly, where the resources for their future mobility will come from. In the 1940–1970 period the struggle to gain equal access to *expanding* public services controlled by whites welded Blacks and Latinos together; now the decline of the public sector is polarizing them in zero-sum competition over public employment and community development funds .... In the face of a dying public-sector economy, and with Anglo wealth and power fortified in seemingly unassailable enclaves, the new majority's search for equality threatens to derail and fragment into permanent ethnic strife (Davis, 1993b: 45, emphasis in the original).

The way ethnicity is politicized today favors a sharpening of conflict along the major "ethnic" boundaries. Class and occupational issues combine with questions of political representation, the depth of the historical presence of different populations within the United States, and visible "racial" markers, to foster conflict of this kind in an era of deepening immiseration. Nevertheless, the prospects for greater "Latino" unification on the principal of "segmentary opposition" remain uncertain. The history of relations between Chicanos and Mexican migrants has been one of relative animosity, fostered by Anglo manipulation. As we have seen, the IRCA has made yet further contributions to fostering divisions and promoted a yet greater demonization of the undocumented.

I have noted some evidence for intermarriage across community boundaries within the recent Mexican migrant population, but many migrant communities still retain strong identifications with particular regions, and may recreate them within a new politics of difference premised on economic insecurity and competition within labor markets that are only regulated in ways that serve capitalist interests. Such developments might be even more destructive than a shift towards individualism and attempts to identify with the dominant society against other groups of immigrants. The boundaries created by kinship and *paisanaje* may be functional for migrants at one level, but they do not necessarily aid the establishment of cross-cutting ties with other countrymen or people from other countries in similar class situations, particularly when they are reinforced by social distinctions premised on ascriptions of racial difference. The fact that "refugees" may find themselves without privileges in the labor market does not necessarily stop undocumented migrants from seeing them as privileged. The formation of individual friendships or even kinship bonds does not, in itself, have any great impact on the processes of category creation and maintenance, at least until it becomes so extensive that boundaries cease to have meaning.

The picture is not, however, entirely one of fragmentation. The other side of the coin of the transnationalization of class relationships is the transnationalization of politics. *Neocardenismo* found a natural constituency in California amongst people who had strong feelings of victimization at the hands of both the Mexican state and a hostile "host community," many of whom were displaced professionals and unionized skilled workers who exported their organizational experience (Dresser, 1993: 98–99). Human rights campaigners and Chicano activists also identified with the PRD's Californian project, and the implications of the NAFTA for labor on both sides of the border drew the movement into dialogue with the U.S. trade unions (Dresser, op.cit.: 101). Nevertheless, Dresser notes that the PRD's attempt to form a "rainbow coalition" in California has been dogged by the same kinds of factional conflicts as have afflicted the party within Mexico, whilst its focus on the overriding issue of democracy in Mexico does not pay sufficient attention to the concrete and specific local interests of its constituency (op.cit.: 102). Some Chicano organizations feel that the PRD's intervention is distracting energy from advancement of Mexicans within U.S. society (Dresser, op.cit.: 108). Furthermore, the PRI itself was not slow to respond to the threat posed by the PRD's demands that this sizeable constituency be allowed to vote in national elections without returning to Mexico. It made substantial efforts to make the more "respectable" Mexican-American organizations interlocutors for its economic strategy, displayed a new interest in providing services to its migrant citizens, and stepped up consular involvement in human rights issues. Given the implications of Salinas's economic policies, the extent to which the regime could reach out to migrant workers in general was limited, and most of its new programs appealed mainly to better-off Mexican Americans and relatively privileged immigrant workers (Dresser, op.cit.: 104). Yet even if these processes merely replicate the tactics of selectivity practiced by the PRI in Mexico, they will foster divisions and reinforce the problems caused by divisions over the balance to be struck between empowerment in the United States and reform in Mexico.

Among long-term residents of California, and in particular young Mexican-Americans who enter higher education, alternatives to building identity on the basis of European origin are debated, in response not only to reflection on the continuing political disempowerment of Latinos, but to the rise of Black studies as part of the institutional curriculum. Identification with the "indigenous" rather than European side of being Mexican also offers a new generation of aspiring political leaders an opportunity to distance themselves from the older style of Chicano politics. "Culture politics" of a kind are also visible among groups lower down the social scale. Some migrant farm workers' organizations had already adopted a populist-*campesino* identity in the incongruous circumstances of the North by identifying themselves with the symbol of Lázaro Cárdenas before 1988, and other groups have organized themselves by reconstituting specific ethnic identities which can also be manipulated politically within Mexico itself, as I noted in Chapter Four. These new forms of "identity politics" are not, however, free-floating constructs which can be entirely divorced from the politics of class and the structuring of political life by states.

I can illustrate this point with a brief discussion of developments in South Texas during the 1980s. Throughout this chapter I have focused largely on California, because it remains the principle destination of the majority of Mexican migrants from my study region, but there are interesting differences between California and parts of South Texas, highlighted in the study by Foley mentioned above (Foley, 1988). Foley's study community, North Town, lies in an agricultural region which today produces fruit and vegetables under an increasingly mechanized regime. The politics of the region's Mexicanos remain highly fractionalized, but the intense political and racial conflict associated with the rise of the Raza Unida Party in the Seventies gave way to what at first sight looks like an impressive demonstration of the flexibility and pluralism of the American political system, with Mexicanos competing successfully for public office and delivering the ethnic vote to the Democrats. Foley argues, however, that what happened in North Town actually reflects the specific class character of its grassroots political struggles.

Mexicanos first began to emerge as political actors as growers shifted, from the Thirties onwards, towards a regime based on migrant labor, and used local Mexicanos as "a kind of labor aristocracy of permanent field hands, managers, machinery operators and contractors" to manage "a broader base of illegal, *bracero* and less fortunate local Mexicanos" (Foley, op.cit.: 273). By the fifties, the value of these brokers to Anglo political machines, their importance for controlling the migrants the system continued to draw in from the South, and their achievement of some social mobility, were laying the basis for what Foley calls "a process of sponsored political enfranchisement." Yet the rise of an activist Mexicano political leadership was underpinned by the growing combativity of ordinary workers, manifest in work stoppages and social disorderliness (Foley, op.cit.: 274). Different kinds of petty bourgeois leaderships emerged in response to these developments in different parts of Texas, but in North Town, campus radicals were far less significant than small businessmen and growers, and there was no organized workers' movement. Local politics became a process of competition between the brown and white petty bourgeoisie. Foley argues that this ultimately fostered alliances across racial boundaries in a community where politics is highly personalized. In this kind of context, massive "white flight" is much less probable (op.cit.: 277). In contrast to the border communities, North Town did not manifest the development of a strong "Hispanic" elite identity to open up breaches between leaders and people within the ethnic community, because a substantial amount of social segregation was maintained between white and Mexicano elites (Foley, op.cit.: 283), but this seems in the long-term to be proving conducive to the reduced racialization of politics, and an increasing emphasis on class. The mass of Mexicanos who find the American dream failing them no longer tend to see the new brown political elite as *vendidos* (persons who have sold out to the Anglos) so much as persons acting out of the same class interests as their white counterparts (Foley, op.cit.: 278, 284).

Only a quarter of North Town's Mexicanos participate in American democracy as voters, and it would be unwise to infer too much from a single case study. Nevertheless, it does seem important that class issues are still articulated in American politics, even if they are often manipulated in a cynical way, as was the case during the Congressional debates on the NAFTA. In my analyses of both Mexico and the United States, I have highlighted the many structural barriers to pursuing an effective class-based politics today. The transnational character of contemporary class processes seems to add to the difficulties, but the restructuring of relations between capital and labor across national boundaries also highlights the interdependence of the problems faced by workers in different countries, and offers new possibilities for the organization of resistance. In conclusion to this study, I will offer a final synthetic assessment of the specific implications of neoliberalism and transnationalization for rural society in Mexico, and argue that it is necessary to reject the claim that "there are no alternatives" to present patterns of development.

8

Neoliberalism and Transnationalization: Assessing the Contradictions

I have argued that the social costs of crisis and structural adjustment in the Eighties were compounded by the policies adopted by the Salinas administration to secure the NAFTA. In the case of rural society, however, the worst may be yet to come, since the full implications of Salinas's moves to restructure Mexican agriculture will work themselves out during the Zedillo sexennial. Although predictions of the rapid displacement of thirteen million people from the countryside may be exaggerated, it is difficult to be optimistic about the prospects for improvements in rural living standards for those who remain in rural communities. Yet it is equally difficult to regard international migration as an unproblematic way out for Mexico's *campesinos*.

In comparative terms, Mexicans have not suffered as badly as the people of some other Latin American countries. The Peruvian economist Manuel Lajo estimated that 15 million of his 22 million countrymen lived below the poverty line in 1993, as compared with 8.4 million in 1983. Seven million of them lived in "total misery," unable to secure minimum calorie and protein requirements despite spending their entire family income on food (*Latin American Weekly Report*, WR-94-21: 244). It could be argued, however, that avoidance of such "total misery" is generally easier in the countryside, and that it is still possible to devise ways of increasing subsistence production, even in landscapes which are marginal and ecologically devastated. Rural poverty may also be extreme, although families may experience it in aggravated forms because men react to their condition by heavy drinking. The thin upper arms of the migrant cane cutters from indigenous communities in Guerrero I met in 1991 indicated that they were less well nourished than local *mestizos*, and there were a few local *jornaleros* who would be happy to work for an *ejidatario* in return for a square meal. It is not, however, immediately clear that the alternatives the medium-term future may hold are any better for the poorest layers of rural society.

As the world enters the next millennium, population pressure will demand major transformations of global food production systems, and the scale of the economic restructuring to come may well dwarf that we have witnessed over the past two decades. Yet the increasing fiscal burden of paying European farmers not to grow anything seems to exemplify the social irrationalities of the capitalist organization of production just as much as the burdens of financing peace-keeping and refugee programs in the proliferating war zones of the New World Order—where the supply of means of destruction to the combatants has been increased by the restructuring of the post-communist economies of Eastern Europe, and the increasing participation of Newly Industrialized Countries like Brazil, with western brokers acting as agents for all parties. Even the most superficial reflection on these kinds of issues reveals the limited scope for today's nation-states to resolve their problems in isolation. The collapse or transformation of the "actually existing socialisms" could itself be taken as evidence of the overriding importance of global power networks in shaping human possibilities in the late twentieth century. Nevertheless, the transnational character of contemporary class relations which I have emphasized in this book offers opportunities as well as constraints from the point of view of seeking an amelioration of the human condition, and it would be premature to conclude that the realities of global power close off all options within national units.

Transnationalism as Resistance and Accommodation

As Roger Rouse has pointed out in his writings about international migration from the *municipio* of Aguililla, Michoacán, the traditional bipolar model of migration processes tended to view social consequences in terms of wholesale "adaptation" (or failure of adaptation) to a new social environment (Rouse, 1991; 1992). Its behaviorist theoretical underpinnings not merely failed to recognize the possibility that migrants could maintain active involvement in two societies even when they settled relatively permanently in the North, but marginalized the cultural dimensions of the processes involved in movement from one type of class system to another (Rouse, 1992: 26–27). Rouse demonstrates that Aguilillans who become long-term residents in Redwood City in northern California maintain involvements in the *municipio*, holding on to property and investing savings in houses and land, contributing to construction, transport and commercial enterprises run by parents and siblings, and keeping up contacts with more distant relatives and friends. At the same time, short-term migrants developed some involvements in Redwood City, so that the "transnational migrant circuit" as a whole became the space in which Aguilillans "orchestrated their lives" and "developed and maintained social ties" (Rouse, 1992: 43–45).

Yet the social space of Aguililla and the social space of Redwood City remained qualitatively distinct. Aguililla was remote from the centres of regional and national power and a relatively marginal area in agricultural terms. When international migration began, in the 1940s, its way of life revolved around small-scale ranching and peasant agriculture, within the kind of social and cultural framework I have associated with *ranchero* culture. It remained free of the agribusiness penetration characteristic of the region of Apatzingán to the North, and only experienced state economic intervention in its more benign forms. In Redwood City, migrants were subject to the disciplines of proletarian labor and an entirely different organization of social space. The two forms of life clashed with each other in fundamental domains of value, such as gender relations, and they also clashed, as Rouse stresses, as class cultures. Furthermore, the life world of Redwood City itself varied along the lines of class, as the migrants themselves realized in reflecting on the different expectations *gringo* society held of proletarians, on the one hand, and professional and managerial workers, on the other (Rouse, op.cit.: 34).

Rouse's analysis of the cultural politics of class transformation within the Aguilillan "transnational community" reveals what he terms a kind of "bifocality" among Aguilillan men. At one level, they appear to have become habituated to the disciplines of proletarian existence in the United States, and to have interiorized and accepted the values of its hegemonic culture. In their home communities, where independent family enterprise was the ideal and collective mechanisms for dispute arbitration and physical protection were weak, everyday life was focused on the maintenance of effective boundaries around the family, its property and the bodies of its members, especially women. Houses were meant to be unassuming and presented a forbidding appearance to the outside world, whilst women avoided make-up and dressed demurely. The place of women and children was in the home or other "safe" havens such as the Church, whereas men moved freely in public space (Rouse, op.cit.: 32).

In Redwood City, the appearance of both homes and women was radically transformed, to signal economic success to the outside world. Life gravitated around a fundamental opposition between workplace and home, which increased the mobility of women and children in the public domain. Children went to school and women became potential workers. The state claimed a right to regulate the domestic sphere over and above the rights of fathers, whose own movement in the public domain was subject to new restrictions. The home and workplace were complemented by a third "dangerous" space of bars, gambling clubs and brothels, sanctioned by hegemonic values as areas which undermined the sobriety and discipline of labor (Rouse, op.cit.: 33). A fourth spatial domain, that of leisure activity, the cinema, shopping malls and theme parks, appeared public, but differed from Aguilillan public spaces by being privately owned and not exclusively male (op.cit.: 34). The inculcation of proletarian disciplines and capitalist consumer culture was reinforced as an unplanned by-product of the specific technologies of surveillance to which migrants were subject. The *migra* and the police were less likely to pay attention to those who dressed smartly, drove nice cars, or moved into single-family dwellings. Migrants were wary of spending too much time in the third "street" domain, since this was subject to greatest vigilance by the immigration authorities. Because men spent more of their leisure time in the relative security of their homes, they invested in stereos and televisions (op.cit.: 35). Rouse suggests, as does Mike Davis (1990) for the case of Los Angeles, that the entire infrastructure of urban zoning and public transport provision in the United States facilitates the monitoring and surveillance of the migrant proletarian population: the daily exigencies of movement through space reinforced more direct controls and the discursive transmission of hegemonic values through the media and the workplace, underpinning a subtle process of habituation. The men Rouse interviewed displayed pride in their achievements as both workers and consumers, placing particular emphasis on their value as "family men" who eschewed involvement with the dangerous spaces of street life (op.cit.: 38).

Yet the same subjects also offered a second discourse. They contrasted the freedom and independence of economic life in Aguililla with the disciplines of proletarian labor, and expressed aspirations to recover economic autonomy. The role of good family man dutifully restricting movement to the journeys between home and workplace diminished their manhood. Proletarianization was feminization (ibid.). These themes are again consistent with the picture I presented earlier for *rancheros* and Nugent's observations on the Namiquipenses. The rest of the Aguilillan discourse resonates with material discussed in Chapter Six: it concerns the threats to male authority posed by the state's penetration of the domestic sphere, and the dangers inherent in the "liberty" inscribed in the American way of life. In particular, Aguilillan men argued that the breakdown of the boundaries which allotted fathers absolute domestic authority and the transfer of responsibility for moral education to the public school system were responsible for the growth of drug use among the young (op.cit.: 39–40).[1]

Rouse's point is that the existence of this second discourse is not a product of cultural inertia, but reflects the active maintenance of contradictory dispositions in a subaltern social situation which he defines as "chronic, contradictory transnationalism" (op.cit.: 46). It is not a phenomenon of transition for the reasons I discussed in the previous chapter. Aguilillan men are responding reflectively to their perception of the negative implications of transformations in global capitalism (and U.S. society) for future prospects of upward mobility in the North, especially for their

---

[1] Drugs are also a concern within Michoacán, where marijuana consumption is regarded as a major youth problem in communities close to the local production areas. It is commonplace in communities like Guaracha, but seen as a pathology imported from the North. Drugs are always seen as a threat imposed on rural communities by outside forces. This makes symbolic sense, but has an element of literal truth, since the forces which promote and control the trade lie outside the peasant community. Two Guaracheños have died violently in the past five years as a consequence of trafficking in drugs. The number of migrant workers who become involved in trafficking in the North, generally as couriers, is small. Most are terrified of the violence associated with street life, and anxious to avoid police attention. The role of the police and army also make involvement in the drug economy perilous in Michoacán, although it may be equally hazardous to refuse to cultivate marijuana.

children (op.cit.: 43). The meaning of "life back home" will itself continue to be defined, and redefined, in terms of those evolving understandings of the American pole of the transnational migrant circuit, and *vice versa.*

As Rouse concedes, the particular shape of the Aguilillan transnational migrant community and the types of involvements of Aguilillans do not represent a universal pattern, although this is also far from being a unique case. The differing nature of local intimate class cultures is clearly one major variable, along with the objective possibilities of building an alternative life world which is meaningful at the Mexican end of the transnational circuit. In some cases, migrants will have great difficulties building an alternative to proletarian forms of existence in their home communities, particularly if agribusiness takes over the local land base and there are few opportunities to invest in other kinds of businesses. They may, of course, be able to build new lives in another community, as several Aguilillans had done in Los Reyes, including the chief of the traffic police, who had returned after thirteen years in the United States to raise his family in a community he found culturally congenial, and had already forged cordial social relationships with other town notables. Chief Eduardo had built up a thriving bakery business whilst he was in the North, from the smallest of beginnings selling bread door to door. He continued to be a man of enterprise, but his case serves to highlight the obvious point that there is some differentiation in the way individual migrants experience the class transformation involved in settlement in the United States itself. Actual class differentiation among Mexican immigrants within the United States is less significant than in the case of some other migrant populations for reasons I have already explored. Recent developments are also tending to homogenize social situations more, in the direction of levelling down, as evidenced by the growing presence of long-established, legalized workers with families resident in the United States in the market for casual laborers and the squatter camps. Nevertheless, social differentiation within transnational migrant communities does have some signifi-cace, particularly where relative success as a migrant is the basis for achieving a more substantial position of social advantage at the home community end of the circuit. This may well amount to a difference of class position.

One respect in which differentiation may be significant is the field of politics. More economically successful expatriates may be wooed by governments as investors in "development" (Glick Schiller, Basch and Blanc-Szanton, 1992: 3–4). Those who do invest may actually prove significant change agents in local com-munities, and they may prove powerful allies for neoliberal regimes in a number of fields, including their political promotion abroad. The other side of the coin is the backing better-off expatriates may give to regional or "ethnic" political movements against the national regimes of their home countries, the phenomenon Benedict Anderson (1992) has termed a "long distance nationalism" which may exercise a decisive contribution to the growth of conflict, without suffering any of its damaging consequences. There is, however, also the prospect of political impacts from the ranks of the less fortunate. As I noted in Chapter Four, Kearney has highlighted the way proletarianized Mixtec migrants recuperate symbolic capital in the form of "ethnicity," as they strive to (re)construct community in an age of transnationalism (Kearney, 1991: 64). Although the Mexican countryside is littered with minor public works which express the desire of absentees to make their name live in their home communities, the compression of time and space brought about by modern transport and communications technologies does make it possible for local movements to receive not merely material support, but also some active direction from members whose main residence is in the North. It is in this context that the cultural politics of class transformation within transnational communities might be able to provide some resistances to the neoliberal project, by asserting the possibility of "alternative modernities" which defend the environment and alternatives to proletarianization, as I noted earlier. Nevertheless, a certain realism is to be recommended here, and not merely because the state may be able to accommodate such movements to some extent without abandoning its general program. As Glick Schiller and her co-authors point out, transmigrant actors themselves may simultaneously both resist and accommodate to their subordination within the global capitalist system, acting as union militants in the circumstances of the metropolis, but investing their savings in property and becoming a landlord at home (Glick Schiller et al: 12).

It is evident both from my discussion in the previous chapter and from Rouse's discussion of Aguilillan "bifocalism" that the transnationalization process does effect transformations of the world-views of the social subjects wrapped up in it, even if they do not become the model subjects of national hegemonies or global capitalist discipline. So far, however, I have restricted my discussion largely to the way transnationalism generates tensions at the ideological level, rather than its impact on the actual practices of local social life.

Class, Politics and the Decline of Community

Case studies have often highlighted the way in which even those who come to spend most of their lives in the United States continue to play a significant role in community affairs back in Mexico, sponsoring *fiestas* and financing social projects which benefit local people. In some cases, such as the indigenous community of Tarécuato (Schaffhauser, 1990) or its mestizoized neighbor, Tingüindín, the return of the *norteños* is the festive focal point of the year. In principal, it seems possible to argue that international migration is not merely consistent with the maintenance of local community cultures and traditions, but might actually help to perpetuate, or even to revive them, in at least two distinct ways. Access to work in the North can provide economic resources to sustain community ritual (or even allow its elaboration), and transnationalism may foster attachments to homeland, especially when it is underpinned by continuing intense social ties and a subaltern position in the metropolis which is reinforced by practices of exclusion on the part of the dominant social group.

Yet migration does not necessarily produce a strengthening of "community." In the case of Tarécuato, Schaffhauser notes that some migrants refuse to participate economically in the *fiesta* of Corpus Christi, view ceremonial expenditures as wasteful, and disparage Purhépecha culture in general as a symptom of backwardness. In a sense, this is ironic, since the *fiesta* attracts a good deal of outside interest for its folkloric quality, which has, in fact, changed it into a pastiche of old and new forms.[2] Some returnees and visitors from the North focus on maintaining their ties with family and friends, to the exclusion of participation in community ritual. Others stay on the sidelines, as spectators rather than participants, where they may express a certain disillusion with the changing patterns of life in their *pueblo*. On the other hand, the *fiestas* of Corpus Christi and October 4th are also celebrated in Tarécuato's migrant colonies in the United States.

"Authenticity" is not really an issue at either end of the transnational network. What passes for "traditional" indigenous culture was the product of a complex syncretism, in which "Indians" appropriated European symbols for their own purposes (Gruzinski, 1990). It is quite immaterial whether recently "revived" practices which are said to be quintessentially "Purhépecha" are genuine revivals of forgotten forms, or the inventions of organic intellectual leaderships of the kind I discussed in Chapter Three (Zárate Hernández, 1994). They become ontologically meaningful for people by being incorporated into practices which are oriented towards re-marking boundaries between "indigenous" communities and the wider society, asserting the dignity of indigenous identities, and pursuing political strategies based on the assertion of ethnic rights and the obligations of the state towards indigenous people. Yet objectified notions of "tradition" and "identity" are also linked to discourses about morality and order, in a way which is manipulated in factional claims to represent "legitimate" leadership

In other indigenous communities in Michoacán, such as Zipiajo in the *municipio* of Coeneo, east of Zacapu, sustained efforts over decades to adapt the civil-religious *cargo* system to accommodate economic change are now threatened by the unwillingness of young international migrants to meet the costs of sponsorship that they are best placed economically to bear (Moctezuma Yano, 1992: 222). In the case of Tarécuato, however, it is clear that some migrants were reluctant to put money into the *fiesta* because they were pursuing alternative strategies for acquiring status and power in the community. Migration has had a deeper impact on this community's class structure than that found by Dinerman in her study of the community of Huecorio, in the Lake Pátzcuaro region, at the start of the Eighties (Dinerman,

2 Within local *mestizo* culture, a folkloricized "Indian" style of dress is donned by children at various points in the annual public ceremonial cycle. Both the politicization and commoditization of ethnicity in the wider society have an impact on the practices of people who identify themselves as "indigenous."

1982). In Huecorio, a high rate of emigration primarily allowed households to close the "consumption gap," though it also led to a declining interest in maize farming and a self-amplifying dependence on migration. Gender, family and leadership roles were transformed without stimulating any increase in participation in the "extra-local decision-making process" (Dinerman, op.cit.: 82). In Tarécuato, in contrast, successful migrants have sought to capture political offices, and have converted themselves into a distinct "middle class," within a community which became deeply politicized in the late Eighties. Tarécuato belongs to the municipio of Santiago Tangamandapio, which was captured by the PRD in 1989 largely because of Tarécuato's mobilization of the indigenous *tenencias* against the *mestizo* PRI majority in the municipal *cabecera*, site of the sweater industry analyzed by Fiona Wilson (1990). Yet Tarécuato itself is increasingly divided.

Here, as in other regions of the country, possible local strategies were transformed by the new forms of state economic intervention and penetration of local social life established in the Seventies, which had both direct and indirect impacts on local politics. Holding public offices or positions in the corporate organizations offered access to the greatly enlarged resources of official development programs. This encouraged competition between emergent factions for the patronage and concessions now offered by official agencies and state-level politicians. At the same time, the economic results of the state-led development effort, including its improvement of transport systems and stimulation of new private sector activities, promoted changes in local class structures. The growing use of farm machinery and, in particular, the development of transport and trucking, provided new opportunities for the profitable local investment of capital in a rural economy in which maize production was declining in significance.

Similar developments have also transformed indigenous *municipios* elsewhere, like Zinacantán in Chiapas. Although Zinacantán's transformation into a community of corn farmers was, in fact, a product of agrarian reform, it did become the relatively closed and tightly knit social universe observed ethnographically in the 1960s in consequence, only to be transformed again into a more outwardly connected, class differentiated and politically conflictive community from the latter half of the 1970s onwards (Cancian, 1992). The subordination of the *municipio*'s hamlets to the head-town of Hteklum broke down, in a process of decentralization linked to the development of agrochemical-based farming, improvements in transport systems which drew Zinacantecos into commerce and regional work off-farm, and competition for the jobs and public investment resources, now concentrated under the control of PRODESCH, the Program for the Economic and Social Development of Chiapas (Collier, 1994). During the Seventies, Zinacanteco politics gravitated around the attempts of a rising generation of leaders to secure public resources for different communities by mobilizing followers through traditional relations of rank and patronage, some of the competing factions affiliating to the PAN in the course of the contest (Cancian, op.cit.: 137–42; Collier, op.cit.: 13). During the Eighties, however, Collier charts a fundamental shift in the nature of politics in Zinacantán, as the competing elites, each of which had seized the opportunities presented by state programs to invest in transport, settled their differences and united under the auspices of the PRI against their former lower class followers. Collier argues that this transition from a politics of rank, in which political relations structure economic relations, to a politics of class in which the reverse is true, reflects the way political leadership no longer depends on the ability to claim a large followership (op.cit.: 9–10).

This is reminiscent of Lomnitz-Adler's idea of a shift towards "plutocratic" relations, discussed in Chapter Three, but Collier relates the specific developments in Zinacantán to the growth of what he terms the "politics of exclusion," the general shift under Salinas of PRI politics away from "cooptative and remunerative strategies" towards a stance of total exclusion of the PRD opposition and coercive punishment of dissent, greatly facilitated in Chiapas by new state laws introduced by Governor González Gárrido from December 1988 onwards (op.cit.: 4–5; 17–18). The politics of exclusion have functioned in Chiapas along essentially similar lines to those I have already documented for the case of Michoacán, but Collier's analysis brings out some specific features of change in Zinacantán which may also be pertinent to Purhépecha communities.

He notes that the new trucker elites and youthful leadership of the PRD alike are "new men" who are products of changing relations of production and new articulations between the communities and the larger economic system. Both are challenging the "traditional" power of elders, the difference between the *priístas* and the *cardenistas* being based on the latter's ability to downplay "the differences separating them as young entrepreneurs from their semi-proletarian prospective rank and file," and to champion a collective struggle against the *priístas* as *ricos* allied to political corruption and impunity (Collier, op.cit.: 24). Yet the discourses of political legitimation and contestation of all the factions have consistently involved appeals to "tradition" and the cosmological boundary between the indigenous and *ladino* worlds. The latter includes a strong focus on the illegitimacy of attempts to defeat rivals by resort to the external, rather than community, system of "law," for which one should read not merely litigation, but the repressive use of fines and arbitrary jail sentences (Collier, op.cit.: 31–33). *Cardenistas* and *priístas* alike charge each other with violating *costumbre* and morality. Beneath this apparent continuity in the terms of legitimation, which implies a certain continuity of ritual observance, there was, however, a substantial change of practice: feeling themselves secure in their wealth, and enjoying a power which is guaranteed by the political center, the *priístas* no longer felt the need to maintain patterns of social exchange with lower class people or to gain their acquiescence by the mutual signalling of "respect."

Collier's observations on Zinacantán in the central highlands are intended to provide some insights into the roots of the Zapatista rebellion in the eastern lowlands, by indicating the low-level social resentments which are bred not merely from the direct effects of neoliberal economic policies and the politics of exclusion, but from the more subtle and insidious transformations of the quality of social relations which this political strategy promotes. The extent to which local politics will gravitate directly around class or around reassertions of collective "ethnic" dignity (which may also have class connotations) is, however, clearly influenced by a complex of factors, including the articulations between local elites and national power centres and patterns of migration. Kearney's analysis of the impacts of Mixtec migration to Northern Mexico and California, discussed in Chapter Four, deals with a case where a collective "ethnic identity" is created which did not exist before. The Mixtec migrant population finds itself confined to oppressive enclave situations which inhibit sharp differentiation amongst the migrant population, and the forces promoting the reconstitution of the community at the Mexican end are stronger than those blocking the process, although the local scene is not entirely conflict-free (Kearney, 1986). There are, however, other scenarios which again point us to the way neoliberal economics, the politics of exclusion and "chronic, contradictory, transnationalism" may foster social tensions. They are particularly disturbing scenarios, because they raise further questions about how tensions will manifest themselves in the practice of social life if the conditions established by the Salinas regime are maintained or even hardened under his successor, so that grievances are denied effective expression, let alone redress, through political representation and mediation.

Why the Mexican Is More Cabrón Than the Gringo

Socio-economic change in the peasant communities of the Ciénega de Chapala has created new points of tension in the fabric of social life, both within and between households. Community views on the legitimacy of social differentiation in terms of wealth and power turn on questions of the morality of different routes to good fortune. *Envidia* towards unusually successful migrants is a long-established pattern, along with tensions which arise from the way migration may effect a perceived social transformation of the person. Recent developments with regard to international migration have, however, provoked new contradictions which are exacerbating such intra-communal tensions.

The first problem is the way that, during the scramble to acquire documents to legalize under Simpson-Rodino, young people sometimes knowingly bought the documents of older villagers and even kinsmen, thereby depriving the latter of their own chance of legalization. Secondly, kin who "helped" novice migrants who secured legalization to make their first, undocumented, trip across the border began to press individuals for further payments for services rendered on their return. The backbiting involved in this process is escalating, since the legalized now seem increasingly privileged, even to their own kin, as the number of newcomers who are forced to enter without documents grows. Thirdly, the government's abandonment of the peasant farmer may affect relations between landholders who are permanently resident in the United States and those who remain. *Emigrado* members of the agrarian community were always liable to become objects of resentment, but long-term U.S. migrants with some capital are now amongst the few who can continue to be active in agriculture. The changes in Constitutional Article 27 make it legal for *emigrados* to hold *ejido* land even if they do not reside in the community. Although this is only *de jure* legitimation of a *de facto* situation in the Ciénega de Chapala, it may become more of an issue as poorer farmers go to the wall. Furthermore, some people at the top of the international migrant tree were already subject to criticism for profiting from their role as intermediaries at the time of the legalizations, at the expense of the families which are now increasingly dependent on the support of migrant children. Many feel that a privileged group of migrants, including those who make money in illicit ways, are likely to be among the principal beneficiaries of any privatization of the *ejidos*. Traditional attitudes to professional migration brokers have always been, at best, ambiguous. A smoldering resentment towards a larger range of actors is now apparent in these communities.

Given the state of agriculture in the Ciénega, the local future seems increasingly bleak to young people, but movement to the cities no longer offers an attractive alternative to international migration, and still more significantly, it no longer seems possible to achieve social mobility through education. Yet the young men who are abandoning their studies to leave for the North are not leaving with many illusions. Many talk vehemently about being second class workers and about the racial prejudices of Californians. In one sense this has sharpened their identification with Mexico, but the specific nature of the identification is important. I can best demonstrate this by examining the discursive forms through which young people's concept of "Mexicanness" is expressed.

There is a genre of story which people like to tell which begins with a statement of the form: "The Mexican is more *cabrón*[3] than the *gringo* because..." There follows an account of how the migrant managed to convince a foreman in the North that he really knew how to drive an alfalfa irrigating machine when he didn't. The guy believed him and gave him the work, with which he coped, after a few mishaps. This is the kind of story young Mexican male migrants tell to each other on ritualized occasions when they congregate together, on their own, listening to very loud *ranchero* or *norteño* music. Despite the fact that transnational ties are strong, the young migrants display the same patterns of keeping their own company as Vietnam Veterans: they cannot fully reintegrate themselves into a community which finds them a reproach to its own incapacity to generate a livelihood, and fears that they have brought back the vices of the North. Their stories are those of deracinated, isolated individuals, living on their wits, not stories which emphasize solidarity between Mexicans. As a worker of rural origin the migrant has not been

---

[3] The word "cabrón" is used in the way the inhabitants of the region of England where I grew up use the word "bugger." It can be denunciatory, admiring, or both simultaneously.

able to acquire real skills within Mexico, but still possesses this unique quality of being *listo*, which is Mexican, a product of harsh experience which cannot be taught in school. Mexicans, in the logic of this discourse, rescue their dignity by lying, cunningly, by not showing themselves *pendejo* ("a prick").

The peons and sharecroppers of the old Guaracha *hacienda* sought their identity in a "total" social institution which exploited them. They represented themselves as the real base of the enterprise, and expressed a thinly veiled contempt for the administrators and foremen who were their theoretical superiors and commanded substantial disciplinary power over them. This "oppositional discourse" was as prevalent among those who supported the *hacienda* against the land reformers associated with Cárdenas as the minority who fought for the land. All thereby succeeded in "dignifying" their productive efforts in Porfirian conditions of abuse and social humiliation, living lives which constantly violated their ideas of justice. Yet they did so by a profound form of self-alienation, in which the *hacienda* appropriated its peons as much as the peons appropriated the *hacienda*. In this case, the production of a "counter-identity" on the part of a subaltern group expressed itself in a form which did express a kind of class antagonism, but could readily be manipulated by elites.

The grandchildren of these peons and sharecroppers find their identity in a "national character," formed of necessity in a world of social and economic exclusion. In the example just given, identity forms in opposition to that of the "dominant Other," the *gringo*. It can, however, also form itself with reference to a series of alternative "Others," Indians, *chilangos* (people from Mexico City) or Argentines, taking on a segmental, regional or national character. Such oppositionally based identities may be collective and provide a foundation for solidary action. Some people do tell stories of how they received help from fellow migrants, and not necessarily Mexicans. One young man recounted how he had rescued a Salvadorean who had been beaten up and robbed on the street, and been incorporated into his family. Yet even this story of extraordinary contingency is not a traditional one of "the network accommodating the new arrival." The network itself has been shaken up by the need to compete for work and move into unfamiliar territory to find it. It has been traumatized by incidents of violence against some of its members by migrants from other communities fearful for their jobs, and by the experience of the legalizations already described. It is difficult to quantity the present balance between solidarity in adversity, which still frequently characterizes relations between strangers in the migrant setting, and the forces which set workers and kinsmen against each other, but that is precisely the point: the migrant experience *is* contradictory and ambiguous in multiple dimensions, most of which ultimately reflect the way that migrant workers have been affected by the transition to "flexible accumulation" and by the use of immigration law to regulate the terms of Mexican labor's participation in the U.S. labor market.

One thing seems clear. The *cabrón* discourse is individualist, albeit in a specific, generic sense. What helps Mexicans survive is something in the character of each and every real Mexican. Survival does not depend on Mexicans solidarizing with each other. Being selfless would, in fact, generally be *pendejo*. People who get on are not like that, and the only people who can afford to help others are those who will benefit themselves by doing so. Nevertheless, "being Mexican" has value. Something can be rescued from one's birthright, although it has little to do with the dignified official discourses of the state, the Mexican revolution, or the *políticos* of the opposition.

Such "realism" reflects the situation of the people concerned, who may be forced to compete with each other for access to work even if they also sometimes help others to obtain it. It also fits in with the kind of habitus I discussed earlier in the context of political demobilization and participation in social movements. It is difficult to know how deeply skeptical young rural people who currently see their only future as lying in international migration have become about political action and the possibilities of changing their own society. It is their fathers who are sitting around the villages all year with the time on their hands to devote to politics. Yet older people also manifest the same kind of tensions between ontologies, between a mode of life which depends on solidarity and struggle and one in which everyone should watch their backs, be wary of the envy of kin and neighbors, and recognize that the ambitious and clever who have their own agendas usually come out on top. The ebbs and flows of popular action in Mexico reflect the way that people privilege one or other of these understandings of the world in different conjunctures, as they evaluate what might be gained from different courses of action. Both are validated by experience and remain in unresolved tension.

As I showed in Chapter Three, local identities and political culture in the Ciénega de Chapala bear the historical imprint of the regional culture of social relations. The actors have to come to terms with the categories of regional hegemony in order to locate themselves within any vision of the nation and its history. They may seek to negotiate their dignity whilst implicitly recognizing some aspects of an identity which they accept as impediments to worth: according to context, to be a Mexican, to be a *mestizo*, to be an Indian because you are not fair-skinned, to be provincial, to not have private property, to not have education, may all be need to be balanced against other virtues. Yet these populations are also enmeshed in transnational class relations which are leading to further redefinitions of why people should be valued as Mexicans.

It seems important not to be too optimistic about the long-term consequences of these processes. The transnational community may remain fractured internally and hostile to members of other such communities, such as new undocumented migrants who appear to threaten the livelihoods of families which have settled in the United States. As I stressed throughout the previous chapter, identities and the boundaries of "community" are constructed in a way which responds to the forms of identification and value which others manipulate, including those who dispose of an official or socially recognized "power to name"(Bourdieu, 1991). Carving out a space of dignity and worth in a larger society may involve some acquiescence in hegemonic values even where the stance takes on an oppositional quality. Different subaltern groups may replicate hegemonic points of view in defining their relations with each other and, to use another term of Bourdieu's, "misrecognize" the causes of their misfortune. These issues are, I believe, of some significance for understanding the deeper implications of the impact of neoliberalism on rural Mexico.

Rural Reform, Political Closure and the Future of the Left

The achievements to date of neoliberal reform have been measured largely in terms of the deficiencies of the earlier model of statist development. These deficiencies should not be underestimated. Gabriel Zaid (1987) has provided some striking calculations on the failings of the "presidential economy." By 1987, the portion of government revenue spent on the functions of government (the executive branch of government, legislature and judiciary) had shrunk to 3%, 56% was public debt, and 41% non-governmental expenditure, including public enterprises. Since the debt itself was the product of public financing, 97% of expenditure could be attributed to the state's non-governmental role (op.cit.: 13). Between 1970 and 1983, public sector employment rose 550%, from 4.8% of the total population in employment to 20.4%. Federal employment increased in absolute terms from approximately 522,000 to 3,339,606 persons, only 16% of public employment being in the area of state and municipal administration (Zaid, op.cit.: 20). Between 1970 and 1986, public expenditure rose from 25% of the gross internal product to 45%, the fiscal deficit from 0% to 16%, the internal debt from 11% to 19%, and the external debt from 23% to 74% (op.cit.: 25). The productivity of public investment, measured in terms of growth of gross internal product relative to the share of investment in gross internal product, fell from 34% to zero.

Seen from a peasant perspective, statization helped rural society reproduce itself, but deprived the producer of real prospects for making a livelihood out of farming. As I stressed in Chapter Two, peasants were not the real beneficiaries of statization and the pattern of agricultural modernization introduced under state auspices during the Seventies, and we have already seen how state intervention promoted new forms of class differentiation at the local level. Even peasant families which possessed high quality irrigated land were forced to devise their own strategies for getting on in life. As I argued in Chapter Four, the statized system fostered an industrialization and internationalization of Mexican agriculture which integrated peasant reproduction through the *ejido* with agribusiness transformation in the United States. This enabled the United States to maintain its hegemony in the international food system at a time when that hegemony might have been undermined by the diffusion of new technology to peripheral countries.

Yet it remains unclear that things had to be that way. Even today an argument can be made for the continuing economic viability of family farming. During the era of statization, official attempts to restructure the social sector in Mexican agriculture were often based on the assumption that achieving greater efficiency depended on the realization of economies of scale in production itself. The formation of production cooperatives was favored as a means of securing that goal, but the fact that peasant production cooperatives in Mexico do not have a resounding history of success seems consistent with broader experience, in both socialist and capitalist countries. Yet as they contemplate the problem of reforming the farm sector of Eastern Europe, some economists associated with the World Bank are now arguing that, whilst producer cooperatives may fail to achieve either greater efficiency or greater equality and social justice, the case for promoting the development of large, highly mechanized, capitalist farms is weakened by the absence of significant scale economies in many branches of agricultural production and animal husbandry. Deininger (1993), for example, argues that the real scale economies in the farm sector lie in the purchase of inputs, industrial processing, marketing, and obtaining credit and marketing information, so that service cooperatives could provide a way forward for systems based on the family farm as the unit organizing production. Although service cooperatives confront similar problems to production cooperatives in terms of coping with "free-riders," establishing efficiency incentives, and devising adequate mechanisms for cost accounting and distributing income to individual members, Deininger argues that such problems can be overcome with appropriate systems of public vigilance, a well regulated policy of subsidies and provision of public goods, and educational programs to promote responsibility. The possibility of achieving benign forms of public regulation might appear somewhat utopian in the Mexican context, but Deininger's argument does at least indicate the existence of serious alternative policy options within a framework orientated by criteria of economic efficiency.

There may therefore be some merit to the arguments currently being made to peasants by representatives of the bureaucratic agencies of neoliberal reform in the countryside: small producers could fortify themselves by reorganizing cooperatively, and might, in at least some cases, be able to derive benefits from new forms of association with private capital. Such rhetoric must, however, be tempered by a realistic appraisal of the type and degree of government support which peasants need to realize "autonomy" as economic actors, and of the way political disempowerment and the impact of existing class relations has influenced the apparent economic "disorganization" of many peasant communities. It is clearly unrealistic to talk in a rhetorical manner about new kinds of associations between the social and private sectors in abstraction from the many imperfections which exist in regional, national and international markets for agricultural products, farm inputs and farm credit. These market imperfections are expressions of evolving power relations in transnational space, but they are also reflections of the specific conditions of development of capitalist relations within Mexico's "bipolar" agrarian structure. Within that structure the *ejido* became integral to the accumulation strategies of a variety of capitalist actors. In this sense, it might be argued that past state intervention also reduced the ability of the capitalist sector in Mexican agriculture to adapt dynamically to changing economic conditions.

The debate about *ejido* reform should not, however, be conducted in purely technocratic and productionist terms. It has yet to be established that the social costs of leaving rural development to the free operation of international market forces are lower than the economic benefits to the nation of neoliberal "shock therapy," particularly given the very tight integration with the economy of the United States for which Mexican neoliberalism has opted, somewhat in contrast to the strategy of developing regional markets within Latin America pursued by Brazil and other South American countries. PROCAMPO might be seen as a belated attempt to introduce mechanisms to promote a cushioned transition, but I have argued that, leaving its political motivations aside, its impact on rural poverty and the plight of small producers will be limited. The restriction of cross-border movement of labor by the United States (within a global economy in which barriers to capital movements have been further reduced) limits the possibilities of "market forces" promoting upward movement of wages within Mexico, and the social situations now facing migrants within the United States itself further strengthen the case for instituting rural reform in Mexico within a framework of coherent national planning and more selective state intervention to reduce sudden social dislocations.

Such a framework would have to recognize the specificities of particular regions and the synergies which bind local economies into wider systems. Thought could be given to developing alternative sources of employment, and to supporting innovations in production and commercialization which would bring the best returns relative to costs, including social and environmental costs. Given the chaotic nature of land tenure and the practical difficulties facing the officials implementing the PROCEDE process at the local level, there are few guarantees that any process of restructuring of agrarian communities which ensues from the reform of Article 27 will meet the criteria of either social justice or greater economic efficiency. Yet even within these constraints, the state could do more to assist potentially viable producers to succeed in the market: giving financial and organizational support to service cooperatives would be one way of achieving that goal. It could also do much more to compensate the losers in processes of restructuring, by fostering conditions which provide young people who lose access to land with decently paid jobs in rural areas, and by providing older people who abandon their rights in the *ejidos* with social welfare benefits. Ensuring national "food sovereignty" is not the only reason for wishing to help smaller producers survive and prosper where it is possible for them to do so in the medium-term. Planning change in rural production and employment patterns would be entirely compatible with allowing greater scope to private enterprise: government would merely have to guide the market, provide start-up capital, and use differential subsidies and inducements to encourage private sector actors, including banks, to take a long-term view. This is not simply a matter of allowing for the immediate logic of profit maximization to be overridden by social cost-benefit calculations, but a question of taking a more strategic view of precisely where Mexico's long-term comparative advantages lie.

Mexico's ability to pursue such a strategy is, however, now seriously impeded by the NAFTA. Furthermore, the simple case for planning which I have just presented and the case for "unfettered market forces" alike abstract from the way social and political power enter into the determination of what actually happens on the ground. The failures of past state intervention reflect the particular relations between state and civil society in Mexico. The present role of the state reflects the new perspectives of a technocratic elite allied to transnational capital, and it is arguably just as interventionist, albeit in different ways. It now seems likely that the politics of exclusion and a process of economic transformation without political reform will be maintained after Salinas, although the long-term political consequences of Ernesto Zedillo's victory in the presidential elections of 1994 remain to be seen. Agriculture was the second largest item in the new administration's first budget plan, after education, and PRONASOL's budget was to be increased by over 7%, to U.S.$3.1 billion, in 1995, although the 4.7% increase in the fourth largest item in the budget, spending of U.S.$3.5 billion on the armed services and other security forces, was less encouraging (*Latin American Weekly Report*, WR-94-49: 578). In the event, however, the peso crisis of December 1994 forced the Zedillo government to introduce a new austerity package, and put its ability even to maintain past levels of spending on social programs in serious doubt.

The PRI's electoral victory on August 21st, 1994, was judged "convincing enough" by the international financial community. At the end of a week in which Zedillo's claimed share of the poll had moved back and forth across the 50% mark, the value of Mexican stocks rose in international markets and financial analysts confidently predicted a renewal of growth and foreign investment. There was even talk of a "new Mexican economic miracle" now that the political conditions for continuing the process of deregulation had been secured, with further privatization of the activities of the state oil company PEMEX high on foreign agendas.

Some financial commentators accepted that the cleanness of the elections was distinctly relative. A few expressed hopes for future judicial and political reform. Business's main concern, however, was simply that the PRI's vote was big enough to make continuity of economic policy viable, and that the PRD would not be able to claim it had been robbed of victory by the defects in the electoral process reported by Mexican and foreign monitors. The elections seemed to demonstrate the continuing viability of the strategy which ran through the entire Salinas sexennial: backstage negotiation with the PAN and marginalization of the PRD. With less than 17% of the vote on official turnout figures of 77.7%—the highest in Mexican history—Cuauhtémoc Cárdenas was not well placed to mount his call for a campaign of civil disobedience to force new elections.

To judge from the reports of the Mexican Alianza Cívica (Civic Alliance) group, the PRI's 1994 electoral triumph was achieved by familiar means. Before election day itself, the PRI enjoyed the advantages already discussed in Chapter Three, in particular its ability to utilize the resources of government for party political purposes. On the day, sixty-five per cent of Alianza Cívica observers recorded that some voters turned up to their polling stations to find their names were not on the register, and were sent to "special" voting stations set up to accommodate people who needed to vote outside their place of residence. They then found that the limit of three hundred persons who could vote in such stations—agreed upon before the elections by all parties in order to prevent fraud—had already been reached (*The Independent*, August 24th and 25th, 1994). This latest variation on the "crazy mouse" (*ratón loco*) technique of fraud was accompanied by the usual "carrousels" of PRI voters, and, according to the monitors, by a substantial amount of direct voter intimidation and pressure from officials and union leaders. Alianza Cívica reported that secrecy of the vote was denied in a third of polling stations. Ten per cent of its observers reported seeing unregistered people voting, eight per cent observed the same people vote twice, and the procedures for marking voters' fingers with indelible ink were circumvented in a similar number of cases (ibid.). There were many reports of personation (*Mexico and NAFTA Report* RM-94-09: 3).

In the case of the gubernatorial contest in Chiapas, held on the same day as the presidential elections, Alianza Cívica judged the victor to be the PRD candidate, Amado Avendaño, with 44.21% to the PRI's 42.57%. Avendaño had been seriously injured during the campaign when a truck collided with his car. Despite reports of more than three hundred irregularities, the State Electoral Commission's preliminary figures awarded the contest to the PRI on a margin of 50.46% to 34.94% (*The Observer*, August 28th, 1994). Yet whatever the truth of the matter in Chiapas, the fact remained that the PRD's national vote could not convincingly be turned into a majority on the basis of "irregularities" on election day. Even from the viewpoint of the combined opposition, any lack of legitimacy in the PRI's victory on this occasion would have to be ascribed principally to the fundamental inequality in the positions of the party of the state and its challengers before voting took place.

The diminishing vigor of the later stages of the campaign of the PAN's Diego Fernández Cevallos and the intemperate haste with which Ernesto Zedillo claimed his triumph do suggest that ruling circles were confident that they had engineered a workable result before August 21st. The fact that the PRI could no longer command the overwhelming majority of the popular vote which it had enjoyed before 1988 was mitigated by three principle factors: by the absolute number of votes claimed by Zedillo on the unusually high turnout, by the fact that his party secured a strong majority in both houses of Congress, and by the fact that the PRI and PAN votes combined did secure an apparently impressive popular majority against the PRD. Whether or not Zedillo allows the PAN a greater participation in government, the latter seems to be drawn towards tacit alliance with the PRI simply by the logic of its own position, as a party which remains unlikely to secure a national majority on its own.

Commentators who interpreted the result as a ringing endorsement of neoliberal policies seem, however, to have little justification for doing so. It cannot be assumed that people see voting for the PAN as a vote for neoliberalism. The party's association with private enterprise and private property is not necessarily seen as equivalent to the neoliberal package by more economically nationalistic small business voters. It may not even be seen as a vote for "capitalism" by lower class *panistas*. The PAN's economic and social policies may also be a less significant electoral asset than its projection of an image of rectitude, and it is interesting to note that some PAN reverses in Michoacán, such as the loss of control of Zamora in the 1992 municipal elections, were associated with a tarnishing of that image. We should also not ignore the PAN's ability to garner the votes of those who simply wish to reject the PRI. Even taking a charitable view of the likely gap between the PRI's official vote and real voter preferences, many of those who did vote for the party of the state willingly may have been motivated more by the fear of violence and disorder, or by dissatisfaction with the alternatives on offer, than by positive enthusiasm for neoliberal reforms. Others voted PRI because it was in their immediate interests to do so, as beneficiaries of the residual structure of patronage networks and cliques controlling career advancement which still lie at the core of an organization which is much more than a political party. It is, of course, true that some voters do support neoliberal policies enthusiastically, and that many ordinary Mexicans genuinely believe that the PRI best serves the national interest. They do not, however, seem to come close to being a majority of the electorate.

All this should be cause for concern within ruling circles, and might force Zedillo to work harder on sustaining the alliance with the PAN. Even before the new economic crisis hit, the sweetness of electoral victory had been diminished by the subsequent assassination of PRI General Secretary José Francisco Ruiz Massieu. The aftermath of this event provided further public evidence of the depth of the divisions within the political class, of the links between politicians and the drug cartels, and of the regime's refusal or incapacity to let legal due process play its proper role in regulating these new tendencies towards political violence. This dark side of the neoliberal transition may yet prove fatal to the continuity of the PRI system, despite its adeptness in the field of the micro-politics of control.[4] Yet as far as the Center-Left opposition is concerned, the outcome of the 1994 elections seems most suggestive of the scenario for Mexico's political future which Cornelius, Gentleman and Smith termed "political closure" (Cornelius et al, 1989: 36–45), confirming Neil Harvey's suggestion that the different scenarios in their

---

4 The ties between politics and drugs suggest ways in which new forms of local power may consolidate themselves among provincial constituencies deprived of significant economic support from the centre, but the role of these "illicit" forms of capital accumulation also takes on a broader significance in an era of globalized capitalism. As the example of Eastern Europe again demonstrates, moving money into international financial circuits permits enterprises built on extra-legal foundations to "sanitize" themselves with a facility unknown in earlier periods. This suggests that the "dark side" is an integral consequence of the new global structures of capitalist accumulation, and a central option for peripheral actors seeking to establish a place for themselves in the restructured world capitalist order.

model need not emerge as discrete alternatives (Harvey, 1993: 5). The election result may give the neoliberal faction in control of the state sufficient confidence to build on the exclusionary and coercive dimensions of *salinista* political strategy to stifle any further popular resistance to neoliberal economic restructuring, despite the fact that the absolute number of Mexicans supporting the PRD opposition is hardly insignificant, even taking the official results at face value. The election result may be used to legitimate an authoritarian politics based on the ("democratic") tyranny of the "silent majority" (Bartra, 1992: 71–77), marginalizing substantial sectors of the working classes in general, and the rural population in particular.

Such a position might well receive support from those elements of the intellectual elite, headed by Octavio Paz, who have recently been decrying all opposition to neoliberal reform as the work of a cabal of ideologically diverse "enemies of modernity" united only by their links to Mexico's barbarous past. Whether it is a wise policy, in the sense that the politics of exclusion may open further spaces for more radical anti-regime movements like the EZLN, must remain an open question at the time of writing. By the end of the sexennial, it was clear that the EZLN rebellion had become the catalyst for a new wave of peasant militancy, not only in Chiapas but in neighboring areas, and that many *campesinos* in other parts of the country, including Michoacán, sympathized with the movement, even if their support was entirely passive and they saw violence as an unrealistic option. Yet although the EZLN had become a symbolic point of reference for a diversity of socially heterogeneous groups and movements, it is important to recognize that the rebellion also provoked a backlash—often manifested in anti-Indian sentiment—in more urbanized regions of the country, particularly in the North, which may well have contributed to the PRI's electoral success. What seems much clearer is that the 1994 election may prove a fatal reverse for the Center-Left position represented by Cuauhtémoc Cárdenas, whose party began to manifest what may prove irreversible tendencies towards division and fragmentation within weeks of the result.

Commenting on the development of the Mexican Left between 1988 and 1991, Barry Carr tentatively suggested that the growth of cross-border party organization, and the NAFTA's promotion of "horizontal relations between labor, community, ecological and political activists," might "partly compensate for the erosion of the Left's 'socialist identity' over the last three years" (Carr, 1993: 98). Assuming that a regime based the informal alliance of the PRI and the PAN can maintain itself in power without provoking popular violence on a scale capable of derailing the neoliberal economic program, and that the program itself does not collapse as a result of the contradictions inherent in its dependence on mobile transnational capital and volatile international financial markets, there would be a case for the Left to follow through the logic of Carr's suggestion, and to concentrate its energies on the social problems created by neoliberalism and transnationalization. As we have seen, the *neocardenista* effort in California might have had greater success if it had complemented its campaign for democratization in Mexico with a greater concern for the immediate and strategic social issues of concern to the Mexican community in the United States. Yet perhaps more than any other Left party in Latin America, the PRD has found it difficult to transcend the ambiguous relationship between socialism and the statist model of development advanced under populist auspices.

The PRD often seems to be engaged in a futile attempt to compete head-on with the PRI, by projecting itself as an alternative which will restore what, from the popular standpoint, seems the positive, inclusionary side of the old populist-corporatist model. The Salinas regime readily defeated opposition attempts to create rival organizations of corporatist stamp, by the simple expedient of denying them official recognition. This was particularly evident in the case of the rival peasant organizations which the PRD promoted during the Salinas administration under the umbrella of the Democratic Peasant Confederation. Few people who already belonged to an "official" organization saw any future in joining one which was denied negotiating rights, if its terms of reference were essentially identical to official organizations, which did at least offer theoretical prospects of negotiating benefits for their members. Little serious attempt was made to give voice to rural workers marginalized by established corporate arrangements. The regional leadership of the PRD in the Ciénega de Chapala, for example, rapidly moved to stop some of its militants organizing invasions of land to be leased on concession following the fall in the water level in Lake Chapala in 1990–91. Militant organizations with different tactics and agendas, such as the *El Barzón* movement, had greater impact precisely because they addressed immediate problems in a way which broke out of the limits set by official channels of representation. Furthermore, the disillusion of the PRD's base increased as its failure to succeed in the game of representation of popular interests drew it towards using "traditional" tactics of political control to maintain its internal coherence.

It is true that the PRD has been able to secure the allegiance of militant grassroots leaderships emerging at the local level in response to socio-economic and generational change, as witnessed by the role of the Zinacantán leaders discussed by Collier and similar change agents, such as the catechists who have been at the cutting edge of radical indigenous politics in southern Mexico and Central America. Nevertheless, the party's focus on electoral politics has limited the forms of grassroots mobilization it has been able to foster, proved of limited viability given the regime's relative success in the practice of the politics of exclusion, and produced the additional contradictions which I discussed in Chapter Three.

The Left's failure to articulate a clear and convincing alternative to neoliberal policies was also a factor in the regime's survival. Yet formulation of clear alternatives is fraught with pitfalls. It is not clear that a strategy of building links with social movements, and allowing the development of the latter to serve as the basis for consolidating opposition politics, is likely to pay rapid dividends, given the regime's proven ability to establish its own selective links with the movements and cut them off from the political opposition. A simple move leftwards towards a more intransigent opposition to capitalism and advocacy of the interests of the poor would alienate some existing support, other things being equal. In the wake of the widespread experience of military rule, it is not surprising that the Latin American Left has, in general, tended to reevaluate its attitude to "liberal democracy," and put political reform within that framework at the top of its agenda during the Eighties, but the PRD's inability to secure either political reform or any prospects for an improvement in the lives of its lower class supporters puts it in the worst of positions. It is frequently argued, however, that the root of the problem confronting the Left today, not simply in Latin America, but globally, is structural rather than conjunctural, the transition to "postindustrial society" and the declining significance of "organized labor" and the classical factory proletariat under conditions of technological change and a capitalist regime of "flexible accumulation."

The old class politics assumed that the social majority would develop a clear class identity, rooted in material conditions of life, which could be fostered by revolutionary politics. We have seen, however, that one type of "class antagonism," concerned with the difference between those who are wealthy and those who are not, remains politically salient in a variety of contexts, in both Mexico and the United States, and does not depend on the precise nature of the labor process in which poorer people are involved. It is also clear that the development of collective organization in various guises remains integral to the struggles of many different kinds of workers under late capitalist conditions, including migrant workers. "Small struggles" to improve the terms of labor's exploitation by capital continue to develop, without any stimulus from political parties, on the part of diverse actors such as women employees in *maquiladoras* and immigrant construction workers in San Diego (Dwyer, 1994: 123–27).

On the debit side, many of these everyday struggles in defence of people's interests as workers have a tendency to set worker against worker. Long-established immigrants in the United States whose security has been undermined by *rodinos* and their undocumented kin and *paisanos* may blame the newcomers for their problems, rather than employers who seek to cheapen their labor costs or the political architects of immigration reform, let alone see the actions of both these agents as expressions of the deeper logic of a global economy organized on a capitalist basis. Although some established workers have seen the formation of new unions as a way of defending wages (and have leaders who are eager to avoid the mistake of leaving the undocumented outside the framework of organized labor), others have sought individual solutions to immediate economic problems, which, as I noted earlier, have ironically often placed them more on a par with undocumented entrants. Flexible accumulation fosters the fragmentation of the working classes, and does so with a vengeance when it is coupled with the kind of hegemonic politics I discussed in the previous chapter, promoting the interiorization of racial models of "difference" on the part of members of subaltern groups. Hegemonic systems often structure the forms which counter-hegemonic movements take in very significant ways, as we saw in Charles Hale's argument about how the politics of indigenous identity today can embody the fundamental premises of state and nation-building.

As David Harvey has argued in his critique of postmodernist celebration of "identity politics" and "fragmentation," no coherent politics can be built on:

> accepting the reifications and partitionings, actually celebrating the activity of masking and cover-up, all the fetishisms of locality, place and social grouping, while denying that kind of meta-theory which can grasp the political-economic processes (money flows, international divisions of labor, financial markets and the like) that are becoming ever more universalizing in their depth, intensity, reach and power over daily life (Harvey, 1989: 116–17).

A viable Left politics cannot, however, be built simply on the rationalist explanation of the common political-economic causes of the problems experienced by fragmented working classes. It must involve concrete proposals for reconciling conflictive interests, in the sense of providing each group with some amelioration of its material and existential problems, within the framework of, minimally, an overall readjustment of the share of national income allocated to capital and labor. The problem is that it may not be possible to provide particular groups with precisely what they want. *Campesinos* who would like to continue pursuing a life-style of family farming with large government subsidies may fall into this category.

The traditional politics of the Left rested heavily on a particular vision of industrial utopia, with the state playing a central role in creating the material conditions for distributive equality, through public ownership and planning of production. Existing social movements were to be won for the party line and subjected to the discipline of the vanguard political organization. An alternative to vanguardism is for a Left party to build itself on the basis of "dual militancy" in social movements and the party, allowing different tendencies to organize themselves within it, on the lines of the Brazilian *Partido dos Trabalhadores*. Brazil offered a more favorable context for such a development than Mexico, because of the way the specific conditions created by military rule influenced the strengthening of social movements. The PRD's relatively "external" relationship to social movements has not helped it to develop the relatively healthy kind of conflict emerging from the base, and the productive clashes between different tendencies tolerated within the party, which fortified rather than weakened the PT.

Even the PT has not been able to purge clientalism and personalism entirely from its internal practice (Moreira Alves, 1993: 234), which is scarcely surprising given the social reality from which it has sprung. It was also forced to compromise on policy in seeking the support of other parties in the electoral arena in the 1989 Presidential Election run-off, and toned down its radical image substantially in the hope of calming the fears of Brazilian and foreign business in 1994. Nevertheless, the PT model does suggest ways in which a focus on mediating and coordinating social movements and labor organizations, without attempting to ride roughshod over them, might offer the basis for broadening popular unity. The PT approach is to bolster the ability of different groups to renegotiate their relations with capital and the state in the first instance, and build social reform from the bottom up.

In Mexico, the PRD faces the problem that the state itself has been able to block its access to key social movements, whilst the regime has also had some, though more limited, success in countering its attempt to mobilize the disenfranchised Mexican population north of the border. Neoliberal policies do, however, create space for new initiatives in the field of cross-border links, if the opposition can focus on the wider social problems related to economic integration, and fight on terrain in which there is some immediate prospect of demonstrating not merely the desirability of alternative policies, but the prospect of producing tangible gains for working people. The striking fall in the share of national income accruing to labor in the United States as capitalist restructuring proceeds clearly creates problems for transnational Left politics, since it can reinforce anti-immigrant sentiment, but it also presents opportunities for those who see the NAFTA combined with control of Mexican migration as an attack on the working classes of three countries.

The Left are often accused of economism as theoreticians, but there is something to be said at the present moment for a strong dash of economism and "trade union" consciousness. It no longer makes sense to pretend that traditional models of state ownership and economic intervention provide an alternative to internationalization of the economy, which advanced considerably during the era of statist development, or guarantee any equitable distribution of the fruits of economic growth among the Mexican people. Populism is not socialism, and recognition of the transnational character of contemporary class relations should refocus attention on the issue at the heart of socialism, that gross economic inequality limits the meaning of the formal freedoms which citizens enjoy, even in liberal democracies.

The "economic miracles" achieved by the "Asian Tigers" were produced by authoritarian regimes, and caused enormous environmental devastation. Nevertheless, economic success has allowed substantial improvements in the living standards of working people in countries like South Korea. I suggested in my introduction to this book that the differences between Mexico and these Asian countries are not simply ones of geographical and demographic scale. The Mexican brand of neoliberalism is reinforcing rather than mitigating these differences. If the Left fails to learn the lessons of recent years, and large numbers of Mexicans are left to interiorize the values of late capitalism without being able to share the fruits of any economic progress that may eventually be achieved, the scenarios for Mexico's future may be grim but undramatic: low-intensity violence, a further erosion of the fabric of social relations, and a growth of the social pathologies which afflict the metropolitan world. As many Michoacán *campesinos* realize, we can already glimpse one image of the neoliberal future. It is called South Central Los Angeles.

Bibliography

Alcocer V., Jorgé. 1991. "Alarma agropecuaria." *Proceso* No. 763, 17th June 1991.

Alvarez, Robert R. Jr. 1987. *Familia: Migration and Adaptation in Baja and Alta California 1800–1975*. Berkeley: University of California Press.

Anderson, Benedict. 1991. *Imagined Communities: Reflections on the Origins and Spread of Nationalism*. 2nd Edition. London: Verso.

Anderson, Benedict. 1992. "The New World Disorder." *New Left Review* 193: 3–13.

Appadurai, Arjun. 1990. "Disjuncture and Difference in the Global Cultural Economy," in Mike Featherstone, ed., *Global Culture: Nationalism, Globalization and Modernity*. Pp. 295–310. London: Sage Publications.

Arce, Alberto. 1993. *Negotiating Agricultural Development: Entanglements of Bureaucrats and Rural Producers in Western Mexico*. Wageningen Studies in Sociology No. 34. Wageningen: Agricultural University Wageningen.

Arias, Patricia and Jorge Durand. 1988. "Santa María de las Esferas." *Sociedad y Estado* (CISMoS, Guadalajara) 1: 5–16

Arrom, Silvia Marina. 1985. *The Women of Mexico City, 1790–1857*. Berkeley: University of California Press.

Arroyo Alejandre, Jesús. 1986. *Emigración rural de fuerza de trabajo en el Occidente-Centro de México: una contribución de información básica para su análisis*. Cuadernos de Difusión Científica 6. Guadalajara: Universidad de Guadalajara.

Auletta, Ken. 1982. *The Underclass*. New York: Vintage Books.

Barkin, David and Blanca Suarez. 1985. *El fin de la autosuficiencia alimentaria*. México, D.F.: Centro de Ecodesarrollo/Ediciones Océano, S.A.

Barraclough, Solon. 1992. "Algunas cuestiones sobre las implicaciones del TLC en el México rural," in Cuauhtémoc González, ed., *El Sector Agropecuario Mexicano Frente al Tratado de Libre Comercio*. Pp. 13–39. Mexico, D.F.: Universidad Nacional Autónoma de México and Universidad Autónoma de Chapingo.

Barragán López, Esteban. 1990. *Más allá de los caminos: los rancheros del Potrero de Herrera*. Zamora: El Colegio de Michoacán.

Bartra, Armando. 1985. *Los herederos de Zapata: movimientos campesinos posrevolucionarios en México*. México, D.F.: Ediciones Era.

Bartra, Roger. 1992. *The Imaginary Networks of Political Power*. New Brunswick, N.J.: Rutgers University Press.

Becker, Marjorie. 1987. "Black and White and Color: Cardenismo and the Search for a Campesino Ideology." *Comparative Studies in Society and History* 29: 453–65.

Blauert, Jutta and Marta Guidi. 1992. "Strategies for Autochthonous Development: Two Initiatives in Rural Oaxaca, Mexico," in Dharam Ghai and Jessica M. Vivian, eds., *Grassroots Environmental Action: People's Participation in Sustainable Development*. Pp. 188–220. London and New York: Routledge.

Bonfil Batalla, Guillermo. 1990. *México profundo: una civilización negada*. México, D.F.: Editorial Grijalbo.

Bossen, Laurel H. 1984. *The Redivision of Labor: Women and Economic Choice in Four Guatemalan Communities*. Albany: The State University of New York.

Bourdieu, Pierre. 1991. *Language and Symbolic Power*. Cambridge: Polity Press.

Browner, Carole and Ellen Lewis. 1982. "Female Altruism Reconsidered: the Virgin Mary as Economic Woman." *American Ethnologist* 9: 61–75.

Bustamante, Jorge. 1988. "Undocumented Migration: Research Findings and Policy Options," in Riordan Roett, ed., *Mexico and the United States: Managing the Relationship*. Pp. 109–33. Boulder: Westview Press.

Bustamante, Jorge. 1992. "La migración indocumentada de México a Estados Unidos vista desde la perspectiva de análisis de 'series de tiempo'." *COLEF I, Vol. III: Frontera y Migraciones*. Pp. 7–34. Tijuana: El Colegio de la Frontera Norte and Universidad Autónoma de Ciudad Juárez.

Buttel, Frederick H. 1990. "Biotechnology and Agricultural Development in the Third World," in Henry Bernestein, Ben Crow, Maureen MacKintosh and Charlotte Martin, eds., *The Food Question: Profits versus People?* Pp. 163–180. London: Earthscan Publications.

Calva, José Luis. 1991a. "Funciones del sector agropecuario en el futuro de la economía nacional," in Juan Pablo Arroyo Ortiz, coord., *El sector agropecuario en el futuro de la economía mexicana*. Pp. 40–52. México, D.F.: Universidad Nacional Autónoma de México, Facultad de Economía.

Calva, José Luis. 1991b. "Política económica para el sector agropecuario," in Juan Pablo Arroyo Ortiz, coord., *El sector agropecuario en el futuro de la economía mexicana*. Pp. 3–13. México, D.F.: Universidad Nacional Autónoma de México, Facultad de Economía.

Campbell, Howard. 1993. "Tradition and the New Social Movements: the Politics of Isthmus Zapotec Culture." *Latin American Perspectives* 20(3): 83–97.

Cancian, Frank. 1992. *The Decline of Community in Zinacantán: Economy, Public Life, and Social Stratification, 1960–1987*. Stanford: Stanford University Press.

Carlos, Manuel Luis, Juan José Gutiérrez and Gaspar Real. 1994. "An Assessment of Processes and Outcomes of Mexican Ejidal Reform: Ejidal Communities of the State of Querétaro in a Comparative Ethnographic Analysis." Paper presented in Session 053/MEX02 Panel at the XVIII International Congress of the Latin American Studies Association, Atlanta, Georgia, March 10th–12th 1994.

Carr, Barry. 1993. "Mexico: the Perils of Unity and the Challenge of Modernization," in Barry Carr and Steve Ellner, eds., *The Latin American Left: From the Fall of Allende to Perestroika*. Pp. 83–99. Latin American Perspectives Series, No. 11. Boulder, Col. and London: Westview Press and Latin American Bureau.

CEPAL (Comisión Económica para América Latina y el Caribe). 1992. *Equidad y transformación productiva: un enfoque integrado*. Santiago de Chile: United Nations Economic Commission for Latin America and the Caribbean.

Chant, Sylvia. 1985. "Family Formation and Female Roles in Querétaro, Mexico." *Bulletin of Latin American Research* 4(1): 17–32.

Chant, Sylvia. 1994. "Women, Work and Household Survival Strategies in Mexico, 1982–1992: Past Trends, Current Tendencies and Future Research." *Bulletin of Latin American Research* 13(2): 203–33.

Collier, George A. 1994. "The New Politics of Exclusion: Antecedents to the Rebellion in Mexico." *Dialectical Anthropology* 19(1): 1–43.

Cook, Roberta, Carlos Benito, James Matson, David Runsten, Kenneth Shwedel and Timothy Taylor. 1991. *Implications of the North American Free Trade Agreement (NAFTA) for the U.S. Horticultural Sector*, in Vol. IV, *Fruit and Vegetable Issues*, of *NAFTA: Effects on Agriculture*. Park Ridge, Illinois: American Farm Bureau Research Foundation.

Cooper, Marc. 1991. "Somos nosotros o ellos, dicen agentes de Los Angeles, llena de negros y latinos." *Proceso* 759, 20th May 1991: 38–47.

Cornelius, Wayne A. 1990. "Los migrantes de la crisis: el nuevo perfil de la migración de mano de obra mexicana a California en los años ochenta," in Gail Mummert, ed., *Población y trabajo en contextos regionales*. Pp. 103–41. Zamora: El Colegio de Michoacán.

Cornelius, Wayne A. 1992. "The Politics and Economics of Reforming the *Ejido* Sector in Mexico: an Overview and Research Agenda." *LASA Forum* XXIII(3): 3–10.

Cornelius, Wayne A. and Ricardo Anzaldúa Montoya, eds. 1983. *America's New Immigration Law: Origins, Rationales and Potential Consequences*. Monographs Series, No. 11. La Jolla: Center for U.S.-Mexican Studies, University of California, San Diego.

Cornelius, Wayne A., Judith Gentleman and Peter H. Smith. 1989. "The Dynamics of Political Change in Mexico," in Wayne A. Cornelius, Judith Gentleman and Peter H. Smith, eds., *Mexico's Alternative Political Futures*. La Jolla: Center for U.S.-Mexican Studies, University of California at San Diego.

Cross, Henry E. and Jorge A. Sandos. 1981. *Across the Border: Rural Development in Mexico and Recent Migration to the United States*. Berkeley: Institute of Government Studies, University of California.

DaMatta, Roberto. 1991. *Carnivals, Rogues and Heroes: An Interpretation of the Brazilian Dilemma*. Notre Dame and London: University of Notre Dame Press.

Davis, Mike. 1990. *City of Quartz*. London and New York: Verso.

Davis, Mike. 1993a. "Who killed LA? A Political Autopsy." *New Left Review* 197: 9–28.

Davis, Mike. 1993b. "Who Killed LA? Part II: the Verdict is Given." *New Left Review* 199: 29–54.

Deininger, Klaus W. 1993. *Cooperatives and the Breakup of Large Mechanized Farms: Theoretical Perspectives and Empirical Evidence*. World Bank Discussion Papers No. 218. Washington, D.C.: The World Bank.

De la Peña, Guillermo 1986. "Poder local, poder regional: perspectivas socioantropológicas," in J. Padua and A. Vanneph, eds., *Poder Local, Poder Regional*. Pp. 275–6. México, D.F.: El Colegio de México/CEMCA.

Deutsch, Sarah. 1987. *No Separate Refuge: Culture, Class and Gender on an Anglo-Hispanic Frontier in the American Southwest, 1880–1940*. New York and Oxford: Oxford University Press.

Dinerman, Ina R. 1982. *Migrants and Stay-at-Homes: a comparative study of rural Migration from Michoacán, Mexico*. Monograph Series No.5. La Jolla: Center for U.S.-Mexican Studies, University of California, San Diego.

Dresser, Denise. 1991. *Neopopulist Solutions to Neoliberal Problems: Mexico's National Solidarity Program*. La Jolla: Center for U.S.-Mexican Studies, University of California, San Diego.

Dresser, Denise. 1993. "Exporting Conflict: Transboundary Consequences of Mexican Politics," in Abraham F. Lowenthal and Katrina Burgess, eds., *The California-Mexico Connection*. Pp. 82–112. Stanford: Stanford University Press.

Dunkerley, James. 1994. *The Pacification of Central America*. London: Verso.

Durand, Jorge and Douglas S. Massey. 1992. "Mexican Migration to the United States: a Critical Review." *Latin American Research Review* 27(2): 3–42.

Dwer, Augusta. 1994. *On the Line: Life on the US-Mexican Border*. London: Latin American Bureau.

Ehlers, Tracy Bachrach. 1990. *Silent Looms: Women and Production in a Guatemalan Town*. Westview Special Studies on Latin America and the Caribbean. Boulder: Westview Press.

Eisenstadt, Todd A. and Cathryn L. Thorup. 1994. *Caring Capacity versus Carrying Capacity: Community Responses to Mexican Immigration in San Diego's North County*. La Jolla: Center for U.S.-Mexican Studies, University of California, San Diego.

Escalante, Roberto. 1993. "La agricultura mexicana en los noventa." Paper presented to the FAO Seminar on Structural Adjustment and Agriculture in Latin America in the Eighties, Institute of Latin American Studies, London, 22nd to 24th September, 1993.

Escobar Lapatí, Agustín. 1988. "The Rise and Fall of an Urban Labour Market: Economic crisis and the Fate of Small-scale Workshops in Guadalajara, Mexico." *Bulletin of Latin American Research* 7(2): 183–205.

Escobar Lapatí, Agustín. 1993. "The Connection at its Source: Changing Socioeconomic Conditions and Migration Patterns," in Abraham F. Lowenthal and Katrina Burgess, eds., *The California-Mexico Connection*. Pp. 66–81. Stanford: Stanford University Press.

Feder, Ernest. 1977. *El imperialismo fresa*. México, D.F.: Ed. Campesina.

Foley, Douglas E., with Clarice Mota, Donald E. Post and Ignacio Lozano. 1988. *From Peones to Politicos: Class and Ethnicity in a South Texas Town, 1900–1987*. Revised and Enlarged Edition. Austin: University of Texas Press.

Fonseca, Omar. 1988. "De Jaripo a Stockton California: un caso de migración en Michoacán," in Thomas Calvo and Gustavo López, eds., *Movimientos de población en el occidente de México*. Pp. 359–72. Zamora: El Colegio de Michoacán and Centre d'Etudes Mexicaines et Centramericaines.

Forbes, Jack D. 1992. "The Hispanic Spin: Party Politics and Governmental Manipulation of Ethnic Identity." *Latin American Perspectives* 19(4): 59–78.

Forbes-Adam, Victoria. 1994. *Profit and Tradition in Rural Manufacture: Sandal Production in Sahuayo, Michoacán, Mexico*. Ph.D Thesis, University of London.

Foucault, Michel. 1979. *Discipline and Punish: the Birth of the Prison*. Harmondsworth: Peregrine Books.

Fox, Jonathan. 1994. "Targeting the Poorest: The Role of the National Indigenous Institute in Mexico's Solidarity Program," in Wayne A. Cornelius, Ann L. Craig and Jonathan Fox, eds., *Transforming State-Society Relations in Mexico: The National Solidarity*

Strategy. Pp. 179–216. La Jolla: Center for U.S.-Mexican Studies, University of California, San Diego.

García Y Griego, Manuel and Monica Verea Campos. 1988. *México y Estados Unidos: frente a la migración de los indocumentados*. México, D.F.: Coordinación de Humanidades, Universidad Nacional Autónoma de México and Grupo Editorial Miguel Angel Porrúa.

Gates, Marilyn. 1993. *In Default: Peasants, the Debt Crisis and the Agricultural Challenge in Mexico*. Latin American Studies Series No. 12. Boulder: Westview Press.

Gereffi, Gary. 1990. "Big Business and the State," in Gary Gereffi and Donald Wyman, eds., *Manufacturing Miracles: Paths of Industrialization in Latin America and East Asia*. Pp. 90–109. Princeton: Princeton University Press in association with the Center for U.S.-Mexico Studies, University of California at San Diego.

Ghai, Dharam, and Cynthia Hewitt De Alcantara. 1991. "The Crisis of the 1980s in Africa, Latin America and the Caribbean: an Overview," in Dharam Ghai, ed., *The IMF and the South: The Social Impact of Crisis and Adjustment*. Pp. 13–42. London and New Jersey: Zed Books.

Giddens, Anthony. 1985. *The Nation-State and Violence*. Cambridge: Polity Press.

Gledhill, John. 1991. *Casi Nada: A Study of Agrarian Reform in the Homeland of Cardenismo*. Studies in Culture and Society, Volume 4, Institute for Mesoamerican Studies, State University of New York at Albany (Distributed by Texas University Press: Austin).

Gledhill, John. 1992. "Movimientos sociales, partidos políticos y las trampas de poder en un mundo transnacionalizado." *Sociedad y Estado* No. 6.: 35–46.

Gledhill, John. 1993. "Michoacán is Different? Neoliberalism, *Neocardenismo* and the Hegemonic Process," in Neil Harvey, ed., *Mexico: Dilemmas of Transition*. Pp. 91–117. London: The Institute of Latin American Studies and British Academic Press.

Gledhill, John. 1994. *Power and its Disguises: Anthropological Perspectives on Politics*. London: Pluto Press.

Glick Schiller, Nina, Linda Basch and Cristina Blanc-Szanton. 1992. "Transnationalism: a New Analytical Framework for Understanding Migration," in Nina Glick Schiller, Linda Basch and Cristina Blanc-Szanton, eds., *Towards a Transnational Perspective on Migration: Race, Class, Ethnicity, and Nationalism Reconsidered*, Annals of the New York Academy of Sciences, Volume 645. Pp. 1–24. New York: The New York Academy of Sciences.

González de la Rocha, Mercedes. 1989. "El poder de la ausencia: mujeres y migración en una comunidad de los Altos de Jalisco." Paper presented to the XI Coloquium on Regional Anthropology and History, *Las Realidades Regionales de la Crisis Nacional*, Zamora, Michoacán, October 25th–27th, 1989 (mimeo).

Goodman, David, Bernardo Sorj and John Wilkinson. 1987. *From Farming to Biotechnology*. Oxford: Basil Blackwell.

Gordillo, Gustavo. 1988. *Campesinos al asalto del cielo: una reforma agraria con autonomía*. México, D.F.: Siglo XXI editores/Universidad Autónoma de Zacatecas.

Gruzinski, Serge. 1990. "Indian Confraternities, Brotherhoods and *Mayordomías* in Central New Spain. A List of Questions for the Historian and Anthropologist," in Arij Ouweneel and Simon Miller, eds., *The Indian Community of Colonial Mexico: Fifteen Essays on Land Tenure, Corporate Organizations, Ideology and Village Politics*. Pp. 205–23. Amsterdam: CEDLA.

Gutman, Matthew C. 1993. "Rituals of Resistance: a Critique of the Theory of Everyday Forms of Resistance." *Latin American Perspectives* 77, Vol. 20(2): 74–92.

Haber, Paul. 1993. "Cárdenas, Salinas and the Urban Popular Movement," in Neil Harvey, ed., *Mexico: Dilemmas of Transition*. Pp. 218–48. London: The Institute of Latin American Studies and British Academic Press.

Hale, Charles. 1994. "Between Che Guevara and the Pachamama: Mestizos, Indians and Identity Politics in the Anti-Quincentenary Campaign." *Critique of Anthropology* 14(1): 9–39.

Hamilton, Nora and Norma Stoltz Chinchilla. 1991. "Central American Migration: a Framework for Analysis." *Latin American Research Review* 20(1): 75–110.

Harvey, David. 1989. *The Condition of Postmodernity: An Enquiry into the Origins of Cultural Change*. Oxford: Basil Blackwell.

Harvey, Neil. 1993. "The Difficult Transition: Neoliberalism and Neocorporativism in Mexico," in Neil Harvey, ed., *Mexico: Dilemmas of Transition*. Pp. 4–26. London: The Institute of Latin American Studies and British Academic Press.

Harvey, Neil. 1994. *Rebellion in Chiapas: Rural Reforms, Campesino Radicalism and the Limits to Salinismo*. Ejido Reform Research Project, Transformation of Rural Mexico Series, No. 5. La Jolla: Center for U.S.-Mexican Studies, University of California-San Diego.

Hayes-Bautista, David E. 1993. "Mexicans in Southern California: Societal Enrichment or Wasted Opportunity?" in Abraham F. Lowenthal and Katrina Burgess, eds., *The California-Mexico Connection*. Pp. 131–46. Stanford: Stanford University Press.

Heer, David M. 1990. *Undocumented Mexicans in the United States*. Cambridge: Cambridge University Press.

Hellman, Judith Adler. 1994. "Mexican Popular Movements, Clientalism and the Process of Democratization." *Latin American Perspectives* 21(2): 124–142.

Hindley, Jane. In Press. "Indigenous Peoples and the State," in Robert Aitken, Nikki Craske, Gareth Jones and David Stansfield, eds., *Dismantling the Mexican State?* London: Macmillan.

Ingham, John M. 1986. *Mary, Michael and Lucifer: Folk Catholicism in Central Mexico*. Austin: University of Texas Press.

Kearney, Michael. 1986. "Integration of the Mixteca and the Western U.S.-Mexico Region via Migratory Wage Labor," in Ina Resenthal-Urey, ed., *Regional Impacts of U.S.-Mexican Relations*. Pp. 71-102. Monographs Series, 16. La Jolla: University of California, San Diego, Center for U.S.-Mexican Studies.

Kearney, Michael. 1991. "Borders and Boundaries of State and Self at the End of Empire." *Journal of Historical Sociology* 4(1): 52–74.

Kennedy, Paul. 1993. *Preparing for the Twenty-First Century*. London: HarperCollins Publishers.

Knight, Alan. 1992. "The Peculiarities of Mexican History: Mexico Compared to Latin America, 1821–1992." *Journal of Latin American Studies*, Vol. 24, Quincentenary Supplement: 99–144.

Knight, Alan. 1993. "State Power and Political Stability in Mexico," in Neil Harvey, ed., *Mexico: Dilemmas of Transition*. Pp. 29–63. London: Institute of Latin American Studies and British Academic Press.

Leacock, Eleanor Burke. 1971. "Introduction," in Eleanor Burke Leacock, ed., *The Culture of Poverty: A Critique*. Pp. 9–37. New York: Simon and Schuster.

Leeds, Anthony. 1971. "The Concept of the 'Culture of Poverty': Conceptual, Logical, and Empirical Problems, with Perspectives from Brazil and Peru," in Eleanor Burke Leacock, ed., *The Culture of Poverty: A Critique*. Pp. 226–84. New York: Simon and Schuster.

Lewis, Oscar. 1959. "Family dynamics in a Mexican village." *Journal of Marriage and the Family* 21: 218–26.

Lewis, Oscar. 1970. *Anthropological Essays*. New York: Random House.

Leyva, Xóchitl. 1993. *Poder y Desarollo Regional*. Zamora: El Colegio de Michoacán and CIESAS.

Linck, Thierry, and Roberto Santana, eds. 1988. *Les paysanneries dù Michoacan au Mexique*, Paris: Centre Nacional de la Recherche Scientifique.

Linck, Thierry, Roberto Santana, Rocío Martinez K. and Jean Damien de Surgy. 1988. "Le boom de l'avocat: les paysans d'Atapan," in Thierry Linck and Roberto Santana, eds., *Les paysanneries du Michoacan au Mexique*. Pp. 117–72. Paris: Centre Nacional de la Recherche Scientifique.

Linger, Daniel Touro. 1992. *Dangerous Encounters: Meanings of Violence in a Brazilian City*. Stanford: Stanford University Press.

Lomnitz-Adler, Claudio. 1992. *Exits from the Labyrinth: Culture and Ideology in the Mexican National Space*. Berkeley: University of California Press.

López Castro, Gustavo and Sergio Zendejas Romero. 1988. "Migración internacional por regiones en Michoacán," in Thomas Calvo and Gustavo López, eds., *Movimientos de población en el occidente de México*. Pp. 51–79. Zamora: El Colegio de Michoacán and Centre d'Etudes Mexicaines et Centramericaines.

Mallon, Florencia. 1992. "Indian Communities, Political Cultures and the State in Latin America." *Journal of Latin American Studies*, Vol. 24, Quincentenary Supplement: 35–53.

Martin, Philip L. 1988. *Harvest of Confusion: Migrant Workers in U.S. Agriculture*. Boulder: Westview Press.

Martinez Fernandez, Braulio. 1990. "Los precios de garantía en México." *Comercio Exterior* 40(10): 938–42.

Martínez Saldaña, Tomás. 1980. *El costo social de un éxito político: la política expansionista del estado mexicano en el agro lagunero*. Chapingo: Colegio de Postgraduados.

Massey, Douglas S., Rafael Alarcón, Jorge Durand and Humberto González. 1987. *Return to Aztlán: the Social Process of International Migration from Western Mexico*. Berkeley: University of California Press.

Maxwell, Andrew H. 1993. "The Underclass, 'Social Isolation' and 'Concentration Effects': 'The Culture of Poverty' Revisited." *Critique of Anthropology* 13(3): 231–45.

Moctezuma Yano, Patricia. 1992. "El cargo de *orhete* en la comunidad de Zipiajo." *Relaciones* 52: 203–24.

Moguel, Julio. 1994. "The Mexican Left and the Social Program of Salinismo," in Wayne A. Cornelius, Ann L. Craig and Jonathan Fox, eds., *Transforming State-Society Relations in Mexico: The National Solidarity Strategy*. Pp. 167–76. La Jolla: Center for U.S.-Mexican Studies, University of California, San Diego.

Moreira Alves, María Helena. 1993. "Something Old, Something New: Brazil's Partido dos Trabalhadores," in Barry Carr and Steve Ellner, eds., *The Latin American Left: From the Fall of Allende to Perestroika*. Pp. 225–42. Latin American Perspectives Series, no. 11. Boulder, Col. and London: Westview Press and Latin American Bureau.

Muller, Thomas and Thomas J. Espenshade. 1985. *The Fourth Wave: California's Newest Immigrants*. Washington, D.C.: The Urban Institute Press.

Mummert, Gail. 1992. "Changing Family Structure and Organization in a Setting of Male Emigration, Female Salaried Work and the Commercialization of Agriculture: Case Study from Michoacán, Mexico." Lecture delivered on March 11th 1992 to the Research Seminar on Mexico and U.S.-Mexican Relations, University of California, San Diego (mimeo).

Nugent, Daniel. 1993. *Spent Cartridges of Revolution: an Anthropological History of Namiquipa, Chihuahua*. Chicago: Chicago University Press.

Olvera Rivera, Alberto and Cristina Millan Vásquez. 1994. "Neocorporativisimo y democracia en la transformación institucional de la cafeticultura: el caso del centro de Veracruz," *Cuadernos Agrarios* 10: 53–69.

Palerm, Juan-Vicente. 1991. *Farm Labour Needs and Farm Workers in California, 1970 to 1989*. Sacramento: Employment Development Department.

Palerm, Juan-Vicente and José Ignacio Urquiola. 1993. "A Binational System of Agricultural Production: The Case of the Mexican Bajío and California," in Daniel G. Aldrich and Lorenzo Meyer, eds., *Mexico and the United States: Neighbours in Crisis*. Pp. 311–67, San Bernadino: The Borgo Press.

Paz, Octavio. 1994. "El nudo de Chiapas." *El País*, Friday 7th January: 14–15.

Petras, James and Morris Morley. 1990. *US Hegemony under Siege: Class, Politics and Development in Latin America*. London: Verso.

Pisa, Rosaria A. 1994. "Popular Response to the Reform of Article 27: State Intervention and Community Resistance in Oaxaca." Paper presented in Session 410/MEX14 Panel at the XVIII International Congress of the Latin American Studies Association, Atlanta, Georgia, March 10th–12th 1994.

Poole, Deborah and Gerardo Rénique. 1991. "The New Chroniclers of Peru: US Scholars and their 'Shining Path' of Peasant Rebellion." *Bulletin of Latin American Research* 10(2).: 133–91.

Portes, Alejandro and Robert L. Bach. 1985., *Latin Journey: Cuban and Mexican immigrants in the United States*. Berkeley: University of California Press.

Powell, Kathy. 1994. "Cambio socio-económico y cultura política en la región cañera de Los Reyes, Michoacán," in Victor Gabriel Muro, ed., *Estudios Michoacanos V*. Zamora: El Colegio de Michoacán.

Powell, Kathy. In Press. "Neoliberalism and Nationalism," in Robert Aitken, Nikki Craske, Gareth Jones and David Stansfield, eds., *Dismantling the Mexican State?* London: Macmillan.

Ramirez, Luis Alfonso. 1986. *Chilchota: un pueblo al pie de la sierra*. Zamora: El Colegio de Michoacán/Gobierno del Estado de Michoacán.

Rello, Fernando. 1986. *El campo en la encrucijada nacional*. México, D.F.: SEP, Foro 2000.

Romo, Ricardo. 1983. *East Los Angeles: History of a Barrio*. Austin: University of Texas Press.

Roseberry, William. 1989. *Anthropologies and Histories*. New Brunswick, N.J.: Rutgers University Press.

Rouse, Roger. 1991. "Mexican Migration and the Social Space of Postmodernism." *Diaspora* 1(1): 8–23.

Rouse, Roger. 1992. "Making Sense of Settlement: Class Transformation, Cultural Struggle and Transnationalism among Mexican Migrants in the United States," in Nina Glick

Schiller, Linda Basch and Cristina Blanc-Szanton, eds., *Towards a Transnational Perspective on Migration: Race, Class, Ethnicity, and Nationalism Reconsidered*, Annals of the New York Academy of Sciences, Volume 645. Pp. 25–52. New York: The New York Academy of Sciences.

Rubin, Jeffrey W. 1990. "Popular Mobilization and the Myth of State Corporatism," in Joe Foweraker and Ann L. Craig, eds., *Popular Movements and Political Change in Mexico*. Pp. 247–67. Boulder: Lynne Rienner Publications.

Rubin, Jeffrey W. 1994. "Indigenous Autonomy and Power in Chiapas: Lessons from Mobilization in Juchitán." Appendix to Neil Harvey, *Rebellion in Chiapas: Rural Reforms, Campesino Radicalism and the Limits to Salinismo*. Pp. 57–62. Ejido Reform Research Project, Transformation of Rural Mexico Series, No. 5. La Jolla: Center for U.S.-Mexican Studies, University of California-San Diego.

Rus, Jan. 1983. "Whose Caste War? Indians, Ladinos and the Chiapas 'Caste War' of 1869," in Murdo J. MacLeod and Robert Wasserstrom, eds., *Spaniards and Indians in Southeastern Mesoamerica: Essays on the History of Ethnic Relations*. Pp. 127–69. Lincoln: University of Nebraska Press.

Salzinger, Leslie. 1991. "A Maid by Any Other Name: The Transformation of 'Dirty Work' by Central American Immigrants," in Michael Buroway, Alice Burton, Ann Arnett Ferguson, Kathryn J. Fox, Joshua Gamson, Nadine Gartrell, Leslie Hurst, Charles Kurzman, Leslie Salzinger, Josepha Sciffman and Shiori Ui, *Ethnography Unbound: Power and Resistance in the Modern Metropolis*. Pp. 139–160, Berkeley: University of California Press.

Sanderson, Steven E. 1986. *The Transformation of Mexican Agriculture*. Princeton, New Jersey: Princeton University Press.

Sassen-Koob, Saskia. 1983. "Labor Migrations and the New International Division of Labor," in J. Nash and M. P. Fernandez-Kelly, eds., *Women, Men, and the International Division of Labor*. Pp. 175–204, Albany: The State University of New York Press.

Sassen, Saskia. 1986. "New York City: Economic Restructuring and Immigration." *Development and Change* 17: 85–119.

Schaffhauser, Philippe. 1990. "Resultados preliminares del estudio sobre prácticas de movilidad y transformaciones de la vida social en México: el ejemplo de Tarecuato." Unpublished report, Zamora: El Colegio de Michoacán.

Schryer, Frans. 1980. *The Rancheros of Pisaflores: The History of a Peasant Bourgeoisie in Twentieth-Century Mexico*. Toronto: University of Toronto Press.

Scott, James C. 1990. *Domination and the Arts of Resistance: Hidden Transcripts*. New Haven: Yale University Press.

Sklair, Leslie. 1991. *Sociology of the Global System*. New York and London: Harvester Wheatsheaf.

Solís Rosales, Ricardo. 1990. "Precios de guarantía y política agraria: un analisis de largo plazo." *Commercio Exterior* 40 (10): 923–937.

Stull, Donald D. 1993. "Of Meat and (Wo)men: Beefpacking's Consequences for Communities on the High Plains." Paper presented in Session 1-090, "Emerging Heterogeneity in Rural U.S. Communities," at the 92nd Annual Meeting of the American Anthropological Association, Washington, D.C., November 18th, 1993.

Trigueros, Paz and Javier Rodriguez Pina. 1988. "Migración y vida familiar en Michoacán (un estudio de caso)," in Gustavo López Castro, ed., *Migración en el Occidente de México*. Pp. 201–21. Zamora: El Colegio de Michoacán.

Ui, Shiori. 1991. "'Unlikely Heroes': The Evolution of Female Leadership in a Cambodian Ethnic Enclave," in Michael Buroway, Alice Burton, Ann Arnett Ferguson, Kathryn J. Fox, Joshua Gamson, Nadine Gartrell, Leslie Hurst, Charles Kurzman, Leslie Salzinger, Josepha Sciffman and Shiori Ui, *Ethnography Unbound: Power and Resistance in the Modern Metropolis*. Pp. 161–77, Berkeley: University of California Press.

UNDP (United Nations Development Program). 1993. *Human Development Report 1993*. Cary, North Carolina: Oxford University Press.

Verduzco Igartúa, Gustavo. 1989. "Las ciudades de provincia, ¿alternativa?" *Demos* 2: 20–22. Mexico, D.F.: Universidad Nacional Autónoma de México.

Vincent, Joan. 1993. "Framing the Underclass." *Critique of Anthropology* 13(3): 215–230.

Wade, Robert. 1990. *Governing the Market: Economic Theory and the Role of Government in East Asian Industrialization*. Princeton: Princeton University Press.

Wilson, Fiona. 1990. *De la casa al taller: mujeres, trabajo y clase social en la industria textil y del vestido, Santiago Tangamandapio*. Zamora: El Colegio de Michoacán.

Wilson, Richard. 1993. "Anchored Communities: Identity and History of the Maya-Q'eqchi." *Man* 28(1): 121–38.

Wilson, Tamar Diana. 1993. "Theoretical Approaches to Mexican Wage Labor Migration." *Latin American Perspectives* Issue 78, 20(3): 98–129.

Wilson, William Julius. 1987. *The Truly Disadvantaged: the Inner City, the Underclass and Public Policy*. Chicago: University of Chicago Press.

Wolf, Eric R. 1982. *Europe and the People without History*. Berkeley: University of California Press.

Zaid, Gabriel. 1987. *La economía presidencial*. Mexico, D.F.: Editorial Vuelta.

Zárate Hernández, José Eduardo. 1991. "Notas para la interpretación del movimiento étnico en Michoacán," in Victor Gabriel Muro and Manuel Canto Chac, eds., *El estudio de los movimientos sociales: teoría y método*. Pp. 111–29. Zamora y Coyoacán, D.F.: El Colegio de Michoacán y la Universidad Autónoma Metropolitana.

Zárate Hernández, José Eduardo. 1994. "La fiesta del Año Nuevo Purhépecha como ritual político. Notas en turno al discurso de los profesionales indígenas purhépechas," in Andrew Roth Seneff and José Lameiras, eds., *El Verbo Oficial: Política Moderna en Dos Campos Periféricos del Estado Mexicano*. Pp. 99–124. Zamora: El Colegio de Michoacán and Universidad ITESO.

Zendejas Romero, Sergio and Gail Mummert. 1994. "Respuestas locales a reformas gubernamentales en el campo mexicano: el ejido como forma de organización de prácticas políticas de grupos locales." Paper presented in Session 053/MEX02 Panel at the XVIII International Congress of the Latin American Studies Association, Atlanta, Georgia, March 10th–12th 1994.

Zepeda Patterson, Jorge. 1987. "Michoacán antes y durante la crisis o sobre los michoacanos que no se fueron de braceros." *Relaciones* 31: 5–24.

Index

About the Book and Author

Carlos Salinas's government drew praise from many academic commentators and foreign governments for its boldness in embarking on neoliberal economic reforms that tackled some of the shibboleths of the Mexican revolutionary tradition and for its supposedly astute political management of change. This book offers a more critical understanding of the economic, social, and political dimensions of Salinismo. Although Gledhill focuses on its impact on the rural sector in the state of Michoacán, he shows that the problems of the region affect the United States as well as Mexico because reform is being implemented within the framework of a longer-term process of transnationalization of class relations and global capitalist restructuring.

Drawing on ethnographic fieldwork and anthropological theory, the book takes a close look at the responses of a regional society to economic change and the political strategies of the Salinas regime. Surveying the local impact of changing agricultural policies, *ejido* reform, and the U.S. Immigration Reform and Control Act, Gledhill distinguishes the positions of different social groups and highlights the larger processes in which the entire region is now caught up. Examining the linkages between rural Mexico and the agribusiness farms and factories of California, he underlines the political and social implications of these evolving relationships on both sides of the border, focusing on questions of hegemony and the role of transnational migrant communities. Only by examining the fractured social worlds of contemporary capitalism and the nature of the politics of exclusion, he concludes, can we assess the true social costs of neoliberal reform.

John Gledhill is Reader in anthropology at University College London.